D1566272

THE USE
OF THE SELF

THE USE
OF THE SELF

Countertransference and Communication in the Analytic Situation

Theodore J. Jacobs, M.D.

With a Foreword by
Warren S. Poland, M.D.

INTERNATIONAL UNIVERSITIES PRESS, INC.

Madison   Connecticut

Copyright © 1991, Theodore J. Jacobs

Library of Congress Cataloging in Publication Data

Jacobs, Theodore J.
    The use of the self: countertransference and communication in the analytic situation/Theodore J. Jacobs; with a foreword by Warren S. Poland.
        p. cm.
    Consists mainly of articles reprinted from various sources.
    Includes bibliographical references.
    Includes indexes.
    ISBN 0-8236-6710-3
    1. Psychoanalysis. 2. Self. 3. Transference (Psychology)
4. Countertransference (Psychology) I. Title.
[DNLM: 1. Countertransference (Psychology) 2. Physicians—Patient Relations—collected works. 3. Psychoanalysis—collected works.
4. Self Concept—collected works. WM 460 J165u]
RC506.J33 1991
150.19′5—dc20
DNLM/DLC
for Library of Congress   90-4926
                                                                      CIP

    ᵀᴾ   Manufactured in the United States of America

To Mickey
and to Ellen, Annie, Nina, Jenny
and the memory of Maggie

Contents

Acknowledgments

All that I have set down in this book was taught to me by others; by my patients, my colleagues, my friends, and my family. It would be impossible to name all of the teachers to whom I am indebted, but I owe special thanks to Drs. Milton Horowitz, Charles Brenner, Milton Rosenbaum, Jose Barchilon, and the late Edward Hornick, each so different, each a remarkable teacher.

Among the many colleagues from whom I have learned so much I want especially to mention Drs. Sander Abend, Michael Porder, Albert Sax, and Martin Willick, co-members of a study group which had a profound effect on my thinking and whose frank and open discussion of case material was a source of stimulation and of fresh ideas. Special thanks, too, go to Drs. Warren Poland and James McLaughlin, whose work has been a continual source of inspiration to me and has paved the way for my own, to my brother, Dr. Daniel Jacobs, who, in many talks over the years, has helped me to clarify often vague and fuzzy thinking, and to Dr. Margaret Emery for her superb editing of the manuscript. My group at The Center for Advanced Psychoanalytic Studies provided an invaluable forum for the discussion of clinical issues and my colleagues in it contributed in countless ways to the development of my ideas.

This book could not have been written without the unfailing support and encouragement of my wife and children and to them I will be forever grateful. Nor could it have been published without the devoted help of Marie Mele, whose patience, good humor, and skill in deciphering my illegible handwriting and in typing the many incarnations of the manuscript have earned my heartfelt gratitude.

I am also grateful to the editors and publishers of the following journals for permission to reprint my previously published papers either in part or in their entirety.

A portion of Chapter 1 appeared in a paper titled "The Corrective Emotional Experience—Its Place in Current Technique" in *Psychoanalytic Inquiry*, Vol. 10, No. 3, 1990, pp. 433–454. Reproduced by permission.

Chapter 3 appeared under the same title in *Psychoanalytic Inquiry*, Vol. 7, 1987, pp. 485–509. Reproduced by permission.

Chapter 4 was published under the same title in *Psychoanalysis: The Science of Mental Conflict: Essays in Honor of Charles Brenner*, edited by Arnold D. Richards and Martin Willick. New York: Analytic Press, 1986, pp. 301–320. Reproduced by permission of The Analytic Press, Hillsdale, New Jersey.

Chapter 5 appeared under the same title in the *Journal of the American Psychoanalytic Association*, Vol. 21, 1973, pp. 77–92.

Chapter 6 was published with minor modifications under the same title in *Analysts at Work: Practice, Principle and Technique*, edited by Joseph Reppen. New Jersey: Analytic Press, 1985, pp. 43–58. Reproduced by permission of The Analytic Press, Hillsdale, New Jersey.

Chapter 7 appeared under the same title in the *Journal of the American Psychoanalytic Association*, Vol. 34, 1986, pp. 289–307.

Chapter 9 appeared under the same title in the *Journal of the American Psychoanalytic Association*, Vol. 31, 1983, pp. 619–642.

Chapter 10 appeared with minor modifications under the same title in the *Journal of the American Psychoanalytic Association*, Vol. 28, 1980, pp. 21–42.

Foreword

Warren S. Poland, M.D.

> It is a very remarkable thing the *Ucs.* of one human being can react upon that of another, without passing through the *Cs.* This deserves closer investigation, especially with a view to finding out whether preconscious activity can be excluded as playing a part in it; but, descriptively speaking, the fact is incontestable.
>
> Freud [1915, p. 194]

Psychoanalysis, with all the bright benefits that have flowed from it, was originally conceived and delivered in the lonely agony of a genius's pained but relentless self-scrutiny. However far we have been carried by subsequent learning, the courage and brilliance of Freud's self-analysis continues to cast its awesome and humbling spell.

Freud's revolutionary breakthrough has both led and misled us. So astonishing and unexpected were Freud's discoveries that we have spent, and spent well, most of the following century extending his search into the unconscious. But for too long as we have struggled with our generations of patients, we have forgotten that our model was a *self*-analysis.

As a result of starting from a self-analysis, Freud was delayed in recognizing in his clinical work the significance of the

transference and the countertransference, the effects that two
different persons have upon one another. Following from
Freud, as analysts we have let too long a time elapse while we
viewed the mind of the patient as if it stood alone, with ourselves
as detached outsiders.

There is no blame to be set for such oversight in the first
half of this century of depth psychology. So amazing and compelling were the wondrous findings, that the first generations
of investigators did not notice the influences they brought with
them in their explorations.

Though progress has been slow, attention has turned at
last to the vital interchange between the *two* participants in the
clinical analytic venture. There is resistance in the progress of
a science just as there is in the progress of an analysis; and the
resistance in part grows from good and sufficient causes in each
instance. The resistance to new attention to "the interpersonal"
arose not only from unyielding conservativism, but also from
a valid perception that "interpersonal" was often used as a sophisticated defense against crediting the power of active unconscious forces. Many of the "interpersonalists" in the middle
of the century, like many in new schools now, saw themselves
as their generation's revolutionaries. Then, like now, new concepts which might have enriched analytic understanding often
served to screen out unconscious forces.

Allegiances led to antagonisms and controversies flared;
such is the dialectic nature of progress. For all of those who
established and defended fixed positions there were others who
strove to integrate. Deutsch, Fliess, Gitelson, Racker, and Stone
are some of the early leaders in extending our grasp of the
dynamics of the dyadic analytic process. Sandler, McLaughlin,
Gardner, McDougall, and myself are a few among the increasing number of those currently examining the hidden currents
in the analytic situation. With his work leading to this breakthrough volume, work that takes us a large step forward, Jacobs
assumes a major pioneering position.

Freud asked the newcomer to the analytic approach to view
his own mind with the same effort to dispassionate objectivity
with which he viewed the minds of others. Jacobs, properly,
demands the same for the analyst in his practice, that he view

himself with the same scrutiny he turns to the patient. The reader will see that the author does not spare himself.

The analytic process no longer consists of the patient's mind being inspected with remote detachment by the analyst, like a scientist peering at the contents of a test tube. Nor is it any longer merely the dynamics of a private two-person small-group therapy, the interaction always relatively close to the surface.

The overriding goal of an analysis remains that of helping someone know himself, know his own mind and how it works, and through that help him increase his peace with himself and the scope of his actions in the world. The study of the patient's mind occurs in the special context of the analytic situation, a unique human relationship in which the trained mind of one person is opened in the service of the other. Fenichel (1941) wrote that the tool of analytic technique "is the unconscious of the analyst which intuitively comprehends the unconscious of the patient. Its aim is to lift this comprehension out of intuition into scientific clarity" (pp. 12–13). The analytic field is, thus, one in which the analyst's mind is both receptive and partially apart, following the words of the patient's associations and the music of emotional reactions, and laboring to use what is perceived both in the other and in oneself, not to enact but to understand.

The analyst works in the service of the patient's pursuit of self-knowledge and self-mastery even, and perhaps especially, when the patient seeks to lure him into hidden patterns of engagement. Inexorably pulled to deal with the patient's subtle eliciting powers, the analyst's self-analysis becomes an inevitable and essential part of his labor with and for the patient.

These pulls and pressures are present even when the analyst seems as if he or she is on automatic pilot; that is, with the self-analytic processing taking place unconsciously or preconsciously, as suggested above by Freud. Yet, whether the analyst attends consciously or not (and consciously is surely preferable), the examination of the patient's mind is realized within a matrix of a deeply buried pair of reciprocal self-inquiries.

Jacobs accepts the primacy of the exploration of the patient's mind as the goal of an analysis. But he repeatedly discovers that what the analyst brings to his work, even when at his best, is the product of his own psychic compromise formations. Even a proper, accurate, fitting interpretation does not arise fully formed like Venus from the sea but is the end product of the analyst's mental processing. All the words the analyst hears are colored by the universe of meanings in the analyst's mind. The analyst's mind may be tamed and unconflicted, and may function optimally in such a state, but it came to that state from its own urges shaped by a lifetime of personal experiences and formed by years of technical training.

Jacobs does not put forth suggestions for a new technique. He certainly does not turn toward wild analysis. He does not alter the appropriate application of the abstinence principle, though he remembers Anna Freud's (1954) caveat that analytic technique was not designed for the defense of the analyst. What he does is hold rigorously to the analyst's equivalent of the basic rule for the patient, the injunction that the analyst privately consider *all* that passes within him for its informational value in terms of the patient. As a result, his portraits of the clinical process are alive, without the pallor evident in case reports drawn in the likeness of an imagined ideal. And as a result we are able to turn to the interactional level of analysis not as an avoidance of depth psychology but with a fuller realization of the implications of unconscious functioning in each of the parties, each with his own unconscious. We are greatly advanced in our efforts to understand how analysis works.

It seems to me that Jacobs' purpose, which he approaches with modesty, is that of observing and reporting analytic engagement in a way as true to life as possible. But I believe that in the process he takes us forward as we try to confront much broader puzzles.

Just what is a human relationship? When two people share an experience, they go through the moment together, yet what each savors is individual, not truly a shared taste of the other's experience. How can it be that no man is an island and at the same time that every man is an island? What does it mean to know someone else, and how vast are the differences from the ways one knows oneself? How does human experience, especially that between people, get internalized; how does one learn or grow?

How a person gets better in an analysis and how an analysis works offer us clues to the greater range of questions with which all people struggle. The dyadic psychoanalytic situation is the best laboratory yet conceived for investigating those questions in practice, providing us with opportunities for controlled deep observations that can carry us far beyond philosophical speculation. Jacobs leads us away from trivial polemics back to the gathering of observations for consideration unclouded by shame, until the matters we watch speak for themselves.

A visitor to Giverny is left to wonder whether Monet was a painter who also gardened or a gardener who also painted. The reader of this volume may similarly wonder whether Jacobs is an analyst who also writes or a writer who also analyzes. His writing is elegantly evocative, free of cant and jargon. His words, with humility and wit, are faithful to the actualities of the clinical work of the analyst as he moves sometimes with and sometimes against the patient, moving as the patient moves, moving from patient to patient, from moment to moment, from hour to hour, from day to day.

Staying true to clinical experiences and true to his search for the unconscious determinants behind those experiences, Jacobs carries us with him through his days with grace and candor, in modest tones exposing the art of analysis to scientific gaze and revealing the incisive wisdom of a sensitive clinician. The "closer investigation" called for by Freud is significantly advanced by Jacobs. This text is a gift from a gifted analyst.

Introduction

This book had its origins some two decades ago when, as a young analyst, I became interested in an area of psychoanalytic practice which had been little mentioned in my training: the experiences of the analyst in the clinical situation.

In supervision and in case seminars the focus of my teaching had been almost exclusively on understanding the verbal material brought by the patient. Very little attention was paid to the nonverbal behaviors that accompanied this material and less yet to the emotional and physical responses of the analyst as he processed and responded to both types of communication. While the general issue of countertransference was acknowledged to be of importance in clinical work, curiously, it was rarely mentioned in case conferences and given little attention in seminars on technique. When, in my own supervisory experiences, a piece of countertransference was noted by a supervisor (an infrequent occurrence), it was rarely discussed as data of importance but was usually handled—and rapidly disposed of—by the tactful suggestion that such and such a reaction of mine might be something I would want to take up with my analyst.

Clearly, teachers and students alike were uncomfortable with the issue of countertransference and, as a consequence, it was dealt with largely through neglect and avoidance. When the subject of countertransference was discussed in class, it was the contributions of Annie Reich (1951, 1960, 1966) that most often were assigned. Written in part as a counterpoint to earlier publications by Heimann (1950) and Little (1951), these articles grew out of Reich's belief that these colleagues had overemphasized the value of countertransference and neglected its dangers. She took the point of view that countertransference, though an inevitable and even necessary component of the analytic situation, nevertheless constitutes an interference with the therapist's proper understanding and technique. Her focus was, primarily, on countertransference as a lens which distorts the analyst's vision and which, through self-analytic efforts or a return to analysis, he is obliged to correct.

Though constituting a major contribution to understanding this important aspect of countertransference, Reich's work overlooked other aspects. Little consideration was given in these articles to the idea that the analyst's countertransference responses could provide data as complex and valuable as that derived from the transference. This perspective, though articulated by Little and Heimann, did not gain general credence among the majority of American analysts for some years after Reich's writings appeared. As a result, the exploration of both countertransference phenomena and the broader issue of the psychology of the analyst as legitimate areas of analytic investigation was slow to develop in this country. This was not true elsewhere. The pioneering work of the Argentinian analyst, Heinrich Racker (1968), published over twenty years ago, was the first comprehensive study of the subject of countertransference and revealed both the complexity of the issues involved and their continued impact on the analytic process.

Viewed from Reich's perspective, countertransference responses inevitably represented some problem of the analyst's that was surfacing in this way. With this point of view prevailing among their teachers, it was difficult for candidates to confront these issues directly and to explore the rich vein of communication contained within them. It was only when they were able to discuss cases with a small group of trusted peers that most students and recent graduates could let down their hair, talk openly of their reactions to patients, and learn from them.

It was, in fact, just such a group, formed in the early seventies, that had a profound effect on my own thinking. Meeting monthly for several years with Drs. Sander Abend, Michael Porder, Albert Sax, and Martin Willick, esteemed colleagues and close friends, I discovered for the first time that I could share with others not only embarrassing mistakes that I had made, but attitudes and feelings toward patients that I had regarded as shameful or inappropriate. In an atmosphere of mutual support and understanding we could talk of the anger aroused in us by certain individuals, of the feelings of frustration and despair that not infrequently we had to contend with, or of our sexual responses to attractive female patients. We felt free to point out countertransference reactions to the presenter of a case when these had escaped his awareness. Included among such responses were not only warded-off and unacknowledged feelings, attitudes, and values, but ways of communicating to patients that expressed these personal reactions. We could also talk about our nonverbal responses, including levels of attention, bodily postures and movements, and physiologic changes that occurred in the course of working with certain patients. These meetings, along with the frank and open discussions that took place in a study group at the Center for Advanced Psychoanalytic Studies in Princeton, New Jersey, helped me in my own work to focus on and begin to explore those covert communications that lay between and behind the spoken words of both patient and analyst, and were having an enduring impact on the analytic process.

A number of teachers were instrumental in helping me appreciate the importance of the transactional aspect of analytic work. In his writing and teaching, Dr. Jacob Arlow stressed the role of fantasies shared between patient and analyst in the treatment situation and in his elegant and convincing way demonstrated the contribution of this phenomenon to the analyst's understanding of unconscious communications and to the genesis of his interpretations.

By emphasizing the fact that countertransference reactions, like other mental experiences, can best be understood as compromise formations containing contributions from various facets of the personality, Dr. Charles Brenner both helped to put the issue of countertransference on an equal footing with transference and other clinical phenomena and stimulated its investigation, not solely as a "problem" of the analyst's, but as an invaluable source of clinical data.

Dr. Milton Horowitz, by stressing the continual interaction of transference and countertransference in his teaching and by illustrating the reciprocal nature of this process with fascinating clinical examples, sharpened my understanding of the interplay of forces that characterizes the analytic situation.

A problem that for some years had troubled and puzzled me concerned certain patients who, though treated by highly skilled analysts whose understanding of these cases was excellent, showed little progress in treatment. Not infrequently such cases were presented in advanced clinical seminars. Listening to the presentations, I noted that patients of this kind rarely responded to the analyst's correct interpretations with the expected confirmatory flow of material. More often these interpretations were met with silence, with protest, with anger, with heightened resistance, and with a decrease in the availability of unconscious material. Nor, in most instances, did a clear understanding and working through of such reactions develop.

It was tempting, of course, to explain such cases as examples of negative therapeutic reactions. From this perspective, their lack of progress would be due in large measure to the factor of unconscious guilt operating silently to undermine the analyst's best efforts. While, no doubt, in certain cases this dynamic contributed in important ways to the stalemated situation, in others it did not fit the clinical data. In them neither the patient's history nor the analytic material supported the idea that unconscious guilt was operating as a factor of prime importance.

Another possibility, of course, was that either the analyst's understanding of the case, his technique, or both, were faulty. While in some situations errors of this kind might have contributed to the problems encountered, it was difficult for me to believe that all of them could be attributed to the analyst's mistakes. These cases were thoroughly reviewed in advanced clinical seminars by senior colleagues and highly respected peers. Although minor differences in approach were often debated and disagreements concerning the handling of particular sessions not infrequently aired, it was rare for serious errors to be found in the analyst's understanding of a case. When such situations did occur, the analyst would regularly make the corrections that were called for. These, however, did not always lead to a more productive analysis.

What, then, was wrong? Why were analyst and patient struggling in a treatment that seemed not to be progressing? My own experiences with a number of cases had been similar. While in several of these situations additional supervision and discussions with colleagues had illuminated errors in my understanding or in my way of working, in other instances, it was difficult to pinpoint the problem. Intrigued by this dilemma, I resolved to pay particular attention to those of my current cases that fell into this category and to focus on the kinds of communication, verbal and otherwise, that were taking place in these analyses.

What increasingly became clear to me as I observed myself interacting with patients was the existence of a dimension of clinical work to which I had paid insufficient attention. This concerned not the words exchanged between patient and analyst, but the underlying messages that accompanied these communications. Often enough, it was these metacommunications, the covert messages sent and received, as much as those conveyed through the channel of speech, that affected the course and outcome of analytic work.

Transmitted through tone and syntax, vocal quality and inflection, posture and movement, are feelings, attitudes, and values of which neither patient nor analyst is consciously aware. This level of communication serves to modify, punctuate, emphasize, or contradict the words spoken by each. It often happens that, despite his outward stance of neutrality, what is conveyed by the analyst on the metacommunicational level are subtle judgments concerning the patient's attitudes and behavior. Also expressed with some frequency are covert messages suggesting that the patient would be well advised to follow a particular course of action. While some patients seek out and welcome these messages, experiencing a sense of security when they are transmitted, others respond to them by engaging in a struggle. This is particularly true if what is communicated by the analyst is subtly critical or otherwise threatens a patient's self-esteem. Then a battle may be formed beneath the surface layer of the analysis that contains the verbalizations of patient and analyst. In time this struggle can lead to an analysis that grinds to a halt. Because the battle is fought out in an arena different from that in which the ordinary exchanges of the analytic situation take place, it often goes unrecognized by patient and analyst. Thus a level of interaction, often of crucial importance in the analysis, is frequently overlooked in clinical work.

Increasingly interested in this aspect of analysis, I began to focus more closely on the metacommunicational dimension of the analytic situation. Eventually I began to set down some thoughts about the interactions of analyst and patient, and the result was the series of articles that, along with some new work, has provided the material for this volume.

Although countertransference figures prominently in these pages, my concern is not with this phenomenon in a narrow sense. It is, rather, with the experiences of the analyst as they resonate with, comment on, and illuminate those of the patient. It is, in short, about the way two people communicate in the analytic situation and about how the analyst, by listening to himself, can better understand that communication.

I

Beginning an Analysis:
Transference–Countertransference
Interactions

1

Communication and Technique in the Opening Phase

A few months ago while flipping through the TV channels in an effort to find a way to avoid some work that I had to do, I came across a quiz show that involved a contest between married couples. One of the pairs was an elderly couple who, although they had known each other for many years, had only recently been married. In a teasing way the M.C. asked the wife why it was that she had insisted on a courtship of twenty years before agreeing to marry her husband.

"It takes a long time," she said, "to get over first impressions."

It is first impressions as they are laid down in the opening phase of analysis that is the topic of this chapter. My emphasis will be on the kinds of communications beyond words, beyond technical precepts and technical interventions that set the stage for all that follows in analysis and that have much to say about its success or failure. I will discuss some factors that I believe make for good beginnings and some that put obstacles —sometimes insuperable ones—in the path of analysis. In doing so, I will offer several clinical examples drawn from the beginnings of treatments to illustrate some of the problems and opportunities inherent in this vitally important phase of our work.

The accumulated wisdom of years of clinical experience has led to the development of certain technical rules or methods of working in the beginning phase of analysis that are part of the armamentarium of every young analyst. Briefly summarized, they include the recognition and early interpretation of resistances; analyzing from the surface downwards; careful attention to analytic tact and timing; the interpretation of mobile and fluid defenses before those more rigidly embedded in character; and the interpretation of affects that are close to consciousness prior to the interpretation of content.

More controversial, and in fact the subject of sometimes acrimonious debate, is the matter of transference interpretation. Gill (1982), for example, has advocated in the strongest terms early confrontation and interpretation of what he calls the patient's experience of the analyst. In his view, it is the understanding of this experience and the myriad ways that the patient may need to defend against the recognition of it that is at the heart of analytic work. One of the cardinal errors in analytic technique, he believes, is the failure to identify and to interpret from the outset of treatment the way that the patient is experiencing the analyst.

Kohut (1971, 1977, 1984) and his colleagues, on the other hand, have stressed the importance, particularly in the analysis of individuals with narcissistic character pathology, of allowing the primitive transferences that evolve in such cases to ripen and take hold. It is only when the self–object or idealizing transferences have had time to develop and become an active part of the patient's psychological experience that they can be meaningfully interpreted in the analytic situation.

While each of these technical precepts, contradictory as they may seem, focuses on issues of importance in analysis and each has made a contribution to technique that has proven useful in particular clinical situations, I do not believe that they speak to the essence of the analytic encounter. To emphasize issues of technique may, in important ways, miss the heart of the matter. This, in my view, lies in the nature of the communications—conveyed through speech and silence, tone and syntax, manner and gesture, movement and posture—that are transmitted between patient and analyst.

If we make the mistake of adhering out of conviction, no matter how soundly based, to a theoretical position concerning the handling of the opening phase, or any other phase, of analysis, we run the risk of not really hearing the patient. Our technique, rather than proceeding out of principles, must derive from our understanding of the moment. Clearly there are clinical situations in which it is of the greatest importance from the first session on to help the patient gain an understanding of his warded-off perceptions and experiences vis-à-vis the analyst. There are other situations, too—not always involving patients with narcissistic disorders—in which it is important not to intervene early but to wait until the transference becomes palpable. When a student, early on in treatment, would try to dig out nuggets of transference from material in which it was solidly embedded, Otto Isakower, a wise and astute clinician, would often point out that there was no advantage in attempting such spadework. Rather, he would say, the analyst, like a doctor treating a boil, must wait for the transference to ripen before lancing it with his interpretations. Otherwise the pus is driven inwards and the lesion hardens.

On the other hand, a situation may arise at the beginning of treatment in which an early and deep interpretation may be necessary to overcome a particularly tenacious resistance. Such moves, when utilized, are frequently the result, not of technical strategy, but of intuition. Receiving messages through the various modalities that operate simultaneously in the analytic situation, the analyst, using himself freely, responds to those communications. Sometimes, if he is attuned well, he simply listens quietly, perhaps grunting at irregular intervals. Sometimes, however, he interprets directly and incisively, bypassing niceties of technique to get to the core of a vital matter. In this regard I am reminded of a story that is told about the master technician, Herman Nunberg. Nunberg was known for his early, and direct, transference interpretations. One day the manifest content of the dream of a young man who had recently started analysis was reported to Nunberg by a candidate in supervision. On the basis of this dream material Nunberg remarked that if he were the analyst in the case he would have interpreted very directly the patient's wish to suck his penis.

"But don't you do that," Nunberg quickly added.

"But why not?" the candidate inquired. "If you would make that kind of interpretation, why shouldn't I?"

"Because I believe it," Nunberg replied.

In short, the core of the analytic work lies much beyond the technical precepts and the technical advice that we are offered from one quarter or another. What Freud said about the later stages of analysis, namely, that the infinite variety of moves and countermoves defies any systematic description, applies, I believe, equally well to the opening phase. According to the particular features of a case and the analyst's intuitive and spontaneous responses to the patient, the way he introduces analysis, and himself as an analyst, may vary markedly from situation to situation. Although in general the analyst may endorse certain basic notions about how one goes about beginning an analysis, in fact he often turns out to be, and perhaps should be, a very different analyst from case to case.

In the opening phase of my work with a nineteen-year-old college student, new to therapy of any kind and terrified that analysis would expose him as a homosexual or worse, I found myself functioning as an analyst in ways that had little surface resemblance to the approach that I intuitively adopted as I began the treatment of a fifty-three-year-old veteran of the analytic wars who simultaneously took on his third marriage and third analyst.

Fundamentally my conscious aims were the same in both cases: to develop an alliance; to work actively with resistances as they appeared; to give the patient a beginning understanding of his patterns of behavior; to interpret transference material when it was serving as an impediment to the flow of material or when, for other reasons, it seemed appropriate to do so; and to help the patient become aware of warded-off affects and conflicts that were neither too far beneath the surface nor too threatening to him. Yet my way of working in the two cases could not have been more different.

Aware of the extent of the young man's anxiety and the conflicts that fueled it and recalling my own fears when, at a comparable age, I began treatment, my interventions were cast in a style and manner that were implicitly reassuring. Although to interpret my patient's defensive style early and actively seemed particularly important in this case, I found myself interpreting in ways that sought to mitigate not only the defenses but his pervasive anxiety. I did not allow silence to continue for long periods. Rather I intervened quickly to bring to the surface the resistances that were blocking the patient. Important among these were the homosexual fears, and although this was in some sense "deep" material and much feared, I found it necessary to interpret these from the outset. I did so in a supportive manner, however, all the time keeping an eye on the patient's self-esteem as well as on his anxiety.

Although if asked to explain my approach I might have come up with a more or less sophisticated rationalization to account for it, it was in large measure intuitive and spontaneous, based on a preconscious reading of the patient. Rationally I was making an effort to reduce resistances and thereby open a path for further analytic work. Less consciously and planfully, I was also seeking to develop a working relationship with the patient by demonstrating to him both that the analytic process could be less frightening and more helpful than he imagined and that I, as his analyst, was allied with him in his struggle to understand his fears.

With the battle-scarred veteran I was quite a different analyst. This patient, incidentally, had failed in two previous attempts at analysis with world class analysts and had initiated this latest endeavor with the remark that his decision to enter analysis a third time represented the triumph of hope over experience. Although in this case, too, I believed it important to build an alliance that could help carry the treatment, the way that I intuitively chose to do so was through another route.

This patient was tough, wealthy, and autocratic. In all of his dealings, both personal and professional, he had displayed a well-developed capacity to manipulate others. I had the impression that in part the failure of his previous treatments could be attributed to his being able to manipulate his analysts. In the opening phase of this analysis, therefore, I found myself functioning technically much more in the model of the analyst who initially listens quietly and observes than I had in the first case. In both situations I focused at first on defenses and resistances and dealt as tactfully as I could with transference issues as they arose, but, without consciously thinking about the matter or deliberately assuming a particular technical stance, my manner with the older man was more reserved, less directly supportive. Responding no doubt to a variety of communications and metacommunications that passed between us, I found myself setting limits as an early and essential basis for our future work. In manner and behavior I was letting my patient know that there would be no manipulation this time; that we were here to do a job, no nonsense permitted, and that I, at least, was intent on doing that job. In sending such a message I sometimes felt as though I was behaving like the teachers in a Bronx junior high school who live according to their fundamental rule: Don't smile until Christmas.

In a third case, my approach was once again somewhat different. Ms. D was a young writer who grew up in a family in which avoidance of the truth, self-deception, and the deception of others were standard operating procedures. Her father, a gifted artist, struggled most of his adult life with an alcohol problem whose existence he could not bring himself to acknowledge until he literally collapsed at work. He also became involved in numerous affairs with both men and women, and although he left ample clues concerning these relationships about the house, they were discreetly ignored by my patient and her family.

Ms. D's father rarely spoke openly about his feelings. He was a self-contained man given more to indirection than to a direct confrontation with emotions. His emotions, however, came through in his paintings which often depicted, in only slightly disguised form, themes from family life. On one level my patient understood these communications, and the ambivalence—and sometimes downright hostility—toward his family that her father evidenced in his art disturbed her deeply. On the level of conscious awareness, however, they did not register. A bit like the fetishist who can hold in suspension two quite contradictory notions concerning truths of anatomy, she knew and she didn't know the truth about her father's feelings.

Ms. D's mother, too, was a denier. Attempting at all times to put the best face on things, she refused to recognize the extent of her husband's problems, the serious difficulties that beset her marriage, or the pain and suffering experienced by her children. She, too, began to act out, having affairs of her own that were as ill-concealed as her husband's and whose existence was as little acknowledged by the family.

Ms. D's own behavior followed this pattern. A keen observer, she took in much, said little, and allowed only a fraction of what she observed to register consciously. Like her parents, she also tended to minimize or deny both the effect that disturbing experiences had on her and the impact that she had on others. At times this quality came through as innocence or naiveté. At others it appeared to be a kind of pseudo-stupidity occurring in someone of keen intelligence and impressive talent.

Ms. D had previously been in treatment with a therapist whose behavior was unorthodox to say the least. Not only did he speak at length about himself and his family, suggesting that his attitudes and values become models for my patient, but he became familiar with her in ways that seemed grossly inappropriate. About this experience Ms. D said little. It was a secret to be protected, very much like certain behaviors of her parents. And as was true of Ms. D's perceptions of her family, much that she perceived about her former therapist was not available to conscious awareness.

It was clear from the outset of her analysis that Ms. D was taking in far more about me than she spoke about—or than she even knew. And what she took in, I realized, was of the greatest importance both in giving specific form and shape to the transference and in providing a nidus for the development of powerful resistances.

If I had followed standard technique in this case, carefully following the patient's associations, identifying and interpreting important preconscious material as it rose to the surface with due consideration for tact and timing, it is unlikely that much progress could have been achieved. For reasons deeply embedded in a network of identifications that had become part of her defensive system, Ms. D's associations did not contain what was most vital at the moment: her perceptions of her analyst and of the analytic situation. I had no doubt that such perceptions were registering preconsciously but they were concealed from both of us.

It was necessary from early on to throw away the book and to go after material that was not readily apparent, or at least showed no evidence of surfacing at the moment. Efforts to follow the more usual method of interpreting Ms. D's defenses, particularly those related to the omission of transference material and to its failure to register in consciousness, proved futile. So entrenched were these protections that I soon became convinced that I could interpret them endlessly without causing the slightest dent in this armor. It seemed necessary to shake up the system, to introduce ideas that Ms. D had not thought of, and to ask questions that initially must have seemed to be the concerns of a demented narcissist. No doubt my patient regarded me as an analyst more bizarre by far than her former therapist and one who, although physically present behind the couch, was clearly floating in outer space.

If, at the beginning of our hour the material that was surfacing was clearly defensive, leading nowhere, I would break in. I would interpret the resistance, but I would then go on. I had noticed, I would say, that Ms. D had been looking at my tie, my haircut, or my unstylish new shoes. In the waiting room, I might add, she seemed to be taking in something about my face; was it that I looked preoccupied, tired, sad—or glad to see her? She seemed also to have noticed my former patient as he left. I wondered if she was not aware of some thoughts about him or about the relationship that he had with me.

All of this, of course, ran the risk of veering off into wild analysis or into a preoccupation with transference perceptions that would make Gill look like a slow-motion Kohutian. Yet I felt intuitively on the basis of what I knew about the patient and what I sensed was happening in her hours that it was essential to bring to Ms. D's awareness what she was clearly taking in about me. Given her history and her own defensive style, such perceptions were of critical importance and had to be dealt with from the very outset of treatment. Ms. D had to be made aware not only of what she took in and therefore "knew" preconsciously about me but, that I, unlike her parents, was aware of what was happening and would not let it pass.

Was this approach intrusive, undiplomatic, neglectful of defenses, or insufficiently respectful of them? Probably. Was it an example of well-accepted technique in the opening phase? Surely not. I doubt if, at the time, I would have presented this case to a technique seminar at my Institute. I had broken most, if not all, the rules of standard procedure. Yet from such beginnings the analysis took flight. At first puzzled and even alarmed by the eccentricity of her analyst, she soon understood what I was about. She began to bring in observations spontaneously and to catch hold of ones that she had made but that were already in the process of slipping away. At one point she even brought in material about me that she had learned from a former patient prior to beginning her analysis. This was material that she swore to herself she would never reveal; material that had already colored her view of me in important ways and that unless openly discussed would have constituted the core of formidable, and perhaps unworkable, resistances.

I end this account with a brief anecdote. One day Ms. D was going on at some length about the intricacies of a book contract that she was negotiating. The attitudes of agent, publisher, and editor were described as were all the fine points of law involved. I was listening as attentively as I could, but suddenly the patient broke off in midsentence; "I can feel that you're restless," she said, "you're not really interested. You know that this is merely filler and you want to know what I'm really thinking, what I've really observed. All right, doctor, I'd like to ask you a question. Is that a noodle on your shoe?" I looked down and my face turned red. Clinging to my shoe was a thin remnant of a quick dinner I had eaten just prior to seeing Ms. D, a scrawny but tenacious piece of noodle. I did not know what to say. Could I acknowledge the truth and suffer total humiliation? There seemed no choice.

"I guess it is," I replied. Then out of nowhere a thought came to mind and before I could censor it, it popped out.

"I'm always using my noodle," I added. Ms. D laughed.

"You're being defensive, doctor," she chided. "In situations like this one has to put aside rationalizations and confront the harsh reality. This is a noodle plain and simple; by the looks of it an egg noodle that has fallen from your plate and has clung to your shoe. My parents might try to avoid the issue but I expect more of you. You have to face the unvarnished truth; there is very definitely and palpably a noodle on your shoe."

Ms. D was having fun turning the tables on me. But in doing so she revealed not only that she understood the issues, but that she accepted the necessity of facing hard truths. Although we had followed a path not usually taken to get there, we had come down the road quite a piece. This was a moment of low comedy, but also, for both of us, a high point in the treatment.

I am well aware that in each of these cases certain reactions that might come under the general rubric of countertransference reactions played a role in influencing my response. I felt keenly for the frightened young student and through memories of my own no doubt identified with him in more than an optimal way. In the case of the older man I experienced a threat of being manipulated and, in addition, was very probably in competition with the senior analysts who had in fact fallen under his spell. Ms. D's situation stirred up memories of certain troubling duplicities in my own family that must have stimulated in me wishes for her to face the truth as I had found useful to do.

Although my technique was influenced by these personal responses, I do not think that this was entirely a negative factor. Reacting spontaneously with responses that inevitably include a mix of some personal as well as more objective elements, the analyst uses his intuitive understanding of the patient's present state of mind and character to make unconscious adjustments in his technique. While no doubt this process of adjustment takes place throughout the course of analysis, it plays a prominent and, perhaps essential, role in the beginning phase of treatment.

In short, it is the messages sent and received by patient and analyst as they begin to work together and enter upon the initial period of mutual exploration that become the basis for the establishment of an unspoken contract that goes beyond formal arrangements or technical procedures. Certain rules and limits are established and certain values communicated. Moreover, each party discovers a good deal about the other. Some of what we learn, of course, becomes immediately enmeshed in transference responses. This is true of the analyst as well as the patient and transferences developing even as early as the first session can have the most profound effect on the course and outcome of treatment. This is a point I will return to shortly.

In all of this the analyst is trying to get the treatment off on the right foot. Concerned throughout its duration about the proper conduct of the analysis, he nonetheless knows that he must pay special attention to the opening phase because of its enduring impact on both participants. While it is true that some good marriages start off badly, it is also true that a good many that begin badly never recover from that bad start. The old saying that the fellow who misbuttons the top button of his shirt is wrong all the way down the line, may apply more frequently than we think in the analytic situation.

I would like to give two examples of such false starts in analysis; beginnings that were influenced not only by communications taking place during the initial interviews, but especially by the metacommunications. While, as I have mentioned, rapidly developing transferences are of the greatest importance to the future course of an analysis, it is not only transference distortions that are important. The clues picked up by each person about the other, clues that register nonverbally as well as by means of the spoken word, can set the tone of treatment, influence the form that transferences take in both individuals, and can exert a far-reaching influence on the analytic process. Sometimes the impressions formed by patient and analyst about the other surface early and become part of the ongoing analytic work. Quite often, however, this does not happen and these impressions go underground. From this subterranean position, well concealed and not easily approachable, these secrets feed the negative transference, strengthen resistances, influence the quality of the alliance, and in other ways put obstacles in the way of effective analytic work.

Such was the case with Mr. N, a man who came to see me after bringing an unsuccessful, and in his mind, horrendous, analytic experience to a close. He had been in treatment with a younger colleague, someone I did not know well, but whose contained, rather stiff manner I found somewhat off-putting.

Mr. N's description of the treatment made his analyst sound
even more rigid and inflexible than I had supposed. By his
account, the analyst repeated endlessly interpretations that had
become sterile, if they were not initially so, and harped on the
transference in ways that sounded thoroughly unproductive.
The analysis had started as a student case and Mr. N had perceived, quite correctly I thought, that his analyst needed him
as a patient so that he could graduate. Soon after his graduation,
the analysis came to a grinding halt.

Mr. N had for some years been living a homosexual life-
style, although he had not fully accepted his homosexuality. It
remained, he said, an area of conflict for him. Listening to his
story, I experienced a mixture of feelings that were not easy
to sort out. On the one hand, I was impressed by Mr. N's
intelligence, his sophisticated and clever use of language, his
seeming capacity for insight, and by his obvious perceptivity.
I thought that in all likelihood his analysis had been complicated
and ultimately undermined by the analyst's inexperience, by
the fact that he was a student and had needs of his own that
interfered with objectivity, and by certain unresolved transference–countertransference interactions. From that perspective
I thought that Mr. N deserved another try at analysis in a
different setting and with someone who might be better able
to handle this complex and difficult man.

That he was difficult I had no doubt. Not only did he have
a perverse symptom, but there were perverse elements in his
character, including much sadism and a wish to be beaten, the
analysis of which promised to be a long and difficult task. There
was no doubt that he needed help and I empathized with his
plight as a person who had not benefited from analysis and
who now found himself out in the cold. There was, however,
something about him that made me uneasy. Perhaps it was the
way he spoke about his former analyst. Sharp-tongued, witty,
and astute, he was also cruel. He could describe every flaw in
his therapist, every mistake he made, and every useless interpretation offered in precise detail. He was a master of the incisive and brutal put-down.

Perhaps because I identified with the younger analyst and
knew well what it was like to stumble and fall in learning anal-

ysis, perhaps because I knew intuitively what would be in store for me in working with Mr. N, I recoiled inwardly at this merciless attack. I began to feel uncomfortable with Mr. N and was aware that the positive feelings that initially I felt toward him were eroding. I wondered, symptoms aside, if I was not dealing with a mean-spirited individual. Moreover, from what I had now heard about the history of his homosexuality, its origins in childhood, its lengthy and unbroken history, and the absence in Mr. N of any sexual interest in women, I became convinced that the perversion was deeply rooted in character and that even a lengthy second analysis had little chance of altering it.

At the same time I realized that, although dramatized and overdone, much of what Mr. N had said about his former analyst was probably true. Perhaps I myself was being unduly defensive for my colleague. Besides, had I not been surprised more than once by seeing seemingly intractable cases prove workable? Could I play God and predict what would happen down the analytic road? Clearly I was having a complex countertransference response to Mr. N, I thought, and to let this kind of reaction unduly color my judgment might be a serious mistake. I decided, after all, to go ahead, to give Mr. N a second shot at analysis, and to see what happened.

To make a long story short, the analysis proceeded ponderously, like an alligator swimming through a pool of molasses, until after two years it slithered to a virtual halt. Much was talked about, much interpreted, and at least, intellectually, much understood, but there was no movement. Neither symptomatically, in the transference, nor in character pathology had there been change in some months. Mr. N and I, not surprisingly, had come to a place not very different from that reached by the previous stalemated effort. And Mr. N, in his acid style, did not hesitate to share with me his opinion both of me and of the entire field of psychoanalysis. He was not, however, only furious. I detected in his attacks a note of pain, and particularly, of hurt. He was wounded. When I inquired about this, he talked at first about the disappointment he felt in his treatment and of his failed expectations for a different and better life. Then, gradually he revealed something else. He talked about how he knew I did not like him from the very first session, that I had

16

been put off by his caustic tongue, and that I regarded his homosexuality as untreatable. He had decided to stay with me, however, because he also felt that I believed what he said about his previous analysis, because I was an experienced person who had helped others he knew, and because he sensed that, despite my feelings, I was trying to understand him. Moreover, he knew he could be obnoxious and that anyone who worked with him would sooner or later come to dislike him. What he did not add, but which also played a role in his decision, was Mr. N's penchant for masochism.

My patient's revelation in this session of what he had perceived about me constituted a milestone in his treatment. Although I rarely share my countertransference feelings directly with a patient or reveal to him what I am experiencing in the course of analysis, I did so in this case. I told Mr. N that he was right, that what he had perceived was true, and that I thought that much of what had transpired thus far between us had been colored by these perceptions. He agreed, and then he went on to relate some observations that he had made about my person that he had heretofore kept to himself.

We cleared the air and in doing so developed a working alliance for the first time. In this new atmosphere I discovered what, intellectually, I knew but had not been able to feel; that Mr. N's less likable qualities, his rage and his sadism, were largely defensive and the products of much suffering. He was a difficult and often exasperating fellow but there were also qualities in him of loyalty, honesty, and willingness to face the truth that I had not appreciated before. With covert feelings no longer coloring the transactions between us, we were able to work together far more productively than before and the logjam slowly gave way. Although I was right about the immutable quality of Mr. N's homosexuality, he came finally to accept this aspect of his life and within this context to develop satisfying relationships. Other things, however, were changeable. Mr. N's sadism abated, he became less defensive—and offensive—and he began to use his intellectual gifts and his gift for observation and mimickry in creative ways. By the time the analysis ended, he was launched on a new career in which he could take advantage of his very considerable talents.

In the case just cited, I have stressed the importance in both analyst and patient of negative feelings developing early on in treatment which remain unspoken and unacknowledged. The same, however, may be true of positive feelings. Such feelings often go unexamined, perhaps because we tend to regard the positive transference as less potentially disruptive to treatment than negative emotions and because positive feelings, despite the pitfalls that may lie, like landmines within them, are often important allies in our analytic efforts. In speaking of positive emotions, I am referring, not only to the positive transference but to qualities actually possessed by an individual; to traits of personality and character that will evoke similar responses in most of those who encounter them.

Mr. R was a man admired and respected by everyone who knew him. A kind, generous person and an artist of high achievement whose germinal work had been an inspiration to a generation of younger painters, he also had the rare quality of being able to grasp intuitively what another person was experiencing and to empathize with that experience. Colleagues sensed this and sought him out, not only as a mentor, but as a confidant.

Before I met him professionally, I had seen and had admired Mr. R's work. Moreover, I admired him for the forthrightness and courage with which he spoke out on social and political issues. A modest and even shy person who avoided the spotlight, he nevertheless was unafraid to speak his mind when he thought his voice could serve the interests of justice and fair play.

I felt honored and humbled when this man, late in life, consulted me regarding a work block that had developed over a period of several years. I was aware, as I saw Mr. R in consultation, that my admiration for him could interfere with objectivity and constitute a problem in our work together. I resolved to, and in fact did, keep this potential danger very much in mind as we began treatment. It was, however, my overt, directly, and readily perceived feelings that I was most alert to. Only later did I realize that the subtle, less apparent, more muted aspects of my positive feelings for Mr. R—and his for me—constituted an equally important problem.

Although Mr. R had been having trouble working for some time, developing detailed and elaborate plans for canvases and not completing them, and despite the fact that it was this problem that, presumably, had motivated him to seek treatment, he did not speak much about his work. Rather he dwelt on his life story, providing much information about his growing up in rural America and about his family. He also spoke at length about his marriage and children and particularly about certain quite devastating losses that he had experienced in recent years.

When Mr. R did mention his art, it was in rather general terms, putting emphasis on the plans he had for current and future work. He did not elaborate on the kinds of difficulties he was having in painting, and when, finally, I asked him about these his responses were rather vague and nonspecific.

I began to think that Mr. R was demonstrating with me the very symptoms that he was struggling with on the outside. He could not get into detailed descriptions of his work just as in his studio he could not come to grips with the specific artistic problems involved in the process of composition. The work block he was experiencing, I thought, might very well be related to a need to avoid certain affects brought to the surface by the act of painting and connected with the shattering recent losses he had endured. From this perspective Mr. R could be said to be struggling with incomplete mourning mixed with a depressive reaction that had gone unrecognized. On the basis of such an initial formulation, on Mr. R's seeming interest in self-exploration, and on his unique capacity for insight, I offered him a trial of analysis.

I won't go into all the details of this case, which would take me too far from the issue at hand, but will merely say that in my understanding of Mr. R I was both right and wrong. Some of the dynamics that I have just mentioned did, in fact, play an important role in his problems and analysis of the underlying conflicts helped both to mobilize an arrested mourning reaction and to aid Mr. R in working through depressive feelings of long duration. It was also true, however, that another factor was of equal importance in contributing to the clinical picture, a factor that for many months I did not understand. From the outset of treatment Mr. R was sending me signals that he did not wish to, and in fact did not dare, explore his work problem in any but the most superficial way. Politely, tactfully, less than consciously, he was warning me off, signaling me to stay away.

I had regarded this communication as an aspect of his symptom, the product of an underlying depression, and in this diagnosis I was not entirely wrong. But what I failed to grasp was that Mr. R's need to avoid investigation of this problem and to maintain the status quo derived from another source. Over the past several years, as he approached the age of seventy, Mr. R perceived in himself some loss of artistic power. His imagination did not seem as rich, his hand not as sure. He no longer approached his canvases with boldness, vigor, and confidence. He felt that his abilities were on the decline, that he could no longer produce the art that his public expected. He dreaded failure, and when an exhibition of oils done in the past decade received only respectful notices, he stopped working. Going to his studio every day and spending long hours there, he nonetheless produced nothing. Forever planning, outlining, sketching, he painted little and what he did manage to get on canvas he soon erased, dissatisfied with one aspect or another of the composition.

Mr. R could not face the idea that he was not the artist of old, that his powers were waning. Somehow I sensed this and because I admired and liked him so much, I wanted to spare him a confrontation with so harsh a reality. Moreover, for my own reasons, I had a need to see Mr. R as immutable, untouched by age or time. I had watched my father become invalided in his later years and lose critical functions. These painful memories were evoked by Mr. R's situation. An old childhood need of mine to be associated with a man of strength whom I could make into a hero no doubt also played a role in the scotoma I had developed. But there was something else as well. At that time my own functioning at work was not up to par. Due to a loss I had suffered I was, like Mr. R, experiencing both mourning and depression. Although I carried a full schedule and found being at work personally helpful, I realized that my mind was not as sharp, not as well focused, as before. Not infrequently I found my thoughts drifting to my own situation and to my own pain.

A perceptive and intuitive man, Mr. R had sensed this difficulty in me. Without quite being able to put his finger on what was wrong, he felt that I was not all there. He said nothing to me, but discreetly made inquiries. Through contacts with former patients of mine, he learned the truth. Mr. R had, before we met, heard good things about me and was predisposed to like me, just as I was primed to like him. We quickly developed a strong rapport and from the outset of treatment Mr. R felt positively about me. He did not want to hurt me and he felt that to mention the observations he had made would do just that. Moreover, having the fresh experience of loss himself, he empathized with me. Less consciously, Mr. R also sensed that to bring up my difficulties in functioning threatened to bring up his own. For that reason, too, he steered clear of this sensitive area.

From my side I also wanted to avoid an issue that was painful and disturbing to me. By focusing on what I saw as Mr. R's temporary and reversible situation, his problem in mourning and his depression, I was also, in essence, reassuring myself. Neither he nor you, I was saying, has suffered a permanent decline. No doubt my patient's reactions would turn out to be transient, as would mine. With proper understanding and with the passage of time both would fade away and we would be restored to our old selves.

In fact, with activation of mourning in Mr. R and with the working through of aspects of his depression, some of the abilities that he feared had been lost now returned. They had been compromised, as I had first imagined, by his depression and by the strong need for self-punishment that accompanied it. Not all of Mr. R's capacities were restored, however, and he had to face certain inevitable changes that accompany aging. He was a man of great resources, though, and when he finally confronted the truth he could make certain adjustments in his approach that allowed him to go on working.

In his process of adaptation I could be helpful. It was not, however, possible for me to be of much help to Mr. R until I had faced and dealt with the full range of my countertransference reactions in this situation. When I finally did some homework and confronted both my own fear of being permanently disabled and my need to see Mr. R as a man immune from aging, I could help him face difficult truths in himself. In doing this we both had to look hard not only at our personal ghosts, but at our reactions to each other. Although it was awkward and uncomfortable to do so, we had to explore the warm and positive feelings that we felt toward each other. Of particular importance in this regard was the way that each of us had made use of these feelings. In a valuable article, Martin Stein (1981) has pointed out that the unobjectionable positive transference can, covertly, contain important negative elements. To this insight, perhaps, can be added another useful finding: that positive feelings arising in analysis, both transference and otherwise, can sometimes function as screens. In that capacity they not only conceal their negative counterparts, but they keep from conscious awareness much that both patient and analyst do not want to see about themselves.

Although we are accustomed to thinking of the opening phase of analysis as constituting the beginning weeks or months of analytic work, sometimes, from the point of view of important transference developments, the beginnings of analysis have their origin at a much earlier time. For certain patients such beginnings go back months or years to consultations done at that time or to periods of psychotherapy that have taken place then. For others, transferences have taken root as the result of other encounters with the analyst. These include public lectures he may have given, presentations made by him at professional meetings, or classes he has taught. Sometimes a casual social contact can provide the nidus for the development of transferences that have far-reaching influence on the course and outcome of later analytic work. The analyst, too, may be influenced in subtle, but important, ways by his earlier contacts with people who later become analytic patients. These may be junior colleagues, students at an institute or residency program, individuals whom he has met in other settings, or even public personalities whose work may be known to the analyst or whose media image has colored his perceptions. Although in all these situations the formal analytic work has not yet begun, in a very real sense the analysis has started. Not only are transferences activated, but fantasies quickly arise and defenses against conflictual thoughts and feelings can be observed. It is quite common today for psychoanalysis to be preceded by a shorter or longer period of psychotherapy, with conversion to analysis being more the rule than the exception. While it is a well-accepted fact that a patient's experience in psychotherapy inevitably exerts a significant, and often enduring, influence on his subsequent experience of analysis, the more specific issues of how such prior contact with the analyst may affect the earliest stages of analysis remains a question that has not, as yet, been well explored. I want briefly to mention a case which illustrates some of the issues that may arise.

When Mr. F first consulted me he was in a state of panic. Recently divorced from a woman who was emotionally unstable and erratic in her behavior, he had left the city he was living in, fled to New York, and found himself totally adrift. The reality of his situation was compounded by fantasies of starving and perishing on the street, long-held ideas that had plagued Mr. F since early childhood.

When Mr. F was seven, his father was killed in an accident and his mother, totally bereft and feeling unable to care for her young child, gave him over to a cousin to raise. This woman knew little about taking care of children and found the task onerous. Often mean and critical, she would threaten Mr. F with banishment, a threat that touched on the child's greatest fears. Mr. F thoroughly disliked this harsh and dictatorial woman and regarded her as the wicked witch of the West. At the same time he needed her and very much feared being cast out. For years Mr. F thought of returning to his mother and of finding a home with her, but in time reality bore in on him and he realized that she was emotionally incapable of providing such a refuge for him. Mr. F harbored deep and long-lasting resentment toward his mother both for her abandonment of him and for her subsequent failure to rescue him from Hades.

My initial work with Mr. F lasted a few months. In his state of mind I did not regard him as suitable for analysis and it was clear that his most pressing need was for therapeutic work that would help him settle down. He did, in fact, settle down rather quickly and when he did, revealed himself to be an imaginative and creative, if highly narcissistic, individual. It seemed to me that he might profit from an analysis at a future time and he agreed that this seemed a good idea. It was clear, though, that he was not yet ready. His life, though less chaotic, still contained many uncertainties. He knew neither where he was going to live nor where he would work. Much remained to be decided.

After Mr. F had been in New York about a month, he met a woman with two children who had recently lost her husband. They immediately struck it off, shared their mutual fright and grief, and within a short time decided to marry. The decision was a sudden one and I pointed out the potential pitfalls of so precipitous a move, but Mr. F, thinking that he had found someone stable, reliable, and generous, was determined to proceed. At that point his remaining symptoms diminished, as did his motivation to seek help, and he experienced a sense of well-being. It seemed reasonable at that point to stop therapy and to await developments. If all went well, perhaps further treatment would not be indicated. If not, analysis might be considered. To continue on with a mixed bag of therapy in the absence of clear need seemed to make no sense. I shared these thoughts with Mr. F and he agreed, rather sadly, that it would be best to bring our work to at least a temporary halt.

I did not see Mr. F again for several years. When I did he was on the verge of divorce. His wife, he said, had turned out to be a carbon copy of his cousin; petty, mean-spirited, critical, and avaricious. She wanted to use him to care for her children, while she gave little in return. She was a totally self-involved person, the second deeply troubled woman that he had chosen. After a brief consultation period, we both agreed that analysis would be necessary if Mr. F were to make genuine progress in resolving his problems, and we began the treatment soon thereafter.

The previous psychotherapy had been characterized by a strong positive transference. Regarding me as wise, informed, and skilled, Mr. F also saw me as a strong, reliable man who could, and would, save him.

Now, in analysis, all those good feelings were gone. From the start of treatment Mr. F experienced me as unreliable, incompetent, untrustworthy, and worse. He complained bitterly about everything I said or did and it seemed as though no working alliance, or even a facsimile of one, could be developed. The analysis was upended before it began. Efforts to investigate Mr. F's negative feelings did not carry very far. He was so caught up in them that he could not gain sufficient distance to utilize an interpretation. All efforts to work with Mr. F seemed quite futile, but I continued to do so in the hope that some breakthrough could be made and some understanding of his intense reaction to me at the start of analysis obtained.

It took more than a year for this negative feeling to dissipate, but slowly it began to lose its force. Then, finally, we could talk about Mr. F's reaction and review what had happened. What became clear was that the analytic situation had evoked a set of powerful memories relating to Mr. F's childhood experience of abandonment. Under the influence of regression stimulated in part by the analytic situation and in part by the stresses of his life situation, Mr. F had begun to relive parts of his childhood trauma. He began to spin out not just a series of fantasies, but an entire scenario in which the key people in his life were assigned particular roles. His wife became the witchlike cousin and her children were fused with his cousin's children whom he believed she favored. I was the mother who had betrayed him by turning him over to the cousin, and he could not forgive me for the injury I had done him. All of this, of course, antedated the beginning of analysis. It referred to the earlier period of therapy and to the fact that I had stopped seeing Mr. F in treatment. In his mind I had cast him out and instead of protecting him, had put him in the hands of a malevolent and mean-spirited person. For this I had to pay. Although Mr. F's reaction, deriving its power from devastating childhood trauma, was unusual in its intensity, the beginnings of analysis are not infrequently colored both by experiences of childhood and by prior contacts with the analyst. In some patients such initial therapeutic contacts, which oftentimes are experienced as more supportive than the ensuing analytic situation, are unconsciously compared to that situation and the comparison evokes memories of early loss or deprivation. This sequence can be responsible for the negative transference reactions, often of surprising intensity, which may develop in an analysis that follows a psychotherapy that has been characterized by the presence of a strong therapeutic alliance.

As a final example, I would like to demonstrate the way that memories of childhood, operating in both patient and analyst, can interact to create difficulties in beginning an analysis. For both people the newness of the enterprise stimulates a storehouse of memories and feelings that have to do with beginnings. New relationships, new schools, new doctors, new teachers, new neighborhoods, new adventures, all are evoked by the new analytic relationship. The unconscious wishes and fantasies arising from both sides of the couch interact and contribute to the transferences in both participants. When such transferences are predominantly negative the analysis may have considerable difficulty getting off the ground. Or if it does, its flight may prove to be a short-lived one.

In the case of Mr. B the lift-off was far from smooth. A bright, imaginative, and verbal young man of twenty-four, he lay for days and weeks on the couch looking miserable, saying very little, and in what he did say hugging the shore of reality.

To his analyst this behavior came as a total surprise—and a severe disappointment. I had expected quite the opposite, a patient who was highly verbal and who would fill the hours with interesting and complex material. Sitting up, Mr. B had given promise of being just such a patient. I had met him on three occasions just before the summer break and we had agreed to start analysis in the fall when I had relocated to a new office. In these interviews, Mr. B spoke easily and articulately, making associative links readily and relating a fascinating life story. Prior to our meeting he had written to me a few times from another city where he had been at school and in these letters had expressed himself with style and grace. I expected him to be a most intriguing person who would take easily to the analytic process.

What had happened then? Had I been entirely wrong in my assessment? It certainly looked that way. Frustrated, angry, and discouraged, I began to doubt if this case could work out and after a few weeks I was contemplating a switch to psychotherapy. My doubts were augmented by the fact that I had no clues as to what had caused so profound a change in Mr.

B. On one occasion, when he entered the office, however, I noticed him looking disdainfully at a lamp that I had purchased. He also scanned the room quite carefully, almost sniffing with contempt at several other new purchases. Although on the couch he said nothing about his observations, I called his attention to his behavior. Gradually, with much resistance, Mr. B revealed how much he disliked my new office. He was critical of every aspect of it from carpet to window blinds. After he had finished his appraisal of the entire room, I was ready to send back the furniture, hire a decorator, and start over.

What Mr. B was expressing in his behavior was, like Mr. F, a set of memories. These had to do with a family move at age nine. Mr. B was bitterly unhappy about the change in school, neighborhood, and friends that was necessitated by the move, and later on in life blamed many of the misfortunes that befell him on that unhappy situation. Although he had said little to his parents about his feelings, in his mind he was highly critical of them for the move and for their purchase of an unattractive new house. His behavior became quiet and withdrawn. For several months he spoke to no one.

In analysis, too, Mr. B kept his own counsel. Saying nothing about his reaction to the change I had made, he simply relived and acted out the severe disappointment in childhood that he had suffered. It was only his nonverbal behavior that provided a clue to Mr. B's feelings.

For my part, my reaction to Mr. B was colored by troubling memories of my own. When I first met him he looked familiar in a way that I could not pin down, and since I could not make a connection to anyone in my past, I let the matter drop. As I struggled later on to understand my own strong reactions of disappointment and discouragement in the face of Mr. B's resistances, I remembered not only who it was that he resembled, but that the two individuals shared the same first name.

The long forgotten figure was a distant relative of mine who, one summer, came from Canada to spend a month with us. This young man, who was perhaps five or six years older than myself, had written several times to me and I found his letters intriguing. I imagined him to be a brilliant and exotic foreigner who would teach me all kinds of wonderful things. I looked forward eagerly to his visit.

Needless to say, I was bitterly disappointed. This relative turned out to be a household drudge who did nothing but eat apples and sit around watching television. He had little to say and what he said was mostly pretentious and inane. I was glad after a few weeks to see him go.

In the analysis similar feelings arose with regard to Mr. B. I had fantasies of his quitting treatment and my being none too unhappy about it. Fortunately, I did not act on these fantasies. Nor did Mr. B act on his strong wish to leave treatment. Rather, in time, we both were able to come in touch with the unhappy memories of new experiences that lay behind our current reactions. When we did so the analysis was able, finally, to lift off from the launching pad on which it had been stalled and, some years later, to complete its mission.

I cite this example, not for its uniqueness, but rather because situations of this kind arise with some frequency. Awareness of the network of associations that are stirred in the analyst by beginning a new case and his efforts to put himself in contact with the memories and fantasies that color his expectations, constitute an important, and sometimes essential, piece of self-analysis. For oftentimes it is those subtle and covert communications extending beyond the realm of interpretation that exert the strongest influence, not only on the opening phase, but on the entire analytic experience.

II

Transference as a Process:
Interactive Elements

2

The Interplay of Enactments: Their Role in the Analytic Process

One of the important advances that has occurred in psycho-analysis in recent years has been our growing recognition of the role of enactments as pathways for communication in the analytic situation. When, formerly, analysts spoke of enactments, they were referring primarily to enactments on the part of the patient. Rarely did the analyst's enactments come in for equal scrutiny. Now, due largely to the pioneering work of Dale Boesky (1982, 1989), James McLaughlin (1988), Warren Poland (1988), and a number of other colleagues, we have come to appreciate not only that enactments flow from both sides of the couch and are very much a two-way street, but that the interplay of enactments between the two participants in the analytic situation provides a rich source of valuable information.

In a thoughtful review of the concept, Boesky (1989) has defined enactments as "experiences or behaviors which have an actualizing intention." By actualization he means "experience and/or behavior which is motivated by wish fulfillment in such a manner that the person is attempting to gratify wishes of which he may be consciously unaware" (p. 3). When an enactment takes place, Boesky points out, the individual who carries

31

it out is seeking, often unconsciously, to persuade himself "that a wish is being gratified rather than only wished for." An essential feature of enactments then, is "the transformation of ideas and fantasies into a performance which seems real. Whether it is the patient or analyst who is creating the enactment," Boesky says, "it is an essential component of his wish that the witness of the performance should join him in the suspension of disbelief." There is, therefore, a compelling quality to enactments, which derives, I believe, from the fact that such behavior is not the outcome of rational thought and judgment nor are significant contributions made to it by the ego's capacities for anticipation, frustration tolerance, or delay. Though a compromise formation which draws on elements from ego and superego as well as the drives, enactments express wishes, fantasies, and memories in ways that have more in common with impulsive behavior than with considered actions. Thus, ordinarily, enactments are carried out before the wishful elements that motivate them reach consciousness. Often containing unconscious fantasies as well as expressing subtle and interlocking dimensions of transference and resistance of which neither patient nor analyst has yet become aware, enactments, properly explored, are particularly useful in providing cues as to the operation of forces in the treatment situation that, although not yet visible, are affecting it in essential ways. From this perspective, then, enactments both reflect aspects of and contribute to the analytic process. The interweaving of enactments, in fact, constitutes an essential, if sometimes overlooked, aspect of that process.

My aim in this chapter is to illustrate the interplay of enactments at various stages in two analyses. I hope to show how these enactments illuminated features of the cases that were not otherwise apparent and how understanding the covert messages contained within them helped to deepen and advance the analytic work.

The first case that I would like to describe is that of an individual whom I found intimidating. Highly intelligent, verbally nimble, flamboyant, and professionally successful, Mr. V, to all appearances, was an engaging and often charming fellow. Beneath the polished veneer, however, there was about him something menacing. Just what this quality was, however, was not easy to define. Although only rarely did he display anger openly, one had the impression that a raging fire burned within him and that, above all, he was not a man to be tampered with.

It was through an enactment occurring at the very outset of treatment that I first experienced the aggression that lay just millimeters beneath Mr. V's surface charm. During the initial consultation interviews he was the soul of cordiality. Thoughtful, capable of insights, and well motivated, he appeared at the same time to be an eminently reasonable, and often witty, man. Nowhere to be seen was the wellspring of anger that emerged as we began the analytic work.

It appeared, in fact, on the first day of Mr. V's analysis. A few seconds after the buzzer sounded announcing his arrival, I started for the waiting room to greet him. I did not get far. When I opened the door of my office, there he was, filling the entranceway, standing not more than a few inches in front of me. Nodding curtly, he swept into the room like a linebacker blitzing the quarterback, took off his jacket and stretched out on the couch. I was stunned. I felt as though I had opened the door to a tornado which, within seconds, had ripped through my office, leaving in its wake a disquieting and eerie calm.

Remarkably calm, in fact, was Mr. V as congenially, almost conspiratorially, he launched into an account of certain events that had taken place in his office. For some time he spoke about an employee who, although deferential in manner, had committed the cardinal sin of infringing on territory that my patient regarded as his own. A chill seized me as Mr. V, speaking in a modulated, controlled voice, disclosed his plan to get even. Like a Mafia chieftain who has been crossed, he would bide his time, wait until the proper moment arrived and, then, with a single deft stroke, eliminate the offender from his life. One had the impression that his victim would not know what hit him. Suddenly, instantaneously, he would be gone, severed from Mr. V's firm and given a half-hour to clean out his desk. Moreover, this man would forever be an enemy. Mr. V would never forgive him his trespass and, in future, would go out of his way to make his life miserable. Mr. V's manner, as he spoke, was companionable, even chummy; what he said was menacing. As I listened, I found myself sitting forward in my chair, my musculature tense, my eyes fixed on the patient as he lay remarkably still on the couch. Watching him I was reminded of the famous painting by Rousseau which depicts a large tiger, eyes burning, lying among high grasses, waiting to spring. But who was that tiger? Viewing the immobile figure in front of me who, in muted tones, spoke of stark vengeance and observing myself, the concealed analyst, listening in a state of tension, poised to interpret my patient's covert aggression, I could not be sure.

Clearly, important transactions were occurring between Mr. V and myself. Swiftly, aggressively, he had moved into the office, pushing past me and evoking in me the feeling that my space was being invaded. Then, lying on the couch and speaking in tones of easy cordiality, he revealed in what he said that he was an angry, vengeful person. Through enactments of my own, expressed in bodily posture and vocal quality, I was responding to him not only with protective vigilance, but with an unconscious need to appease this menacing figure. This latter reaction I recognized through my manner of interpreting. Rationally, I understood that beneath his anger, behind the wish to strike back and hurt others, was a wounded man. Physically and mentally brutalized by a disturbed and vicious older brother, he had been left unprotected by troubled and ineffectual parents. Unable to defend himself, he had also been sexually used by this brother. Hating him and yet drawn to seek his approval, Mr. V sought desperately to wrench from his heart and mind the image of the man who had tortured him and to whom he felt hopelessly attached.

As a child, Mr. V sought to emulate his brother in many ways. Often he would sneak into his brother's room to play with his games or to try on a piece of his clothing. Discovered trespassing by his sibling, he would be beaten, ejected from the room, and the door slammed in his face. His parents, too, shut him out of their lives. Self-involved and anxious people, concerned about their own survival, they could neither hear Mr. V's complaints nor respond to his needs. They clung to each other and let the children drift along on their own. Thus the enactment with which Mr. V initiated treatment, his standing inches outside my door and sweeping into the room, contained within it important facets of his history. Through it he was expressing his determination not to be shut out, not to be the extruded, expendable child but, by force if necessary, to make his presence felt. Clearly this behavior contained an aggressive response to the indifference he felt on the part of both his brother and parents. Being denied access to a room had the unconscious meaning to him of being excluded from the parental bedroom as well as his brother's room, and came to stand for the pervasive feelings of rejection that characterized his childhood.

Related to these perceptions was Mr. V's intense reaction to anyone who infringed on his territory or otherwise crossed him. In his violence and his need for revenge he was expressing not only years of pent-up rage, but an identification with those who victimized and rejected him.

When, in time, I understood this aspect of Mr. V's history, I sought opportunities to bring to the fore not only the anger that smoldered beneath his surface charm but, more specifically, the feelings of hurt that fed it. When I spoke in sessions, my voice was calm, its tone soothing as I tried to convey my understanding of the trauma that Mr. V had experienced. Such an approach to someone who was responding to life with the rage of a wounded animal was, perhaps, not inappropriate. But as I listened to myself, I realized that my voice contained more than simply an effort to convey empathy. It contained a familiar undertone of fear; an attempt to appease and mollify which concealed an unconscious and encoded response to an angry man. It was the protective reaction I had, as a child, to my father's rages.

For the most part a shy and withdrawn man, my father could, when threatened, become a tyrant. I recalled the fear I felt when, at those times, his fury was unleashed and he turned with wrath on those around him. Alone in my room, I would hear him ranting at my mother, his voice on fire and threatening to destroy anyone in his path. Sometimes his rage would be directed at me. At those times I would seek the safety of my room and, shutting the door, hope against hope that he would stay out. Often he did, but sometimes the door would swing open and, bursting into the room as Mr. V had, he would continue his verbal assault. Then I would find myself trying, in tone and manner, as well as with words, to appease him. This was the quality of voice that, unconsciously, I had adopted with Mr. V. Rationally, I was attempting, with tact and empathy, to express my understanding of his hurt; less rationally, automatically, I was reacting to Mr. V with ancient fears, ancient responses.

Recognizing this piece of countertransference helped me gain an understanding of just how menacing I experienced Mr. V to be and how anxious he made me. What I was not yet fully in touch with was the extent of the anger that his behavior mobilized in me. This reaction surfaced in response to a series of enactments carried out by both patient and analyst in the course of treatment.

Both enactments involved magazines and both contained important aspects of memory as well as being expressions of current conflict. One evening after work, when I was straightening up the waiting room of an office to which I had recently moved, I came across something unusual. I noticed that the mailing labels on two magazines had been torn off. Investigating further, I realized that the magazines from which the labels had been removed were ones that had been forwarded from my old office. Several other magazines which contained the correct mailing labels had been left untouched.

I had no idea as to who was responsible for this dastardly crime but I resolved to keep an eye out for the culprit. Within a short time, however, buried under other, more pressing concerns, the incident was forgotten and I thought no more about it.

Then, one day, as I opened my office door to Mr. V, I saw him rolling a small piece of white paper between thumb and forefinger. Quickly he put the scrap into his pocket and, as usual, charged into the office. I said nothing to him then, but after his hour checked the magazines. The label from another magazine, one that had recently been forwarded through the mail was missing. Now I had my man. It was Mr. V.

I was puzzling over how best to raise this sensitive issue with my patient when still another unusual event took place. A subscription to a magazine I had not ordered arrived at my office. This was a special interest publication devoted to a topic about which I had little knowledge. While it is not unusual for me, like many physicians, to receive unsolicited mail, including occasional throwaway magazines, this, clearly, was not one of those offerings. Casually, I scanned the pages, read through the table of contents, and realizing quickly that I had neither sufficient time nor interest to do more than that, I left the magazine in the waiting room for others to enjoy.

I then returned to my office and reviewed some notes while waiting for my next patient, Mr. V, to arrive. It was no more than thirty seconds before he rang the bell that the flash realization hit me: it was Mr. V who had sent me this subscription. The topic that the magazine covered was one of special interest to him and represented one of his few avocations. He had spoken of this interest only a few times in analysis and on each occasion, quite briefly. When he did, however, I had noticed an enthusiasm for the subject which in other aspects of his life was notably absent. Quickly I retrieved the magazine from the waiting room and that night, after work, set myself the task of attempting to understand what I could of the interplay of enactments between Mr. V and myself that, suddenly, had taken the center of the analytic stage.

It soon became clear that the episodes involving the magazines were connected and that each was a beacon signaling the presence in both analyst and patient of affects and fantasies that were being actualized in treatment but had not reached the consciousness of either. From time to time in analysis Mr. V had mentioned the fact that his father's business had folded when he (Mr. V) was an adolescent and that, as a result, the family had fallen on hard days. While he spoke of the shame he felt about his father's business failure and the wide reverberations it had on his family, Mr. V never described exactly what had happened. In fact he avoided specifics, and when this omission was pointed out to him he claimed that the details of that troubled period were lost to memory. In fact, Mr. V had managed to drive out of awareness much that belonged to that turbulent time. And what he did recall he found difficult to reveal.

Now as we discussed Mr. V's behavior in removing the

mailing labels and explored its meaning, memories surfaced which had not appeared before. The fact that his "crime" was dealt with not punitively but with an effort to understand it may have helped him to become more open. In any case, Mr. V spoke of the discomfort he felt when he noticed that some of the mailing labels contained my old address. Seeing unfamiliar faces in the waiting room and concluding I must have some new patients who did not know that I had moved from another address, he felt a sudden impulse to remove the mailing labels that would reveal that fact. Such information was private, he thought, and was no one's business. In acting as he did, Mr. V imagined he was protecting my privacy.

As he described his feelings and the action that he felt compelled to carry out, Mr. V recalled two other occasions when he had behaved in a similar way. The first incident occurred in adolescence and was connected to his father's loss of his business. What Mr. V had not mentioned in his initial description of this event was that his father's decline was the result of his having been convicted of a white collar crime. It was this situation and its consequences that forced the closing of the business and precipitated the family calamity. For several years Mr. V was shielded from the truth and it was only when he inadvertently came across some old legal papers in a desk drawer that he learned what had happened. So shaken was he by the discovery and so angry at being kept in the dark, that he tore the papers to shreds. He then disposed of the fragments and said nothing to anyone about what he had done.

The second incident occurred some years later when Mr. V was working in a government office that dealt with criminal matters. One evening after work, when the office was empty, Mr. V went to the files, removed the folder containing records of his father's case, and destroyed them. He felt a need to obliterate all traces of that crime.

In removing the mailing labels Mr. V was not only enacting an old scenario and reliving pieces of history in the transference, but was expressing both his fantasy that I possessed shameful secrets that I was loathe to reveal and a wish to keep hidden certain impulses and fantasies of his own.

Sending me a subscription to a magazine he valued was

also a complex and multidetermined act. On one level, it represented an apology and an atonement for Mr. V's behavior in destroying the mailing labels. As a youngster he had been tortured by feelings of guilt for having destroyed the legal papers, for secretly regarding his father with contempt, and for the realization of a childhood wish to see him go down in defeat.

In a similar way, Mr. V felt guilty for having tampered with my property, but as was true in childhood, his guilt had deeper sources. Secretly he disparaged my new office, my clothes, and my speech. He regarded himself as superior to me and in his fantasies he often defeated me in contests of one kind or another. Regarding my new office as a stepdown from the old one, he saw in this change evidence of my decline and experienced a sense of triumph. Thus for Mr. V, sending me a subscription was an effort to atone for all of the unacceptable feelings toward me that he harbored. In addition, Mr. V wanted me to know that he was a man of broad interests. Believing that I shared those interests, he wanted to let me know that we had much in common. Indirectly he also wished to let me know that in addition to the negative feelings that he harbored toward me there were also some positive ones, and he wanted me to like him. These positive feelings embarrassed and frightened Mr. V and it was only through an enactment that they could be expressed.

For my part, I was aware, as I have noted, of a certain feeling of tension as I worked with Mr. V and of a vigilance expressed in my posture and mode of listening. The extent, however, to which the undercurrent of violence in him and the subtle ways in which he conveyed his competitiveness and hostility had evoked in me a counterreaction of anger and a wish to strike back, had not surfaced until my behavior in leaving the magazine in the waiting room made clear that I, like his parents and brother, was acting in a rejecting way toward him.

As I reflected on the need I had to modulate my responses to Mr. V, I realized that this reaction had particular roots. Mr. V's attitude toward me in the transference, and historically toward his father and brother, resonated with feelings I had struggled with toward my own father—feelings that I found threatening and that I had tried to keep at bay. Working with

Mr. V had, no doubt, stimulated affects and memories connected with these childhood experiences that were defended against, as they had been originally, largely through repression and isolation, but also by unconscious efforts to minimize their intensity. It was only when I could put myself in close touch with the strength of the emotions stimulated in me that I could grasp affectively, rather than intellectually, the power of Mr. V's rage and his destructive urges.

The working through of these feelings and the thwarted love that helped feed them, which was so essential a part of Mr. V's treatment, depended on their actualization in the transference. From this perspective, the enactments carried out by both patient and analyst were an essential aspect of the process of actualization. Their investigation opened the way, not only to uncovering an essential piece of history that had not yet surfaced, but to bringing to the fore crucial aspects of the interaction between patient and analyst that, arousing anxiety in each and strongly defended against by both, had until then been insufficiently explored.

The second case I wish to describe is that of Mr. N, a patient with whom I worked early in my training and who taught me much about the power of enactments. For a period of about eighteen months, Mr. N had been in twice weekly therapy with a senior analyst. After this time, believing analysis to be the treatment of choice for him, this colleague referred Mr. N to the Treatment Center for student analysis.

At the time, I knew very little about the criteria for analyzability, but having met Mr. N, I wondered whether a man who, had he shed his shoes and donned a pair of overalls, could easily have doubled for Li'l Abner, met any of them. A homespun Southerner who moved and talked as though he were swimming through a pool of molasses, Mr. N sounded like one of the good old boys in a small Mississippi town who sits on the porch of the general store and rambles on about the trivia of the day. When not preoccupied with changes in the weather and their effect on his garden, he focused on the various home improvement projects in which he was forever engaged, describing in minutest detail the size, number, and purpose of every screw, nut, bolt, and hinge employed.

After two weeks of listening to Mr. N's discourse on the arts of plumbing, cabinetmaking, and electrical repair, I began to doubt my sanity in accepting such a case. After several initial interviews with him, I had, in fact, contacted the senior colleague who had treated Mr. N and expressed doubts about his suitability for analysis. Told in reply that Mr. N's problems were neurotic ones and that what he needed to make progress was the powerful tool of analysis as compared with the weaker instrument of psychotherapy, I had suppressed my doubts and had gone along with the recommendation. Now I regarded myself as an innocent who, naively believing in the superior wisdom of senior analysts, was attempting the impossible: to analyze a man whose associations seemed to have been lifted verbatim from the text of a hardware catalogue.

On his side Mr. N was none too happy about beginning analysis. He had liked his therapist, been content with the treatment, and felt that he was making tangible, if slow, progress. In a manner that was characteristic for him, however, he had accepted the recommendation for analysis obediently and without protest. If it was suggested by the doctor whom he so admired and whose expertise he relied on, there was no way that he would question such an authority.

This was the situation as we began: two disgruntled individuals, unhappy with each other and with the idea of analysis, thrown together in a consulting room, and engaged in an unlikely project. It was not an auspicious beginning and it was not surprising, given such a setting, that enactments quickly became an important mode of communication.

The first enactments of which I became aware were played out through bodily postures. Through them, both patient and analyst expressed strong resistances to the analytic process; resistances that, arising from the outset of treatment, found expression in this nonverbal way prior to registering in the realm of word and thought.

Mr. N lay stiffly on the couch, his long legs extending a few inches beyond its end. His hands were clasped behind his head and, fanning out as a protective shield, his arms and elbows formed a picket fence behind his head. Sometimes Mr. N changed positions and turned on his left side. Then he would place one arm across his head so that his face and ear were protected beneath it.

For my part, I noticed, as I listened, that I was leaning back in my chair and that my body was rotated slightly away from the patient. Only intermittently did I look at Mr. N, and sometimes, trying to catch the drift of his associations, I found myself listening with my eyes closed.

All of this was different for me. Ordinarily I observe a patient on the couch, often leaning slightly forward in my chair to do so, and rarely do I listen with closed eyes. I tried to tell myself that this latter behavior reflected my efforts to concentrate without distraction; to catch the faint whisperings of the unconscious that come through in Mr. N's reality-bound narration. But there was more. My listening posture, like Mr. N's posture on the couch, conveyed an important message. Both of us were cautious, both wary. Each, struggling with negative feelings toward the other and toward our joint venture, was revealing through his body language the ambivalence he felt about proceeding with it.

It was these enactments that signaled the presence, in patient and analyst, of unconscious conflicts that had not as yet surfaced. And it was by using the enactments as clues to these conflicts that I was able to learn more about them.

I began to observe my patient more closely, to keep my eyes open at all times, and to see what I could see. What, in fact, I saw when I began to look was something that should have been apparent from the first. As Mr. N rose from the couch and the protective wall of hands and arms was dismantled, I noticed two deep scars behind his ears. In the course of providing some background history in a consultation session, Mr. N had casually mentioned the fact that he had had some ear problems as a child, had become friendly with the doctor who took care of him, and to help pay for his treatment had done some household chores for him. In the analysis Mr. N did not mention these experiences again. They seemed to have slipped from memory. And for reasons of my own I, too, forgot this passing reference to an important experience of childhood.

I had no doubt, however, that at some point in our sessions I had observed the bony defects behind Mr. N's ears (both mastoid bones had been removed) and it had registered, if not consciously, at least subliminally. I realized, in fact, that it was precisely because it had registered that I found myself shifting my body away from Mr. N and not looking at him.

The factors in myself that gave rise to this behavior now began to filter into consciousness. As a young child my brother had developed a severe case of mastoiditis that required emergency surgery. Occurring in the preantibiotic era, the situation was a life-threatening one. I recalled the intense fear that I felt at the time, a fear of mutilation and death (as well, very likely, of death wishes toward an intruding sibling) that were fused with other frightening memories involving illness and operations. As a young child I had undergone surgery without preparation of any kind and was haunted by terrifying residues of that experience. When I was somewhat older, my father suddenly developed an acute illness that required immediate surgical intervention.

In both patient and analyst it was the awakening of traumatic memories involving illness, pain, and threatened loss that we were defending against. Contained within them and expressed by them were anxieties over mutilation, death, murderous wishes, survival, and annihilation that in childhood had troubled each of us and that formed the core of our neuroses. In our adult lives we had managed to keep these anxieties under lock and key and neither of us looked forward to turning them loose. For each of us, then, the analytic process threatened some disruption and through our body language we signaled our intuitive understanding of that fact. It was these enactments, however, that also provided the first clues to the nature of the interlocking resistances that, from the outset of the analysis, blocked its unfolding. And it was the understanding of those resistances that paved the way for an analysis, previously stalled at the starting gate, to finally take off.

Not that there were no further problems, far from it. Mr. N was a man who was terrified of his feelings and of the impulses that gave rise to them. Highly controlled, afraid to need anyone and to feel vulnerable, he remained cautious about revealing himself. Sometimes he could open up, and at those times it was possible to make substantial progress. At others,

especially when Mr. N felt threatened by emerging affects, he
would shut down and a period of drought would ensue. It was
at just such a time that I found myself behaving in a manner
that once again was alien to me.

The way we analyze is as much a function of our personalities as it is of technique. This is a point made by Bert Lewin,
who believed that an analyst's style of working and his special
interests reflect much about the inner man. As an example, he
cited the work of Franz Alexander, who was very much interested in issues of action and acting out and who, in his personal
life, was an athlete and a boxer.

"As for me," Lewin added, "I like to sleep."

Having been a quiet and rather shy youngster, my own
style is to be a relatively quiet analyst. It is rare for me to speak
at length or to offer interpretations of more than a few sentences at a time. At one point in Mr. N's analysis, however, I
interpreted the hidden, deflected aggression that lay behind his
passive behavior in what was clearly a long-winded way. I went
on for some time, explaining what I meant, citing evidence
from the material, and using an anecdote to illustrate my point.
I found it hard to stop speaking and afterwards was reminded
of the story of the Rabbi whose sermon went on for over an
hour and a half. Finally, seeing members of the congregation
dozing off, the Cantor leaned forward, tugged at the Rabbi's
gown and whispered, "You'd better stop now, rabbi." Turning
toward him and looking bewildered, the Rabbi shrugged his
shoulders. "I would if I knew how," he replied.

Curious about this enactment, I thought about it and realized that it contained a complex communication that arose in
response to a subtle communication of Mr. N's. For some weeks
in the analysis he had been hard to reach. After a period of
becoming more engaged he had reverted to a stance that
seemed quite inaccessible. Interpretations seemed not to register, or if they registered, to be ignored. Sometimes it was hard
to know if Mr. N had heard them at all.

This behavior on Mr. N's part followed directly upon a
disappointment in his life which was difficult for him to bear.
Depressed and angry, he unconsciously blamed me for not
making it possible for him to achieve his goals but was unaware

of the anger he felt toward me. He experienced only depression and discouragement. When, in childhood, he had displayed anger he was frozen out by his parents who would not tolerate such behavior. Quickly he would shape up and conceal his feelings, but he would then make repeated errors in carrying out family chores and responsibilities. He got directions wrong, and often acted as though he had not heard them.

I realized my response was an effort to reach out to Mr. N, to make contact with him at a time of discouragement and disappointment, and, unconsciously, to act in a way that was different than the unforgiving parents. But I was doing something more. Without thinking about it, I was reacting to Mr. N's distress by trying to breach the wall that he had set up. In fact, out of hurt and anger, he had turned a deaf ear to me. Previously, I had not recognized the important role that Mr. N's ear problem had played in his passive–aggressive behavior, but now, as I strained to make him hear me, that fact hit home with clarity. His enactment was to be deaf; mine was to shout to a deaf man. Realizing this as I was enacting my part, I was able to show Mr. N what was happening and how his behavior was a characteristic vehicle for the expression of unconscious anger. For the first time he became aware of how he had utilized his chronic ear problem and this insight took him a step along the road toward understanding, not only this important facet of his behavior, but the exasperated responses of other people to him.

Our struggles continued in analysis as Mr. N's fears of letting down his guard and being vulnerable kept him emotionally distant. One day, just before he arrived for his hour, I noticed that the light in a waiting room lamp had gone out. The result of a loose connection, this had happened before and I knew that if I tinkered with the lamp for a few minutes I could get it to work. Telling myself that I had better make an overdue phone call, however, I let the matter drop. When, a few minutes later, I reentered the waiting room to greet Mr. N, the light was on. Noticing that something was wrong, he had discovered the problem and had corrected it.

In the ensuing hour the enactments on both our parts were explored. As we discussed the waiting room scenario, I realized that my action was, in effect, an invitation to Mr. N to play a familiar role. I had set the stage for him to do a chore for me; to perform a task for the doctor who was treating him. He, in turn, had obliged, and in doing so, was reliving an important piece of his own history.

Consciously I was not aware of remembering the nugget of history that in an offhand way Mr. N had related in a consultation session; that as a youngster he had done household chores for a doctor to help pay off his medical bills. Clearly, however, the information had registered and now, with my initiating the scenario, each of us was playing our parts. Why had I acted in this way? What message was my enactment trying to convey? For some time I pondered over this question and, slowly, gained some understanding of my behavior. I was seeing Mr. N for no fee and for me analyzing him constituted a substantial sacrifice of time and money. Although I had undertaken this as part of my training, I realized, as I reflected on the matter, that I often felt frustrated and ungratified by my work with him. In fact Mr. N was not a very gratifying patient. After sessions I often felt emptied and depleted. I wanted something more from him. Thus, unconsciously, I had set up a situation so that he could do something for me. He could pay me as he paid his former doctor.

By inviting Mr. N to act this way, however, I was also doing something else. Unconsciously I was creating a situation in which he could be the giver. Momentarily he could be the knowledgeable expert who could fix things and not the dependent, needy patient. In this way I was expressing through an enactment my intuitive sense of the pain and humiliation that Mr. N felt at being a patient. He had never expressed this openly, always showing gratitude at being accepted for analysis, and at all times acting in a deferential manner toward his analyst. However, Mr. N was a man who, in the outside world, prided himself on doing for others. He had become a pharmacist and was forever offering advice, guidance, support, and suggestions about medications and home remedies to his customers. He was a dispenser of balms, both emotional and physical, and his own neediness was well concealed behind this altruistic attitude. My action, I realized, was another effort to reach out to Mr. N and to build a bridge between us. By offering him a momentary opportunity to reverse roles and to provide for me, I was intuitively attempting to meet some of his self-esteem needs. I was also trying, by giving Mr. N an opportunity to feel more of an equal partner in our undertaking, to build a stronger alliance between us.

Whatever therapeutic value such enactments may have, as bits and pieces of the numerous "corrective" interactions between therapist and patient that are an inevitable aspect of any therapy, including analysis, they also provide an opportunity for both patient and analyst to gain insight into aspects of their relationship that may not previously have come into focus. This was the case with Mr. N. My actions alerted me to an aspect of his conflicts over issues of dependency and neediness and the reaction formations he had developed against these wishes that, although previously recognized, had not been sufficiently worked with.

There was another dimension to the waiting room enactments that was also important and that remained concealed beneath its more obvious layer. As I reflected on what had happened, a memory of someone I had not consciously thought about for decades arose in my mind. This was Cal, a young handyman, who worked in the apartment building in which I grew up. Cal was amazing. There was nothing he could not repair; nothing he could not set working again. In addition he was a builder of wonderful model airplanes with miniature motors that took off from fields in Riverside Park and circled, like hawks, in the sky far above the Hudson River. My own father was all thumbs, could repair nothing, and had no interest in building models of any kind. I yearned to learn these arts and for a while Cal became a surrogate father to me.

My relationship with Mr. N had stirred up some of these old yearnings which, in part, I enacted in the lamp incident. I had not before been aware of how powerful a need he had to care for others, to be the fixer and repairer of bodies and souls. Now, through the evocation of old wishes in myself, I felt this power. I also became aware that there was a growing bond between Mr. N and myself; a bond that, as one of its aspects, contained fantasies on his part to take care of me and on my part to be taken care of. This realization alerted me to a dimension of our relationship that I had not been aware of before; a dimension that in time could be fruitfully explored. Its investigation led, ultimately, to an understanding of the way that Mr. N's yearnings for a man's love was quickly turned by him into his being the provider and source of help and comfort.

The final enactment I want to describe occurred in the termination phase and, like the earlier one, conveyed something important about the relationship of patient and analyst. When Mr. N arrived for his appointment one day, a new patient of the colleague who shared my suite struck up a conversation with him. This patient was a loquacious fellow and he soon began describing the misery he was experiencing in an unhappy love affair. Ordinarily Mr. N sat quietly in the waiting room, avoiding eye contact, and not inviting conversation. If he interacted with others it was usually to do something helpful; to pick up an object that someone had dropped, to open a window when the room was stuffy, or to pass a magazine to someone sitting out of reach of the rack. On this occasion, however, despite the fact that Mr. N was suffering with severe lower back pains and a heavy cold, he conversed with this agitated young man, listening attentively to his story, and then making a few comments aimed at easing his tension.

In the ensuing hour I noticed how uncomfortable Mr. N was. His back was clearly causing him much pain and it was difficult for him to find a way of lying on the couch that did not increase his distress. Despite this problem, Mr. N spoke easily and fluently, recounting the events of the waiting room and doing so with a certain pride.

As I listened to Mr. N and observed his discomfort, I was aware of a wish to ease his pain. In fact, as I listened I began sketching some doodles on a notepad. Now I looked at what I had drawn. Hidden within a doodle, but clearly decipherable, was the name of the muscle relaxant that I had taken when, some years before, I had been incapacitated with lower back pain. As I focused on the name I had written, I realized that my action conveyed a wish, not yet conscious, to provide Mr. N with some medication. The fantasy which then surfaced more clearly was that at the end of the hour I would go to the medicine chest, get several of the muscle relaxant pills that had helped me, and give them to Mr. N.

In the waiting room, then, Mr. N, the pharmacist, had played the role of the understanding psychiatrist to a fellow patient. In the office I had imagined and had begun to enact the role of the pharmacist, dispensing medication to Mr. N. In fantasy and in our enactments, we had switched roles.

For some time I was at a loss to understand the meaning of this behavior. Then, one day, walking toward my car after work, I recalled an incident which Mr. N had related early in the analysis. In pharmacy school he had made friends with a Jewish student from New York. They liked to tease each other about their respective backgrounds and especially to fool others who had stereotypic views of ethnic groups. Once, as a practical joke, they went to a well-known establishment restaurant where Mr. N, the Southern cracker, ordered a corned beef sandwich and his friend, the New York Jew, ordered hominy grits. Their joke conveyed much about their relationship; not only that worlds of tradition and history divided them, but that an affectionate bond united them. This was the message that, at the end of the treatment, Mr. N and I were sending to each other. We did it at that moment not through words, or conscious thoughts, but through enactments related to a specific and meaningful memory.

This is the way with enactments. As communications of the greatest importance in analysis, they often express what is not yet otherwise expressible. As nonverbal conveyors of rising memories, concealed resistances, and fantasies waiting to see the light of day, they are avant garde messengers that anticipate and signal what is to come. As such, enactments play a vital part in clinical work. Along with other cues, both verbal and otherwise, that arise in the treatment situation, they function as signals that we rely on to tell us what is stirring just beneath the surface of the waters; and, as such, they serve as indispensable guides in our efforts to explore the subtle and pervasive interactions between patient and analyst that form the core of the analytic process.

3

Notes on the Unknowable: Analytic Secrets and the Transference Neurosis

Although generally regarded as the quintessential element in the analytic process and among its most distinguishing features, the phenomenon known as the transference neurosis remains an area whose full dimensions have yet to be explored.

In this chapter I will discuss one of those dimensions. My focus will be on certain covert interactions between patient and analyst that, communicated in subtle and often unconscious ways, may constitute essential, if often overlooked, aspects of the transference neurosis.

The importance of secrets in family life and in child development is well known and has been the subject of recent papers by Caruth (1985), Michaels (1985), and Rustin (1985). In chapter 10 (Jacobs, 1980) I discuss their role in the analytic situation and note that it is not rare in analysis for secretive collusions to exist between patient and therapist. In what follows I will take up another aspect of the problem of secrets and illustrate how they may enter into the formation of the transference neurosis. In doing so I will discuss secrets kept not only by the patient but also by the analyst and how the interplay of the mutual need for secrecy may affect the development, uncovering, and working through of aspects of the transference neurosis.

Appreciation of the transactional dimension of the analytic situation and in particular of the analyst's contribution to the form and character of the transferences has, in recent years, been the focus of interest of a number of authors. Among the most articulate spokesmen for a more comprehensive view of transference has been Sandler (1976) who has expressed what he believes to be a commonly held dissatisfaction with earlier formulations: "Nowadays many analysts must have the conviction (or at least the uneasy feeling) that the conceptualization of transference as the patient's libidinal or aggressive energic cathexis of past objects being transferred to the image of the analyst in the present is woefully inadequate" (p. 44).

In Sandler's view, transference "need not be restricted to the illusory apperception of another person but can be taken to include the unconscious and often subtle attempts to manipulate or to provoke situations with others which are a concealed repetition of earlier experiences and relationships" (pp. 43–44). Central to the analytic process in his view is the effort of both participants in that situation to impose an intrapsychic role relationship on the other. Thus, for Sandler, the forms that transferences take are influenced not only by historical factors, but by current transactions between analyst and patient. Under the sway of his need to repeat certain interpersonal as well as intrapsychic experiences the patient attempts by subtle means to prod the analyst into behaving in particular ways. Then in unconscious response to the analyst's behavior he scans those reactions and adapts to them. Although Sandler's focus is primarily on the patient's side of the equation, he also points out that parallel processes take place in the therapist. The analyst's identification and interpretation of this unconscious interplay, in fact, is one of his most important functions.

Pick (1985), makes a similar point in a paper focusing on the working through of countertransference reactions. She believes that there exists in humans the psychological equivalent of the mouth of the infant "that seeks a breast as an inborn potential" (p. 157). This innate psychological trait is "a state of mind which seeks another state of mind" (p. 157). In the analytic situation she views the patient as attempting to elicit an enacting response from the analyst. On his side the analyst has an impulse to respond in just this way, and a part of this tendency will be expressed in the form of interpretation. In one phase of Pick's treatment of a deeply troubled patient the latter's wish for mothering mated with a part of the analyst that wished to mother, while at another point in the treatment the patient's need to avoid recognition of certain deeply rooted fears mated with the analyst's wish not to confront her own fear of death and other human vulnerabilities. For Pick, as for Sandler, transference and countertransference are in continual dynamic interaction, each shaped by and giving shape to the other.

Stolorow, Brandchaft, and Atwood (1983) hold that psychoanalysis is neither a science of the intrapsychic focused on one isolated mental apparatus nor is it a science of the interpersonal "investigating the behavioral facts of the therapeutic interaction as seen from a point of observation outside the field under study" (p. 118). Rather "it is a science of the intersubjective focused on the interplay between the differently organized subjective worlds" of patient and analyst (p. 118). From this perspective neither psychopathology nor the therapeutic action of psychoanalysis can be understood apart from the intersubjective field in which they occur.

In their paper on the phenomenon of gas lighting, Calef and Weinshel (1981) cite a number of clinical examples characterized by the efforts of one individual to exert influence over another by causing the latter to doubt the accuracy and validity of his or her own perceptions and judgments. In these situations those who were the targets of such behavior revealed a tendency to incorporate and to assimilate what others externalize and project onto them.

In the analytic setting, too, analogous phenomena may occur. The ambiguities fostered by the analytic frame contribute to the difficulties experienced by some patients in differentiating inner from outer, self from object. In this atmosphere the analyst's countertransference reactions "may facilitate the distortion of the patient's perception or impose his own perceptions on the patient" (p. 54).

On the other hand, analysts may become the victims of gaslighting maneuvers. Inevitably they become the "targets for the patients' disavowels, defenses and externalizations. Patients try to transfer their unacceptable feelings and conflicts onto analysts. Since those feelings and conflicts are often universal, analysts may not always find it easy to separate what the patients wrongly ascribe to them from what truly belongs to them" (p. 54). Such interactions, Calef and Weinshel note, "are commonplace and by no means limited to the more disturbed patients" (p. 55).

Writing from the perspective of child analysis, Kestenberg (1972) has observed that in treatment children may play out scenes that they have witnessed but whose reality is denied by parents. Influenced by such denials, the analyst may, initially, regard the play as representing wish and fantasy rather than memory. Thus he may ally himself with the parents' gas-lighting behavior. Successful treatment depends on the analyst's recognition of the accuracy of the child's perceptions and that it is the parents who are distorting the truth.

These and a number of other recent contributions have emphasized the importance in analysis of the interpersonal as well as the intrapsychic dimension. Such a perspective inevitably influences the way that the transference neurosis is conceptualized. No longer is the essence of that phenomenon viewed as the development of a new neurosis with the analyst playing an essentially passive role in that process. Rather, the transference neurosis is seen, as is transference itself, as a development that is strongly influenced by current interactions between patient and analyst as well as by displacements from past object representations.

In what follows I will focus on one aspect of this view of the transference neurosis. I will try to demonstrate by means of several clinical examples the existence in certain cases of a covert aspect of that phenomenon. I will try to show how this hidden dimension may be played out in analysis, the roles in the drama taken by both participants, and the relation of the analytic secret to secrets in the lives of both patient and analyst.

The first example concerns Mr. C, an intense young man of twenty-six, who entered analysis because of a long-standing inability to choose a vocation. A man of intense passions, Mr.

C felt his emotions strongly, and what he felt was often anger. Rarely could a session pass without his ventilating rage against someone—friend, acquaintance, or analyst—who, by failing to understand his needs, had managed to complicate an already embattled existence.

Mr. C's family was the target of much wrath. Both his older brother and mother came in for substantial criticism as tight-fisted, withholding types who gave little of themselves to anyone, but it was for his father that Mr. C reserved his most scathing attacks. His father, he said, was a sham. Self-important and pompous, he habitually played the role of the great man with friends and family while, in fact, he had the mind of a civil servant. Like the rest of the family, he was self-involved and shared little with his children. In fact, Mr. C complained, he did not really know his father. The latter had never let anyone be close to him. He functioned as an isolated, self-contained unit, and when it came to matters of a personal nature, he stonewalled all efforts to learn about those parts of his life. There was, as it turned out, another side to Mr. C's feelings about his father, but this could not surface until certain transference issues, played out behind the scenes, could come into the open.

With Mr. C's long-standing history of antagonism toward his father, it is not difficult to imagine the kinds of transference that early on dominated the analysis. Quite rapidly I became the distant, ungiving father whom Mr. C disparaged but with whom he was also quite competitive. Attacks on me filled the hours as Mr. C left no part of my person unscrutinized. My appearance, my manner, my speech, my behavior, all came in for sharp criticism. He regarded me, from top to bottom, as an anachronism—a Freudian who had lost touch with the times, and who, in fact, belonged to another era. He exhorted me to give up my anonymity and to step into the twentieth century as an analyst who communicated with his patients. In fact, Mr. C insisted that there was nothing wrong with my discussing my personal life with him. It would only give him more to fantasize about.

While the dominant transferences centered on me as the father, with whom Mr. C struggled in myriad ways, other transferences were not absent. Sibling rivalry entered the picture as Mr. C envied certain personal attributes of mine, competed with me intellectually, and coveted a number of my possessions. In time, too, transferences that had their origins in Mr. C's relationship with the mother of his early years and with his oedipal mother, entered the analysis. In short, there developed a full-blown transference neurosis that had multiple roots. Focused in large measure on the oedipal father, it also involved other object representations and, interwoven with these, representations of the self. There appeared, then, on the analytic stage a rich and complex mix of memories and fantasies involving multiple objects interacting with contributions from various aspects of the personality.

Given this picture, which unfolded over several years, I had little doubt that a transference neurosis in all its manifestations had evolved in this analysis and that gradually it was being worked through.

Had it been pointed out to me at that time that an important, even essential aspect of that phenomenon had been neglected, I would have responded with puzzlement, if not incredulity. Such a situation seemed quite impossible. Yet this is precisely what had happened. There was a dimension of the transference neurosis that, because it was involved in conflict for both patient and analyst, had imperceptibly been enacted beneath the surface. Clues to it became visible from time to time but were not picked up and utilized by either participant. Rather, a collusion between patient and analyst took place—a collusion unconsciously designed to avoid confrontation of an issue that was highly charged for each was tied to a network of memories and experiences.

The issue which gave rise to this situation is one that is familiar to all analysts and that has, for years, plagued our institutes. It involves the status of the analyst and, in particular, whether or not he is a training analyst. This question, which proved to be a crucial one in Mr. C's case, arises from time to time in the course of some analyses. Most often it does so in situations in which the patient is a professional colleague; but it may also become important in the treatment of others who, for one reason or another, have a keen interest in matters of status and position.

If the therapist is not a training analyst, as was true of my own situation during Mr. C's treatment, this issue often can stir in him strong emotions which, subtly or otherwise, may affect his ability to deal effectively with the question and with all that it may mean to the patient. Certainly this was the case in my work with Mr. C.

It so happened that although he never spoke openly about the matter, Mr. C had more than a passing interest in my status at the Institute. In fact, with the precision of a radar operator he had tracked my every move. Although he had no direct connection with the field, Mr. C had friends who were analytic colleagues of mine and from whom he managed to elicit some information about me and about the Institute's hierarchies and promotion procedures. He knew, for instance, not only that I was not a training analyst and that I might at any time be evaluated for such an appointment, but approximately when during the year such appointments were made. His intelligence gathering, carried on furtively, was worthy of one of John Le Carre's double agents.

For my part, the training analyst issue had become a source of embarrassment and discomfort. I knew through the grapevine that on a couple of occasions my name had come up for consideration but that I had failed each time to gain the necessary votes to be appointed. I was at that juncture feeling about as popular as a Turk in Armenia and was discouraged about the entire state of affairs.

One spring, learning that new appointments were soon to be announced, Mr. C surreptitiously began to observe me closely in the waiting room in the hopes that he might thereby pick up clues as to my fate. Being, by that time, a veteran rejectee, I thought that I managed to conceal the latest disappointment well.

No doubt I was wrong. Something in my manner, perhaps a hint of dejection revealed in posture or facial expression, must have given me away. Mr. C guessed the truth. He thought to himself that I had not made the grade. The material of those hours contained indirect allusions to these ideas. Mr. C spoke of a book about Churchill that he had been reading. It dealt with the great leader's early years and related how, as a young man, he had failed the entrance examinations for Sandhurst. Mr. C also referred indirectly to a medical colleague who, having failed his licensure examination, was contemplating a second try. These associations passed me by. I have no doubt that preconsciously they registered, but I was not prepared to deal with them. To do so would have been to bring to the surface feelings of shame, humiliation, and anger that I was all too willing to suppress.

Why it was that Mr. C had so intense an interest in my career and at the same time was unable in any direct way to acknowledge that interest was a mystery whose investigation ultimately became a core issue in Mr. C's analysis. When, through my coming to better terms with my own situation and therefore being able to hear the messages that were contained in Mr. C's associations I was able to explore that question with him, I learned that his concerns represented the reactivation of a critically important piece of past history that had not as yet surfaced. This experience and its consequences became embedded in a family secret that ultimately was enacted as an analytic secret.

For many years Mr. C's father held a position as a vice-president of a large industrial concern. The ruling ambition of his life was to succeed to the chairmanship of that company and he fully expected to do so. When Mr. C was a young teenager, however, his father failed to obtain a key promotion that would have put him in line of succession. The job was given to a younger man.

For the father, this rejection was a crushing blow. The hopes and dreams of the entire family, in fact, rested on the realization of his ambitions. A stern and proud man, the older Mr. C kept his suffering to himself. He shared his feelings with no one. Both the mother and brother followed suit. They rarely spoke of the family disappointment and, when they did so, it was in an oblique and indirect way. Mr. C's efforts to learn the facts of the situation were met with avoidance. What had happened was regarded as a matter of deep shame that was not to be talked about.

The entire episode became a family secret. A face-saving story about the father's decision to seek early retirement was quickly invented and circulated among friends and relatives. This became the official story and was the one that Mr. C soon came to adopt. Over the years the truth about his father was buried, and by the time he entered analysis as a young adult Mr. C had quite forgotten the entire incident. He had managed to banish it from consciousness.

Part of the reason for Mr. C's need to forget was that these traumatic events in the family led to a much diminished view, not only of his father, but of himself as well. As an adolescent, Mr. C's self-image was closely linked with that of his father. To him, his father was a hero, the big and powerful boss who was to rise to the leadership of an international company. In his imagination the boy would follow in his footsteps. Made of the same clay, he too would one day sit in the chairman's chair and direct far-flung operations.

Now he had to revise his picture of his father and see him in a new light as someone who was vulnerable, who had been passed over, and whose limitations could not be ignored. Since, in his unconscious, Mr. C was his father, a similar fate awaited him. No longer could he aspire to great heights. Now he, too, would have to settle for a second rung position. All this, of course, was depressing to a youngster and Mr. C wished to rid himself of such thoughts as quickly as possible. Like the others, he grasped at and clung to an explanation that spared himself as well as his father.

All that Mr. C remembered of that period were endless quarrels with his father and his disparagement of the older man. He recalled thinking of him as shallow and self-important and remembered his wish to have a different kind of father. At that time he distanced himself emotionally from this parent, subsequently giving many rationalizations for this behavior. The sense of betrayal he had suffered, however, and the accompanying narcissistic injury, remained for some years out of awareness. This was the secret that in a new version was played out beneath the manifest aspects of the transference neurosis. Mr. C's overriding interest in my career, the sleuthing that he did, and his strong but silent reaction to my failure to be promoted constituted a reliving in analysis of the traumatic experience in adolescence and of the family secret.

Its recovery in analysis was important in several ways. First, it highlighted an aspect of the transference neurosis that is often overlooked, namely, its relation to adolescence. Traditionally and most commonly the transference neurosis is regarded as a revival in a new version of the infantile neurosis. Its childhood roots are emphasized and developmentally later editions of the same neurotic conflicts often ignored. In fact, the period of adolescence, which involves a reactivation and reworking of the infantile, and especially oedipal conflicts, plays an essential role in giving new shape and form to those conflicts. This leads to the neurosis of adolescence, an entity no less important than its forebears. What is revived in analysis in the form of the transference neurosis often relates more directly to the remodeled neurosis of adolescence than it does to the childhood version. This way station is often overlooked and, with it, a critical period in the patient's development.

In Mr. C's case, uncovering the early adolescent experience and the decisive influence that it exerted on his future development proved essential to the understanding and working through of aspects of his neurotic conflicts that had not previously been accessible. Reexperiencing the disappointment and betrayal that lay at the root of his negative feelings toward his father and in the transference toward his analyst, Mr. C was able to gain new perspective on those attitudes. Also clarified was an important source of Mr. C's negative self-image. Important in this respect was not only the identification with his father but guilt of a high order. Consciously Mr. C criticized and disparaged his father; unconsciously he lacerated himself for his betrayal of the man whom he had once loved. Understanding this aspect of the father–son relationship proved to be of great importance to Mr. C. Feeling alienated from his father for many years, he was surprised and deeply moved to discover how much, as a child, he had loved and admired him.

This discovery, in turn, opened new paths to the oedipal conflicts of childhood. While, in the transference, these had appeared in the form of criticism and competition with me, a dimension was missing. For some years Mr. C's positive feelings for his analyst and the disappointment in love that he experienced in analysis had been concealed as had the oedipal disappointments involving both parents that lay behind the later adolescent experience. These central conflicts could not surface and be worked with until the defensive cover provided by the adolescent secret could be exposed.

Clearly the difficulty of bringing to light so important a part of the transference neurosis was a two-way street. While from my side the surface aspect of the problem concerned the issue of training analyst appointment, its roots went deeper. Like Mr. C, I experienced disappointment in my father in adolescence and, feeling hurt, I, too, moved away from him. Like my patient, I had to contend both with the effects of an identification with my father and with guilt which I sought to rationalize and avoid. Thus, in some respects, Mr. C's story resonated with my own history and for me threatened to awaken troublesome ghosts. Patient and analyst, then, each for his own reasons, formed a conspiracy that had as its purpose the avoidance not only of current conflicts but of memories rooted in parallel life experiences. This is not as unusual a situation as one might imagine. Correspondences between the lives of the two participants in the analytic situation occur with some frequency, and memories and fantasies of the therapist's that interlock and interweave with those of the patient can prove to be an important source of the analyst's resistances. It is just such resistances that, interweaving with those of the patient, contribute so importantly to the formation of analytic secrets and to the concealment of those aspects of the transference neurosis that are embedded within them.

The second case that I wish to discuss is that of Mr. M, a young professional man, who also shared with me an analytic secret. In this situation, however, that secret was screened by another, more obvious one.

This more palpable secret centered on an incident that occurred in the early months of the analysis. I had missed a session and had been unable to notify Mr. M of my absence. Starting out from home for my office at the usual time, I had been caught in a massive traffic jam and had spent the hour sitting motionless on a parkway.

At the next session, Mr. M was completely understanding. He had figured something like that had happened, he said, and he had left after waiting no more than half an hour. He dismissed the episode as unimportant and in subsequent sessions did not return to it in any direct way.

It was indirectly, however, that Mr. M spoke of it. Over the next several months his associations contained allusions to the incident. Mr. M hinted that he was more troubled by what had happened than he had let on.

Regarding this matter as of some importance both in terms of the experience itself and Mr. M's handling of it, I was assiduous in picking up these clues. I interpreted what I thought to be my patient's hidden feelings and attempted to explore his need to keep them secret. What I came to understand only gradually was that by offering hints and clues that he knew would interest me, Mr. M was attempting in subtle ways to set the analysis on a particular path.

In these efforts Mr. M was seeking unconsciously, to avoid exploration of another incident that had occurred some months later and that he hoped both of us would forget. What had happened then was that one noon hour Mr. M spotted me at a nearby restaurant conversing with a young woman resident. On occasion I use my lunchtime for supervision and that day, in the midst of doing so, I looked up and saw Mr. M observing us from a seat at the far end of the counter.

It was not the first time that he had been there. Twice before as I entered the restaurant following a midday session with Mr. M, I noticed him having lunch at the counter.

Since Mr. M failed to mention these episodes in subsequent hours, I introduced the subject several times in the hopes of tapping into some important material. These efforts were frustrated by Mr. M's response. Immediately he became defensive and guarded. He emphasized the reality of the fact that on those days he had been pressed for time and that there was no other decent place in the neighborhood to grab a quick lunch. He expressed hurt at my bringing up the subject which he took to mean that I did not want to associate with him in any way. Efforts to explore this reaction met with a stone wall. Mr. M's response to having observed me with the resident was the same.

He said nothing about it. This time, however, I did not introduce the topic and gradually, buried under the weight of other pressing material, it faded from the consciousness of both patient and analyst.

Some time later I recalled the rationalization that I used to justify my willingness to let the matter slip by. In light of Mr. M's sensitive reaction to my previous attempts to raise the issue, I thought it inopportune to interject the matter once again. This seemed especially so in view of the fact that Mr. M was experiencing quite considerable marital difficulties at the time and sessions were preoccupied with that problem. Only when, later in the analysis, still another incident took place was I more effective in confronting Mr. M with his behavior and in exploring its meaning with him.

This last event was similar to the others in that once again Mr. M observed me outside of the office. It differed from the previous situations in one not unimportant respect. This time I was with my wife. Once more the setting was the familiar restaurant, but on this occasion the time was not the lunch hour but after work.

I had just seen Mr. M in one of the two evening appointments that we had scheduled at that time and had arranged to meet my wife at the restaurant for a quick dinner before going out for the evening. As the two of us were standing on line waiting to be seated, I spotted Mr. M again sitting at the far end of the counter. He seemed to be keeping an eye on the entranceway.

This time when Mr. M failed to mention the episode in the next hour, I did not hesitate to bring it up. Although, initially, his response to my intervention was to protest as before, I continued to return to the matter and focused on his secretive behavior both within and outside of the hours. Due, perhaps, in part to this more active confrontation, but also because important analytic work had been done in other areas of Mr. M's life, including his marital difficulties, he was finally able to discuss the restaurant incidents. When he did so an important secret of Mr. M's childhood, revived in this piece of acting out, came to light. The secret related to Mr. M's mother, an attractive and coquettish woman, who was many years younger than his father. When Mr. M was ten, his mother arranged for the two of them to take drawing lessons at a local art school. Two afternoons a week mother and son would make the half-mile trip to the school and once there go their separate ways, Mr. M to a children's class and his mother to work privately with Mr. L, the artist in charge.

What troubled the boy and aroused his curiosity was that after her lesson his mother would often emerge from the studio looking flushed and distracted with her makeup uncharacteristically smudged. One day when the occasion presented itself, he slipped away from his own class, walked the few steps to the adjacent room, and listened at the door. He heard low moans. Peeking through a crack in the door, he saw his mother lying on a mattress in the center of the room wrapped in the arms of Mr. L.

For several weeks Mr. M said nothing about what he had witnessed. Then he could contain himself no longer and confessed to his mother. Although she was quick to explain her behavior as an innocent effort to comfort Mr. L, who had become upset, she also made clear to the child that no one, least of all his father, would understand. He would accuse her of all kinds of terrible things and there would be hell to pay.

Mr. M got the message. He was to say nothing. This was to be a secret between himself and his mother. And so it was. Although many times he was tempted to tell his father what he had witnessed and rid himself of the terrible burden that now weighed on him, he never did. He was too afraid. The father had a violent temper and more than once, in a fit of rage, he had struck his wife. Mr. M was terrified that if his father discovered the truth he might kill her and himself as her secret accomplice.

From the time that it became his silent and ever-present companion, this secret had a profound effect on Mr. M's development. Not only did it create unspoken tensions between himself and his parents and stimulate resentment that could neither be articulated nor well understood, but it fostered guilt in Mr. M for being his mother's accomplice in deceiving his father. It also contributed in Mr. M to the development of an image of himself as a sham and an imposter and, because the secret was so quickly caught up in the process of acquiring knowledge, it led to the development of learning difficulties.

This secret lay behind the analytic secret. Mr. M's curiosity about my life was acted out via the restaurant scenes, and when he observed me there with a young and not unattractive woman he was convinced that he had caught me in the act of having an affair.

This secret he could speak of no more than he could the childhood one. In fact, he attempted to cope with the unwelcome emotions stirred in him by his troubling discovery in the same way as he had done originally; by an effort to sequester the information in a corner of his mind and not think about it. What he could not manage in this fashion, he rationalized in ways that protected his positive image of me. He also attempted, quite unconsciously, to divert me from pursuing the matter in analysis by dangling hints about his response to the first secret, the missed session, as a decoy.

This was a tactic that as a youngster Mr. M had often employed to throw his father off a dangerous trail. If the father grew suspicious of his wife's relationship with Mr. L and began to query his son about the art school, the boy would frequently manage to change the subject by hinting at a matter that he knew troubled his father.

This situation, like the one that occurred in analysis, also involved a missed appointment. On this occasion it was the father who was the culprit. After reluctantly agreeing to take Mr. M to a basketball game and arranging to meet him in front of the arena, he never showed up. Summoned by his boss to a dinner meeting at the eleventh hour, the father could not get in touch with his son and left him standing cold and angry on a street corner.

Mr. M's reaction to this event was characteristic for him. He was understanding and forgiving and readily accepted his father's apology. After that he did not bring the matter up openly. However, it was not lost on the child that his father felt extremely guilty over what had happened. Something of an amateur psychologist, the father was concerned about possible untoward consequences of his defection and he observed his son for signs that such a reaction might be taking place. Know-

ing this, Mr. M had developed ways of taking advantage of the
situation that in time became quite automatic. He would allude
to having felt rejected and unloved for some time, scarcely
needing to make the link to the unfortunate incident. The
father, out of his feelings of guilt and worry, would do the rest.
This is the way Mr. M managed to throw his father off the track
and at the same time get back at him for what he regarded as
persistent neglect.

The father was a busy professional man, meticulous and
obsessional, who often seemed preoccupied and aloof. Mr. M
felt as though he were little more than an afterthought in his
father's life and he resented him for this attitude of indifference. The father knew this and from time to time would make
short-lived efforts to remedy the situation. In the minds of both,
then, the basketball game episode came to concretize their long-
standing failure to connect.

In analysis, Mr. M's concealed references to the appointment I had missed thus had wide reverberations and in the
transference served multiple functions. The ambivalent relationship with the father was relived and became a central part
of the transference neurosis. Mr. M felt that I, too, was preoccupied with my work, cared more about my professional obli-
gations than I did about him, and regarded him, essentially, as
just a patient who could be easily replaced. In his imagination
my missing the appointment stood for all of this.

Conflicts concerning the mother, too, were prominent in
the transference. A sometime actress, she was a self-involved
woman whose relationships had little depth. In ways more subtle than obvious she manipulated people behind a veneer of
charm and graciousness. Part of Mr. M's feeling that I was not
really connected with him constituted a reliving of his tenuous
relationship with his mother. His conviction, too, that I valued
him only for his achievements and for what he produced as a
patient reflected his belief that his mother's primary interest in
him was as a talented child who through his accomplishments
would enhance her self-image.

Thus, in the case of Mr. M, as in that of Mr. C, there
developed in the analysis a transference neurosis that on the
manifest level seemed rich and complex. What was concealed,

however, was the secret shared with the mother. And embedded in his secret was a side of Mr. M's relationship with her—and indirectly with the father—that contained the essence of the child's sexual yearnings and fears. As in the former case, one of the unconscious functions that the secret came to have in the child's psychology was to screen from awareness a constellation of love–hate conflicts involving both parents that had to be warded off. Because this complex of fantasies and memories was concealed behind the analytic secret as well as the childhood one, until the former surfaced only a portion of the transference neurosis, and not its core, could become the focus of analytic work.

Interestingly, I was able to explore Mr. M's acting out of his wish to discover my secrets only after he had seen me with my wife. What I came to understand about this rather curious fact was that being in the company of my wife unconsciously represented for me a legitimate situation as compared to the earlier experience of being observed. Although I was not aware of it at the time, the previous incident, which involved my having lunch with a young and attractive woman, must have been experienced on some level, if not as a liaison, at least as a pleasant date. I will not comment on the wishful aspects of this situation but will note only that I remember thinking that the particular supervisory hour in question was an unusually good one.

Mr. M's belief that the scene he witnessed was part of an affair must have resonated with feelings of guilt stirred up in me and that guilt had a deeper core. As I reflected on the situation, I came in touch with certain memories of childhood. These involved long hours spent in private kitchen table talks with my mother from which my father was excluded but upon which, anytime after the eleven o'clock news, he might intrude. These memories represented in shorthand form the oedipal wishes and guilt with which I had struggled in childhood and which I had long repressed. The supervisory incident, which involved my being observed in a private talk with a woman, must have connected with memories of these childhood experiences and stirred anxiety in me which I unconsciously defended against.

One way of doing this was to offer myself rationalizations for not exploring Mr. M's behavior and his perception of what he had seen. This contrasted sharply with my ability to confront these issues later on when Mr. M spotted me on line with my life. The difference, I suspect, lay in the fact that in the latter situation I experienced no guilt and hence had no need to defend myself through avoidance.

Thus, in this situation, as in the former one, the collusive interaction of patient and therapist served to exclude from analytic investigation material that constituted an important aspect of the transference neurosis.

My final example concerns another, less common, but not unimportant pathway for the enactment of covert aspects of the transference neurosis. This route involves not only the spoken word but the written one.

As an aspect of the clinical situation, the written word is rarely discussed, but in certain circumstances it can play an important part in the interactions between patient and analyst. Dreams that are written down; notes taken by the analyst and diaries or records of the analysis kept by patients; insurance forms filled out by one or both participants; handwritten bills and checks and the analyst's manner of endorsing the checks he receives; written communications concerning appointments and other matters; and the writings, professional and otherwise, of analyst and patient that are read or—as significantly—not read by the other. All of these have communicative value and, at times, may convey important messages that do not appear in the verbal material.

Such was the case with Mr. D, a middle-aged professional man, who utilized the written word—or more precisely, allusions to the written word—as a means of communication with his analyst. As a young adult, he had written a story about the devastating impact on an adolescent of the discovery of a family secret. This story had appeared in an obscure magazine which later became defunct. At the time that he began analysis Mr. D was planning to rework this story into a novel. For reasons which he rationalized in terms of fear that analysis could prove disruptive to his creative efforts, Mr. D spoke very little about his writing. On occasion he made reference to the published story but never revealed its theme.

Prior to his entering analysis, Mr. D had learned from a colleague who had previously been a patient of mine that except in unusual circumstances I made it a practice not to read the published work of authors whom I was currently seeing in treatment. Learning about this policy played some role in Mr. D's choice of an analyst. It reverberated with aspects of his own past history and his need to relive aspects of that past.

In analysis the messages that Mr. D conveyed about his writing represented just such an unconscious repetition. He gave consistently mixed signals. On the one hand he revealed very little about his work; on the other, by alluding to the short story that he had written, he was inviting me to discover and read it. In this way I would learn not only about the theme of his fiction but about the family secret that he had referred to in analysis but had not openly discussed.

In this behavior, it became clear, Mr. D was enacting an identification with his mother. An aspiring writer, the mother left notes for articles and stories as well as fragments of stories everywhere in the house. They were open for anyone to read and, when he was eleven, Mr. D took advantage of the opportunity. What he read, however, was extremely troubling. Using only the thin disguise of a fictional heroine, the mother revealed that for many years she had been romantically involved with another woman, a cousin once removed who was much younger than herself.

This revelation was shocking to Mr. D; so shocking, in fact, that consciously he could not allow himself to take it in. He acted as though the fiction was just that—fiction that had nothing to do with his mother. Preconsciously, however, he understood. In fact, he repeatedly hinted to his mother that he knew what was happening and wanted to understand the situation.

In analysis, Mr. D played out the role of the mother. He left clues for me to find in the hope that without his being responsible for revealing it, the secret would be brought into the open.

At the same time, through enactments that involved a second secret, Mr. D relived another facet of the childhood situ-

ation. An avid reader of psychoanalytic material, he had come
across an article of mine published some years earlier. In that
article, to illustrate a countertransference issue, I alluded to a
personal loss that I had suffered. Although Mr. D never mentioned this article directly, references to it, and specifically to
the information about me that it contained, appeared in his
associations. In this way he enacted in analysis another familiar
role; that of the child who hints to a parent that he knows that
adult's secret but cannot speak of it without permission.

All of this material clearly had its roots in Mr. D's relationship with his mother—one that in many ways was carried
on through secretive communications. In analysis, however, he
spoke very little about her. He was preoccupied, rather, with
his father and, initially, the transference material centered on
that powerful figure in his life.

With his father Mr. D had for years carried on a running
battle. Dominant, strong-minded, and inflexible, the father
sought to exert his will on all those around him. From Mr. D
he demanded, and on the surface received, unwavering obe-
dience. Behind the scenes, however, another scenario was
played out. Quietly and in his own way, Mr. D waged guerrilla
warfare. Through covert withholding, convenient forgetting,
and other passive–aggressive means, he fought an underground battle. In a variety of ways he also tried to please his
father, however, and the result was behavior that oscillated
between compliance and concealed rebellion.

In analysis similar struggles were carried on as Mr. D's
behavior reflected a conflict between his wish to win my love
and the contradictory attitude of wanting to defeat me—and
the analytic process. This conflict seemed to form the core of
the transference neurosis as it unfolded in Mr. D's treatment.
Although oedipal issues and their derivatives were clearly central to it, positive feelings about Mr. D's mother seemed
strangely absent from the material. Instead Mr. D railed against
her, regarded her as cold-hearted and unapproachable, and
wanted little to do with her.

When Mr. D was fourteen his parents were divorced. Using
his knowledge of his wife's illicit relationship as a weapon, the
father obtained custody of his son. Thereafter it was he who

raised Mr. D. Contact with the mother diminished over the years partly because of her lack of persistence in the face of obstacles, and partly because Mr. D, like his father, had become hostile to her.

Behind Mr. D's conscious attitude toward his mother lay the love for her that he could not acknowledge. As a young child he had been exceptionally close to his mother and they shared much together. He adored her. This affection, however, could not survive the discovery of the mother's secret relationship and the subsequent breakup of the marriage. Mr. D felt crushed by these events and he blamed his mother for them.

Mr. D's affection for his mother and the world of early childhood experience that it represented was not approachable through the transference for some time. It existed, though, in an unspoken way as an undercurrent of warm feelings for the analyst combined with the conviction that we shared similar ideals and values. This silent spring of emotion with its source in deeply felt oedipal love constituted an important, if concealed, part of the transference neurosis. Although, in time, Mr. D became aware of his warm feelings for his analyst, they could not be meaningfully related to his buried love for his mother until the secret that helped bury it, and that subsequently blocked access to those feelings, could be shared in analysis and its reverberations explored.

For many years Mr. D believed that the cause of his alienation from his mother lay entirely in her attitude toward his father and himself. Although he recalled the episode of coming upon his mother's story, he had managed to isolate the ideational aspects of that memory from the emotional chaos that he experienced at the time. Sequestered with those emotions were the ones of early childhood which contained Mr. D's deep and abiding love for his mother.

The barriers to uncovering the analytic secret were created in this case, as in the others, not only by the patient but by the analyst. In holding fast to the policy of not reading the work of authors in treatment, I was playing into a powerful resistance. Mr. D experienced me as an inflexible and controlling parent who was insensitive to the needs of others. Moreover, he regarded me as unwilling or unable to pick up clues concerning information that he wanted me to have. In this respect I was experienced as the mother who refused to hear the message about the secret that he was transmitting.

As I came to understand these reactions, I realized that my policy of not reading the work of authors in treatment, justified as it had always seemed by the necessity of avoiding extraneous influences on my perceptions and judgments, also represented identifications with my former analyst and teachers. Unconsciously, I had adopted their attitudes and methods. In this regard, I am reminded of a recent observation made by Joyce MacDougall (1979).

"The garnering of analytic knowledge has been accomplished and [is] deeply impregnated with transference affect, and thus tends to carry an in-built resistance of its own, making it difficult for us to hear all that is being transmitted" (p. 302). I realized, too, that this policy contained within it a hidden identification with Mr. D. Much to my consternation at the time, my own analyst had thought it best not to read anything I wrote. I was, therefore, in my own conduct as an analyst, identifying with both aggressor and victim.

When I was able to abandon my rigid posture and convey to Mr. D my willingness to read his story, it no longer became necessary. The transference battle was at an end. Partly for this reason and partly because by then a fair amount of analysis of Mr. D's defenses had taken place, he was able to discuss the theme of his creative work.

A more specific piece of countertransference also contributed to Mr. D's inability to reveal aspects of the analytic secret for some time. This had to do with my reaction to Mr. D's having read my article. Concealed in his associations were clues that revealed his keen interest in the personal reference it contained and to the fact that he had pieced together the truth about that situation.

For some time, however, I did not receive the messages that Mr. D was sending. To do so would have meant for me the revival of painful memories that I was not prepared to deal with at that time. As a result I screened out what I could not tolerate hearing. In fact, when I was finally able to understand Mr. D's wish for me to give him permission to reveal what he knew, it took a number of sessions before I could offer that interpretation. I had first to reflect on what I was experiencing and attempt to come to better terms with the residual feelings connected with my own situation. As in the previous cases, the analyst had to accept the exposure of his own secret before the patient's secret could come into the open. And it was through the analytic secret that access could be obtained, not only to the earlier secret, but to the infantile neurosis that it so effectively screened.

In the foregoing examples it becomes clear that the transference neurosis, often described as though it were a unitary entity whose development and resolution constitutes the essence of the analytic process, is, in fact, a highly complex phenomenon. Well understood at present are the amalgam of mental representations, self and object, past and present, that enter into its formation as well as the contributions made to it by the various aspects of the personality. Less well appreciated is the fact that the transference neurosis may be composed of multiple levels.

As was true of the cases I have cited, the covert aspect of the transference neurosis is often related to, and represents, a reliving in analysis of a secret that has played a role of critical importance in the patient's development. In many such situations the secret has remained untouched and unexplored since its inception. It exists as a silent force in the personality, affecting its bearer in multiple ways. Prominent among these are its defensive uses. Since by definition a secret draws around it a curtain of silence and of mystery, it can serve as a magnet to draw under its protective shield much not directly related to it that must also be forgotten. Included in this catalogue of things unrememberable are not only family myths that must be preserved and troublesome aspects of object relations, but memories of certain wishes and fears of childhood that stimulate anxiety. Central to these, but by no means limited to them, are the oedipal conflicts that form the core of the infantile neurosis. Having under ordinary circumstances a secretive quality, these conflicts can achieve further defensive cover by coming under the protective umbrella of a secret that develops in later childhood or adolescence.

When it develops in the course of treatment, an analytic secret serves a function analogous to the original one. Just as the later secret conceals the earlier infantile ones, the analytic secret forms a third layer and screens the others. In analysis the process of uncovering proceeds from the surface and, to reach the underlying secret, must deal first with the secretive aspect of the transference. As is often true of family members, however, the analyst, for his own reasons, may convey to the patient his need to avoid exposure of the secret. When this happens, a collusion develops between patient and analyst that may have as its outcome the failure to explore an important aspect of the transference neurosis.

4

Transference Relationships, the Relationships Between Transferences, and Reconstruction

In this chapter I wish to discuss an aspect of the phenomenon of transference that thus far has received little attention in the literature. I refer to the relationships that exist between the multiple and shifting transferences that emerge in the course of every psychoanalytic treatment and to the fact that in certain instances investigation of these relationships can yield valuable clues in the process of reconstruction.

That every analysis contains within the experience of transference a panoply of transferences that interact and interweave in diverse and complex patterns has been appreciated by a number of observers. Blum (1971) has noted that clinical transference is overdetermined with regard to object representation and past experience. He has compared the coalescence of images and experiences in transference to "the manifest content of a dream deriving from contemporary day residues and memories and fantasies of childhood" (p. 49).

Greenacre (1959) has spoken of "a constant panoramic procession of transference pictures merging into each other or momentarily separating out with special clarity in a way which

is frequently less constant than the symptoms and other manifestations of the neurosis itself" (p. 485). She has made the
suggestion also that analysts pay consistent attention to the special forms, variations, and movements within the transference
relationship itself.

Stone (1967) regards the phenomenon of transference in
analysis as being composed of two different elements; the primordial transference which derives from the effort to master
the earliest experiences of separation from the mother and
whose aim is renewed contact with her, and the mature transference which is displaced from the parent of early childhood
and which "tends toward separation and individuation" (p. 25).
These two elements of transference are in constant interaction
with each other.

Bird (1972) regards transference as one of the functions
of the ego, which, as such, may be counted on to possess many
characteristics of such a function.

"The ego's ways of reality testing, for instance, its responses
to internal and external stimuli, its uses of defense mechanisms," he writes, "may all reveal much about the basic phe-
nomenology of transference" (p. 299). He also suggests that
much may be surmised about transference's functional vicissitudes by assuming that transference "suffers the same general
developmental and neurotic deficiencies, distortions, limitations and fixations to which various other functions of the ego
are susceptible" (p. 299).

Brenner (1983) shares Bird's belief that the commonly held
views of transference as a simple projection or repetition of the
past do not do justice to the complexity of the psychological
processes involved. He points out that every instance of transference contains not only elements of drive and defense but
superego components as well. The resultant of multiple forces,
transference, in his view, should always be regarded as a compromise formation.

Kohut (1971) has stressed the importance of self–object
transferences in disorders of narcissism. In analytic work with
such patients he observed that such transferences, derived from
the infantile period when self and object were not yet clearly
distinguished, tended to emerge earlier in treatment than those

more familiar transference configurations whose essential feature is the displacement onto the analyst of object representations of childhood.

Although Kohut was the first to utilize the term *self–object transferences,* the phenomenon which he described is a familiar one to all psychoanalysts. Decades of clinical experience have shown that it is not only patients with narcissistic disorders who may develop transferences of this kind. To the contrary, patients of all types may, at various stages of treatment, develop transferences that contain not only a mixture of perception and memory, ego and superego, drive and defense, but aspects of self and object representation as well.

Although modern perspectives on transference in the clinical situation have emphasized its complexity and its multiple roots, the question of the forms, manner, and sequences in which transferences develop in analytic treatment has been comparatively little explored. Of particular interest are the problems of how the various transference pictures relate to one another, how the relationships between them may convey forgotten pieces of history as well as be utilized currently for the purposes of defense and of working through of residual trauma, and how understanding these relationships may assist the analyst in his reconstructive efforts. It is these issues that, by means of several clinical examples, I wish to illustrate in this chapter.

The question of why it is in any given case that transferences emerge in the way they do is a matter to which comparatively little attention has been paid. It is clear, however, that the factors that influence the form and manner of their appearance are multiple. Among these are the character and life situation of the patient and the particular conflicts that are psychologically active; the manner in which he experiences the analyst and the memories and fantasies, both conscious and unconscious, that these perceptions evoke; the state of the patient's resistances at any given time; the intensity with which extra-analytic transferences are currently experienced, and the manner of their interaction with the transference proper; reality considerations concerning the analyst (age, gender, appearance, and personal style, including the extent to which these may be, in fact, a physical or behavioral resemblance to an important figure from the past); the analyst's countertransferences and the particular techniques that he employs.

As a result of the influence of these and other factors, the sequences and timing with which the various transferences appear in a particular case may, and often do, follow a pattern that is quite different from that which characterized the development of the corresponding self and object representations in childhood. It is also true, however, that for certain periods in some cases and for rather extended times in others, it can be shown that the form and manner in which transferences emerge and the patterns that they evolve are meaningfully related to aspects of an individual's psychological history.

In what follows I would like to cite several case examples to illustrate these relationships. In doing so I will focus primarily on those aspects of transference that relate to object representations, although it is true, of course, that in each example cited the transference paradigm that developed was a highly complex matter containing contributions from several aspects of the personality. If, in light of the foregoing discussion of transference as containing multiple and complex elements, my own descriptions of it seem naive if not simplistic, I will ask the reader to understand that to illustrate the thesis of this chapter I must deliberately focus on one narrow aspect of the phenomenon, for to do otherwise would be to obscure the central issue.

Some years ago I undertook the analysis of a bright and capable young woman whose relationships to others were marred by attitudes of wariness and suspicion. Born to a family of aristocratic background, Ms. L was raised in an environment in which social position was a matter of overriding importance. Her mother was a forceful, energetic, and highly ambitious person whose never ceasing involvements in luncheons and charity balls made her almost a caricature of the society matron. Ms. L's father, an inhibited, anxious, and vain man, seemed to have as his primary ambition the wish to play the role of attendant and social companion to his wife.

Early on in treatment it became clear that part of Ms. L's difficulties in relating to friends and colleagues was attributable to the fact that she regarded herself as an imposter. Quite convinced that if she allowed others to become close to her the essential falseness and disingenuousness of her character would be revealed, she avoided intimate relationships. The reasons for this belief were not at all clear. Far from being an unreliable person or a devious one, Ms. L was, on the contrary, totally trustworthy.

Why it was that Ms. L held to a view of herself that was so patently false was a mystery to which there were few clues. So far as I knew there was no one in the family who could be described as an imposter or as having behaved in a deceitful manner. Nor could I discover in Ms. L's case either a historical event that might have thrown light on the origin of her beliefs, unconscious fantasies that might have explained it, or pronounced guilt feelings, conscious or unconscious, that might have contributed in a significant way to such a distorted self-image. The closest that I could come to an explanation of this problem centered on Ms. L's masturbatory conflicts. For some years in adolescence these had been intense and she blamed the frequent skin problems that she had at that time on this evil habit. I had no doubt that this conflict played some role in Ms. L's view of herself as devious and a sham, but I questioned whether, by itself, it could have had so enduring effect as to account for the puzzling symptom at hand. For some time, though, I had to be content with this explanation as it was the only one that I had.

From the outset of treatment it was my hope that some of the unconscious factors that were at the root of Ms. L's symptoms would be revealed through the transference. In this expectation I was not disappointed, but because the clues to deciphering this puzzling clinical picture depended on understanding not only the individual transference pictures that emerged but the relationships between them, it took several years for my hope to be realized.

Initially, and for quite some time, the dominant transference centered on the mother. Ms. L experienced me, as she did her mother, as an active, energetic, socially ambitious person whose burgeoning schedule allowed precious little time for her. She treasured the hours set aside for analysis and from early on appealed to me to increase them. In silent protest, and with resentment, she observed the comings and goings of other patients and fantasized my greater attention to them. She imagined me busy each night with some social engagement and when an important charity function was to be held at the Plaza or 21 Club, she took for granted that my wife and I were among the sponsors.

Convinced that I, too, regarded her as false and devious, Ms. L initially did all that she could to show herself to be a reliable person and one of good character. Always prompt for her hours, she regularly paid her bill as soon as it was rendered; and on the rare occasion when it was necessary for her to miss a session, offered to pay me in advance.

This behavior reflected Ms. L's tireless efforts as a youngster to be the daughter that she imagined her mother wanted—a well-behaved, obedient, and reliable child who made a point of being aware of the needs of others. It reflected, too, her method of competing with the parade of friends, acquaintances, and committee people who sought her mother's attention. Less obvious in the early months of treatment, but increasingly so as time went on and the extent of Ms. L's ambivalent feelings toward her mother became evident, was the defensive aspect of her behavior. Concealed behind it lay powerful feelings of resentment that, in childhood, she did not dare to reveal to her mother and that now, with equal tenacity, she concealed from me.

The initial transference constellation held center stage in the analysis for approximately three years. Then, abruptly, without a hint of what was coming, it underwent a change. Still Ms. L sought to please me, but now she did so by deliberate efforts to play up to me as a man.

All at once she had kind words for my ties, my haircut, the quality of my voice. Shifting in so rapid a manner that, at first, I was rather bewildered by the transformation, the prevailing object representation in the transference was now centered on me as the father—a father whose devotion to his tailor was exceeded only by his attachment to his Porsche.

That a development of this kind had taken place was not, in itself, so surprising. To the contrary, in view of the fact that for several years the transference focus had been on the mother and that not insignificant work had been done on the working through of competitive feelings with her, progression toward beginning to deal in the transference with sexual feelings for me and with the frightening oedipal feelings that lay behind them, seemed a natural development.

The reawakening of such feelings, in fact, did play a role of importance in the change that occurred. There was, however, something more to this sudden shift in transference focus. Hidden in it was the reliving of a piece of Ms. L's forgotten history. Of crucial importance in her development, this experience, however, could not be clarified until the transference had taken still another turn.

Once again the change occurred rapidly. In this instance, though, the shift took place only a few months after the predominant transference had centered on me as the father. During its short life this transference constellation had been a complicated one. While Ms. L's need for me to respond to her as an attractive woman was strong and her behavior, initially, was teasing and flirtatious, negative feelings toward her analyst soon became prominent. Surfacing at first in an oblique manner as a piece of mockery in a dream or as the innocently quoted remark of a critic of analysis, Ms. L's hostility gradually became more palpable. Within a few months after this phase of the transference had set in, her attacks became sharper and more direct. When, at one point, she spotted me getting into a taxi and imagined that I wished to avoid her, her angry accusations were followed by pronounced feelings of depression.

It was at this juncture that the second transference picture receded. It faded, it seemed, as quickly as it had come, replaced now by the reemergence of a transference in which Ms. L related to me primarily as her mother. The second mother-dominated transference, however, was, in significant respects, different from the first.

No longer was Ms. L the good, responsible child forever seeking affection. Now she was contained and aloof. Still polite and outwardly respectful, she nonetheless maintained a kind of formality and distance that I had not seen before. Apparent for the first time were both the insular quality and the sense

of wariness that, in later childhood and adolescence, characterized her relations with others.

To me the shifts that had occurred in the predominant
transference paradigms—and particularly the rapidity with
which they came on—were as puzzling as they seemed important. I knew from prior experience that in certain individuals
the particular form and manner in which transferences unfold
constitutes an unconscious living out of specific psychological
experiences of childhood or adolescence, but in Ms. L's case no
material had yet surfaced to suggest that sudden or unexpected
alterations in her life situation or in her self or object representations had, in fact, constituted an important aspect of her
development.

In the hope that the patient herself might provide some
clue to these puzzling developments, I drew her attention to
the phenomena that I have been discussing. Intrigued by the
overview that she now had of this aspect of her analytic experience, and as interested as I was in the idea that the particular
way in which it unfolded might have some meaning, she was
equally perplexed as to what that meaning could be. It was at
that point that Ms. L began to question her mother about her
childhood; and it was the mother, ultimately, who clarified
matters.

At first, however, she was reluctant to do so. She possessed
certain information that could clear up the mystery, but she
had serious misgivings about sharing it with her daughter. It
concerned a long-held secret in the family that the mother did
not want to unearth. Fortunately, however, she had recently
entered therapy for feelings of depression and she discussed
her dilemma with her therapist. That he must have helped
clarify the situation was evident, for, one afternoon, after returning from a session, she summoned her daughter to the
library and revealed to her the nature of the secret. It was not,
however, the first time that she had done so. This discussion
had taken place once before, when the patient was slightly over
three years old. How long Ms. L had remembered the facts that
were disclosed at that time is unclear, but it was apparent that
for many years they had been banished from consciousness.

What her mother revealed was that Ms. L's father was not,

in fact, her natural father but her stepfather. The parents had been divorced soon after Ms. L's birth, following her father's desertion of his wife in her sixth month of pregnancy. For a short time thereafter he kept in touch with the family but gradually his contact diminished and he vanished from the scene. Ms. L never knew him.

Within a year the mother remarried and her new husband adopted Ms. L. So far as Ms. L knew, this man was her father. The name of her natural father was never mentioned in the house and, in fact, it was a condition laid down by her stepfather prior to marriage that this rule be strictly enforced.

In all likelihood Ms. L would never have known the true circumstances of her birth but for the intervention of the family pediatrician. This doctor knew the full story and he prevailed on the mother to discuss the facts with her child lest in later life she discover the truth and suffer irreparable psychological damage.

Under this pressure the mother reluctantly told Ms. L about her natural father. This was, however, to be a secret between mother and daughter, and, in fact, the mother conveyed still another message. It was a secret to be forgotten. Except for an incident which occurred several months later, the matter was never mentioned again. On this occasion Ms. L and her mother were walking on the street when the mother spotted her former husband in a crowd. Spontaneously she pointed him out to the child who strained to see him. Before she could get close enough to get a good look, however, he hailed a taxi cab and was gone. For some time this experience remained in memory. According to the mother, Ms. L played it out repeatedly; then, in time, it faded. It was revived in the analysis when, by chance, she once observed me getting into a cab. Coming, however, at a time when she consciously knew nothing of the family secret, its significance could be grasped neither by patient nor analyst.

In discussing with her daughter the long forgotten events of childhood, Ms. L's mother recalled the child's reaction to being told the truth about her father. She had said nothing, remained subdued for several hours, and then, without a further word, resumed playing as before. For some time thereafter, however, the mother noticed a marked change in the girl. No longer did she seek out her mother for attention and affection. Now she turned to her stepfather and with all the seductive charm of a three-year-old, sought to win his favor.

The stepfather, though, was an exceedingly controlled man, embarrassed by open displays of affection, and he did not encourage the child in such behavior. She, in turn, took his reaction as a rejection. When, repeatedly, she could not obtain from him the response that she wanted, she gave up the effort. In the course of doing so she displayed increasing anger at the stepfather and when, in an unhappy incident, he severely disappointed her, she turned on him with an outburst of tearful rage.

For some weeks her stepfather had promised to take Ms. L to a puppet show. When the appointed time came, however, he reneged. Claiming as an excuse urgent business matters, and with the child watching glumly from the doorway, he drove off to the office. This disappointment, combined with the feelings of rejection she had been experiencing, caused Ms. L to turn away from the stepfather. Thereafter her interest in him seemed markedly diminished.

Once again Ms. L turned back to her mother as the primary parent, but now their relationship took on a different quality. No longer was she the good child, forever eager to please. She had become more distant, more wary. Her manner seemed to convey a fear of being hurt and disappointed.

Once this forgotten piece of Ms. L's childhood surfaced and could be integrated with the rest of her history, the forms and transformations of the transference, at first so puzzling, were now comprehensible. Clearly the shifts and changes that occurred constituted, in large measure, a reactivation and re-living of memories of a crucial phase in Ms. L's development. Motivated by a need to repeat and to master the psychological traumas of that period and guided by the workings of the un-conscious sense of time, she recreated in the analytic situation not only the content of particular childhood experiences, but their essential form as well.

Reproduced were not only aspects of the child's early re-lationship to the mother, the shift to the stepfather and the shift back again, but elements of fantasy and memory that related to the natural father. Thus, Ms. L's behavior toward me as the frustrating stepfather contained within it not only the revival in memory of the disappointments she experienced at his hands, including the specific memory of his failure to keep his promise about the puppet show and his driving off without her, but the earlier memory of the natural father disappearing into a taxi cab. This memory, which apparently was worked over and elaborated rather extensively following its occurrence, became fused with the later experience. Thus Ms. L's anger at her stepfather—and at me in the transference—concealed within it long repressed rage at her natural father for his abandonment of her. It was this covert anger that in later years contributed to her wariness, not only of her stepfather, but, unconsciously, of all men.

Clarified, too, by recovering the forgotten piece of childhood history was the meaning of Ms. L's view of herself as an imposter. Learning that the person she knew as her father all of her life was, in fact, no blood relation and that her natural father had deserted her produced the idea that she, too, was not the person she thought she was. It was as though she was someone else. Moreover, Ms. L's mother had deceived her and could no longer be trusted. She, too, was someone other than who she claimed to be. And if her mother was not an honest person, Ms. L developed the fantasy that as her mother's child she must be equally untrustworthy. It was this unconscious identification with the mother as an imposter that played a significant role in Ms. L's distorted view of herself. There was, in addition, another piece of reality that, in all probability, played a role in the development of Ms. L's self-image. This was the fact that as a young child she had participated in a deception. Having learned the truth from her mother, she joined with her in concealing that knowledge from her stepfather. Although, over the years, this secret became thoroughly repressed and was lost to conscious awareness, it surfaced in another way; as a significant contributor to Ms. L's feeling that she was an imposter.

In another case, that of Mr. A, study of the emerging transference was instrumental in gaining insight into a particular type of resistance that he utilized: the defensive use of one transference against another. It also fostered understanding of the way that, in childhood, Mr. A utilized a shifting investment in object representations to defend against anxiety.

From the outset of this analysis a dominant transference note was struck. Before the first hour had come to an end it was clear in what role I would initially be cast; that of an omniscient mother. A strong-willed, articulate, and self-assured woman, Mr. A's mother never lost for him the image he had of her as a child; that of a powerful, invasive, and overbearing presence who was absolutely necessary for his survival.

It was not surprising, then, that early on in treatment Mr. A experienced me as he did; a controlling individual whose unspoken intent was to have him do my bidding and whose guidance he both needed and resented. For some months this transference dominated the scene, with Mr. A alternately disputing my every word and behaving as though without my assistance there was little chance of his surviving from one hour to the next.

During this time references to the father were infrequent and transference perceptions of me as a father figure were fleeting. On occasion Mr. A complained that I was indecisive and lacked assertion—traits that in his mind characterized his father—and once or twice reported a fantasy that I, like his father, was undoubtedly a Milquetoast of a husband who was thoroughly browbeaten by my wife. For the most part, however, the predominant transference centered on the reawakening of Mr. A's relationship with the mother of his early years. While, clearly, this was important in its own right, the extent to which this transference prevailed struck me as significant both in terms of current resistances to experiencing me as the father and in terms of historical factors in Mr. A's childhood. It was not, however, until additional transference configurations made their appearance that the overall picture could be clarified.

Mr. A had two brothers, one several years older, the other a few years younger. Little material concerning them surfaced in the early months of treatment. Initially they remained, like the father, shadowy figures. In time, however, they came into view both in terms of Mr. A's current interactions with them and in the transference. The sibling transferences, in fact, had a special quality. Each gained prominence at particular, and ultimately predictable times in the analysis; when pronounced anxiety was stimulated in Mr. A by the emergence of threatening impulses connected with the predominant transference of the moment.

This unconscious maneuver, clearly used in the service of resistance, became initially most evident in terms of the older brother. I noticed, on more than one occasion, that in the course of responding to me as a parent, and when his feelings were running high, Mr. A would, in a sudden shift, begin to refer to me as though I were this brother. These were, to be sure, not the only times that he perceived me in this way. On these other occasions, however, there was no sudden shift from one central transference configuration to another. The fact, though, that such shifts did occur at times when the prevailing transference stimulated anxiety-provoking impulses in Mr. A, lent particular importance and interest to such occurrences.

It was not unusual for feelings of aggression to constitute a large component of Mr. A's reaction to me as the dominant and overbearing mother. While rarely absent when this transference was in the ascendancy, the extent of these aggressive feelings varied within a considerable range. When they grew in intensity and Mr. A was in a fury at me for what he perceived to be my wish to control his every action, he would, after experiencing much anxiety, shift gears and begin to talk to me as though I were the older brother to whom he could complain about their mother. This defensive shift occurred at other times, too. It took place not only in connection with Mr. A's threatening aggressive feelings toward his mother (where clearly it served an object sparing purpose), but also in response to his libidinal ones. Though hidden behind his rages at and denunciations of his mother, such reactions were not entirely absent. When, in fact, they were stimulated by positive feelings in the transference and memories of incestuous wishes began to surface, it was quite predictable that a perception of me as the brother would soon make an appearance.

The sexual feelings stirred up in the transference, however,

were not limited to maternal ones. Yearnings toward me as the
father whose love Mr. A wished for were also mobilized, and
it was these, even more than the forbidden wishes toward the
mother, that had to be defended against.

Mr. A's relationship with his father was more complex and,
in some respects, richer than had first appeared. As a young
child they were quite close. For the first two years of Mr. A's
life, in fact, they were inseparable companions. Later on, largely
because of repeated depressions, the father withdrew emotionally from the family and the mother became the dominant parent. Mr. A's focus shifted almost exclusively to his mother, not
only because of the changed relationship that developed between them, but for defensive reasons as well. By concentrating
in so exclusive a way on his mother, he could avoid recognition
not only of his competitiveness with his father and his guilty
triumph at feeling himself the center of his mother's universe,
but of his frustrated longings for his father's love. And in his
efforts to protect against these feelings, he utilized not only his
relationship with his mother but that with his older brother as
well.

This brother, in fact, clearly became a substitute for the
father. In turning to him in this manner, Mr. A accomplished
two important goals. He was able to obtain at least a facsimile
of the loving response that he yearned for from his father and,
by concentrating interest and attention on the brother, was able
to screen out both the rage he felt toward his father and the
longings for him, that, because of their homosexual implications, were threatening.

Thus, in the transferences that emerged in Mr. A's analysis,
the representation of the older brother could, when needed,
serve for him a defensive purpose analogous to that which was,
at times, accomplished by their real relationship. But as was also
true of that relationship, the brother transference became
caught up in conflict. And when that transference stimulated
sufficient anxiety, a shift to another transference configuration
regularly took place.

This transference had as its central figure the younger
brother. It came into focus whenever Mr. A, experiencing his
analyst as the kindly and supportive older brother, felt unu-

sually close to me. This shift reflected a movement from one brother to another that occurred with some frequency during Mr. A's adolescent years. Like the defensive focus on the older brother described above, its aim was to protect against anxiety. As was the case with the father, this anxiety was generated by Mr. A's wish for love from the older brother and from me in the transference. Unconsciously this brother and the father were equated, and the patient's yearnings for affection from one extended to the other. In the case of the brother, however, the situation was complicated by the fact that during his latency years Mr. A had joined him in several episodes of mutual masturbation. The wish to repeat this exciting and frightening experience, which remained as a residue of these episodes, broke through to consciousness in adolescence and was reactivated in the analysis.

In life Mr. A had responded to this threat by a familiar expedient. Finding reasons to avoid his older brother, he focused instead on the younger one. Since frightening sexual feelings of the kind mentioned above played no part in Mr. A's relations with the younger brother, he represented in this regard an island of safety. Moreover, he provided an ideal vehicle for the living out of Mr. A's need to identify with his powerful mother. Thus Mr. A's relations with this brother were characterized by the domineering and overbearing attitude to which he himself had been subjected.

In the analysis the protective shift to a transference dominated by the younger brother took a characteristic form. Feeling threatened by feelings of closeness to me, Mr. A would, at first, seek to distance himself through an attitude of aloofness and indifference. Then focusing on some area of business about which he imagined I had little knowledge, such as the stock market or real estate transactions, he proceeded to show up my deficiencies. Then, as a sophisticated businessman, he would proceed to instruct me in the fundamentals of those fields. For a matter of several weeks behavior of this kind, with which he regularly harassed his younger brother, characterized his relations with me. Then, when his anxiety had been reduced and sufficient distance obtained from the threatening feelings that had aroused it, perceptions of me as the older brother would once more find their way into the transference.

Thus by following the shifts and changes in the transference pictures that emerged in Mr. A's analysis, it was possible to uncover some of the unconscious roots of the persistent difficulty that characterized his relationships, not only with friends and family, but with colleagues as well. Understanding the way that, when feeling threatened, he defensively altered his perceptions of me threw light on the similar unconscious displacements that had both taken place in the past and that were still active in his relationships with others. It provided insights that served as a first step in his efforts to improve these troubled relationships.

As a part of his reconstructive efforts the analyst sometimes finds it valuable to trace out the longitudinal aspects of object relationships and the way that, over years, they have undergone change. Intimately connected with shifting self representations and with unconscious fantasies that have contributed to symptom formation and to character development, the history of an analysand's changing perceptions of centrally important figures in his life is a rich field for analytic investigation. In this effort the close study of the relationships that exist between transferences can prove a useful tool.

This was the case in the analysis of Mr. R, a successful and energetic professional man in his midthirties. Unlike Ms. L, whose neurosis took the form of imagining herself to be an imposter, Mr. R was, in many respects, a sham. Quite striking was the way his polished style, youthful good looks, and unusual ability to ingratiate himself with clients concealed the fact that he was far from the expert in his field that his outward manner suggested.

Mr. R's need to play out the role of the charlatan despite good intelligence and considerable talent, however, shared symptoms and an unconscious dynamic with Ms. L's difficulties. In each, identification with a parent who was perceived as dishonest played a central role. In the case of Mr. R, however, this perception had in reality a more substantial basis.

A shrewd and ambitious entrepreneur who was given to marginal business practices, Mr. R's father, on one occasion in the patient's youth, overextended himself and was unable to pay his debts. As a consequence, he lost his business and the family fell on hard days. Although his parents tried to conceal from him the true reason for the abrupt decline in their fortunes, Mr. R discovered the truth. That discovery, as well as subsequent developments to which he reacted strongly, had a profound effect on his attitudes toward both his father and his uncle, the father's younger brother, who was also involved in the business. The transformation that took place in the way Mr. R viewed both men—views that were a mix of perception and fantasy—were reflected in the analysis in changing transference pictures.

For Mr. R, his father had always been a hero. From the patient's earliest years he regarded this parent as a powerful and magnetic figure whom he wanted to emulate. The uncle, too, was much admired, although in a very different way. While the father was viewed as the stable force in the family, the director-general, the uncle was a bon vivant. His good looks, dazzling clothes, and adventurous spirit became, in turn, attributes to be emulated. When trouble developed in the family, however, Mr. R's views of both men, and, as a consequence, of himself, underwent marked change.

In the initial months of the analysis two transference pictures took center stage, one related to the father, the other to the uncle. There was, between these dominant transferences, constant shifting and interweaving, so that at one point Mr. R would perceive me as the powerful father, at another as the dashing uncle. Not infrequently, mental images of the two men overlapped, as they often did in Mr. R's childhood, so that a view of me as solid and stable, charming and debonair, father and uncle, captured Mr. R's imagination. For some months he regarded me as all but flawless, the perfect analyst who was not only reliable and perceptive, but who, he imagined, drove a Mercedes sports coup.

I was perfect, that is, until Mr. R found out through the grapevine that I no longer held a certain academic position with which he had associated me. Then his view of me changed. Clearly he was disappointed, perceived me as a much diminished figure, and had to struggle to retain a positive image of me.

To do this he developed the idea that I was a victim, that I had been forced to relinquish my rightful place, and that to keep the peace in my department I had allowed myself to be sacrificed. From an initial reaction of rage and disappointment, Mr. R's attitude gradually shifted to one of solicitude and concern. At the same time that part of the transference that related to the uncle seemed to fade away. Rarely was he mentioned now and on the few occasions when some aspect of my person called forth memories of him, Mr. R's voice took on a sarcastic tone.

This state of affairs persisted until another change occurred in my life; I was forced to relocate my office. To this move, Mr. R responded with much distress. In his mind it was a setback, a sign of my professional decline. Disapproving of both the new location and the space I had obtained, he viewed the change as a sign of my economic failure. Once again I became a disparaged figure, but now Mr. R's attitude toward me contained scarcely concealed contempt. To him I had become a loser, a rather pitiful figure whose efforts to maintain the image of a successful practitioner were now revealed for the charade that they were.

At the same time positive feelings toward the uncle were revived. In fact, during this period the only positive transference notes that were struck in an otherwise persistent refrain of negative comments about his analyst related to those aspects of my personality that Mr. R could view as sharing something in common with his uncle.

Of particular importance to him were qualities that, in his mind, marked me as an assimilated Jew. While I was criticized for my ineptitude as a businessman and for my inability to earn an adequate living, the fact that I did not speak with a Bronx accent and that in neither dress nor manner did I call attention to being Jewish came in for praise. In fact, at one point, Mr. R was quite convinced that in my private life I made determined efforts to conceal my ethnic background.

The shifts that took place in the evolving transferences and in Mr. R's views of me as father and uncle represented the reactivation in treatment of object representations that were closely connected to historical events in his childhood and adolescence. And it was by means of them that certain centrally important memories and fantasies relating to these two most influential figures in his life—and to perceptions of himself —could be reconstructed.

Following his discovery of his father's troubles and the truth about the loss of his business, Mr. R was thrown into a turmoil. No longer could he believe in his father's strength, his judgment, his business acumen. The man whom he had adored and whom he had looked to as a model for years had turned out to be a cheat and a failure. Despite the irrefutable evidence that this was so, Mr. R found the idea impossible to believe and, in fact, he did all that he could to prove to himself that it was not true. As had occurred in the transference when he discovered certain unacceptable facts about me, Mr. R concocted an explanation of the events that cast his father in the role of a victim. It was other relatives in the business who were the true culprits, he believed. Were it not for their greed the financial crisis that precipitated the trouble would never have occurred. He convinced himself that it was his father's wish to avoid a bitter disruption in the family and his willingness to protect others at his own expense that led him to shoulder the blame.

As part of the process of protecting the father, devaluation of the uncle took place. He, too, was classified among the guilty. His expensive life-style and the inflated salary that he demanded to support it had, in Mr. R's mind, contributed to the problem. For some time thereafter Mr. R lost interest in his uncle and when they met treated him, to the latter's amazement, with a coolness not unmixed with sarcasm.

This attitude toward the uncle, however, did not persist for long. Although, temporarily, Mr. R had managed to salvage from the collapse of his world a positive image of the father, this view could not survive a second disappointment. Further disillusionment occurred when the father attempted to establish a new business. Without the requisite capital and unable to borrow money, he was forced to set up shop in the back room of a dilapidated warehouse. Neither the location of his new venture nor the fact that within a matter of months the business was on the verge of bankruptcy did he reveal to his family. In fact, when as the result of a relative's slip, the truth came out and Mr. R went to see where his father worked, he was crushed. A final illusion was destroyed. As part of his personal rehabilitation of his father Mr. R had pictured him dictating letters in the office that he had visited as a child; a darkly paneled room complete with a large executive desk and a dictating machine. Now he found him closeted in a dingy back room without a proper desk or secretary. The disparity between reality and fantasy was overwhelming. To Mr. R it confirmed his worst fears about his father; that he was a loser and that the image of a dynamic, aggressive businessman that he tried to project was nothing but an empty facade.

In desperation, and in an effort to fend off the feeling of depression that accompanied this realization, Mr. R turned once again to the uncle. Seeking a man in the family of whom he could be proud, he tried to recapture the old image of the uncle as a charismatic figure. Part of Mr. R's reason for this was that in contrast to his father who had never recovered from the blow he had suffered, the uncle had prospered. He had become the star salesman of an industrial firm and with the money to indulge his expensive tastes lived a flamboyant life-style. He became the family success story.

Along the way, however, something else had happened to the uncle. He turned his back on his religion and acted the part of a Christian. At work he tried to give the impression that he had been a lifelong Episcopalian. When, once again, Mr. R came under the uncle's influence, the latter encouraged him to follow his lead and to shed outward signs of his Jewish identity. For a period of a year Mr. R sought to pass himself off as a Protestant and when he entered a new school he registered as such. This was a year in his life that Mr. R had completely blotted from memory. It was only in the course of analysis that it was recovered.

The final shift in Mr. R's view of his father and uncle took place in late adolescence and was reflected in transference attitudes that appeared toward the end of the analysis. No longer was Mr. R enraged at me nor did he condemn me for my failings as a businessman. Rather, toward them he adopted a tolerant and even indulgent attitude; an attitude that, after much inner turmoil, had evolved toward his father.

Transferences centered on me as the uncle no longer surfaced very much, but on the few occasions when they did, Mr. R responded with a kind of amused detachment that did not preclude positive feelings. In reality the uncle more or less disappeared from view during Mr. R's young adult years. When their paths met it was with the attitude described above that he perceived the man who had played a role of such importance in his life.

In fact, although by the time he entered analysis Mr. R had developed perspectives on both father and uncle that were quite well attuned to reality, it was the residues of the unconscious identifications that had taken place many years earlier that were at the root of certain of his difficulties.

Already mentioned was Mr. R's need, in his professional life, to live out the role of the charlatan, a role that caused him innumerable difficulties and that, on one or two occasions threatened him with total ruin. Clearly operative in the formation of this symptom was not only an identification with the father as criminal, but unconscious guilt of a high order. While these feelings of guilt related in large measure to the contempt that Mr. R felt toward his father at the time of his decline, it also contained important oedipal roots that had been buried under the impact of the later experience.

As an adult Mr. R also displayed certain character traits that he did not find compatible with his conscious ideals. Among these was a penchant for expensive clothes and cars and for a more lavish life-style than, in fact, he could afford. Even more troubling, however, was Mr. R's attitude toward himself as a Jew. He was ashamed of being Jewish and although he disliked himself for this quality, he often attempted, particularly when making a new business acquaintance, to conceal this fact. It was not until the uncle's anti-Semitism had come to light and Mr. R's unconscious identification with this attitude was clarified, that he was able, finally, to free himself from this tendency.

In Mr. R's case the emerging transferences and the patterns that they formed contributed not only to the reconstruction of particular object representations but also to the understanding of the vicissitudes of certain self representations. Closely linked to his perception of his father and uncle, Mr. R's self-concept fluctuated with the particular images that he had of these central figures. When, in the transference, he viewed me as the powerful, effective father, he too felt powerful and effective. When he experienced me as a failure, he was very much diminished. He, too, felt like a failure and he became depressed.

Similar transformations in Mr. R's self-regard occurred via the uncle transference, although to a lesser extent. When he saw me as the exciting, magnetic uncle, he identified with this image and his view of himself was temporarily inflated. When, in his mind, I took on some of the negative qualities of his uncle, superficiality, greed, and a disregard for the value of money, he experienced himself as similarly tarnished. Although, clearly, multiple factors contributed to Mr. R's view of himself at any given time in the analysis, including the mobilization of sexual and aggressive wishes, superego responses and resistances that were active, a meaningful correlation could be consistently made between Mr. R's current self representation and changes in the prevailing transference configurations. Thus it was through observing these shifting transferences and the relationships that existed between them that fantasies and memories relating to crucial experiences in Mr. R's development over a period of a decade or more could be recovered. These fantasy-memories involved not only shifting views of the men who had played so large a role in shaping his early years, but of himself as well.

In the foregoing examples, study of the shifting and changing transference pictures that emerged in the course of analysis, including the temporal and sequential relationships between transferences, could be meaningfully related to aspects of a patient's history. In each case the manner in which the transference unfolded followed patterns laid down in childhood and, in some cases, reproduced rather closely the vicissitudes of particular object representations. Why it is that in these cases repetition of the past, an unconscious process central to the creation of all transference phenomena, included significant aspects of form as well as of content, remains a matter for further investigation. As discussed above, this is not always, or even usually, the case. In many analyses (including substantial periods of time in the ones cited here), the manner in which the transferences emerge bears no clear relationship to the unfolding of the original object representations. Why, then, is history repeated in quite specific ways in some cases and not in others? Although the definitive answer to this question must await further research, one idea suggests itself on the basis of the foregoing clinical material. In each case trauma of a not inconsequential kind played a significant part in childhood. In the case of Ms. L it centered on the discovery of the truth about her father; in that of Mr. A on a troubled relationship with a disturbed mother to which was added the early loss of the father through depression and seduction in adolescence by the older brother. In the third case, that of Mr. R, knowledge of his father's illegitimate business activities followed by his steady decline had a profound effect on the boy's development.

Analytic experience has shown that when trauma of this kind has occurred, a tendency for it to be repeated in life, as well as in the transference, develops in certain individuals. It may be that in some instances part of the reliving of the experience includes the repetition of the forms and sequences in which fantasies, memories, and perceptions were laid down as well as their content. Included also would be temporal relationships which are unconsciously linked to these emotionally important experiences. Like anniversary reactions, memories of certain traumatic experiences seem to be linked to the unconscious sense of time as well as to registration of the sequential order in which they occurred. It is these formal qualities which, along with content, are not infrequently reproduced in the course of reliving such memories in analysis. When this occurs, the forms that the transferences take and the relationships between them will appear as integral parts of the process of repetition.

III

Uses of the Analytic Instrument

5

Posture, Gesture, and Movement in the Analyst: Cues to Interpretation and Countertransference

From their earliest days, psychoanalysts have been interested in the nonverbal as well as the verbal aspects of human communication. As a keen clinical observer, Freud (Breuer and Freud, 1895) was well aware of the way in which facial and bodily movements could convey unconscious mental attitudes. Readers will remember the graphic description of his first meeting with Frau Emmy Von N., written with the novelist's eye for evocative detail:

> This lady, when I first saw her, was lying on a sofa with her head resting on a leather cushion. She still looked young and had finely-cut features, full of character. Her face bore a strained and painful expression, her eyelids were drawn together and her eyes cast down; there was a heavy frown on her forehead and the naso-labial folds were deep. She spoke in a low voice as though with difficulty and her speech was from time to time subject to spastic interruption amounting to a stammer [pp. 48–49].

In his account of the obsessional neurosis of the Rat Man,

Freud (1909) emphasized that it was the patient's facial expression which provided an important insight into the unconscious satisfaction associated with the dread obsession. "At all the more important moments while he was telling his story his face took on a very strange, composite expression. I could only interpret it as one of horror at pleasure of his own of which he himself was unaware" (pp. 166–167).

Freud's observations on the importance of nonverbal behavior as a communication were elaborated on and advanced by Wilhelm Reich, who in many ways can be considered one of the founders of modern kinesics. In his famous concept of character armor, Reich (1933) described the manner in which defensive processes and character traits are revealed in muscular tension, body posture, voice, and movement.

> Apart from the dreams, associations, slips and other communications of the patient, their attitude, that is, the *manner* in which they relate their dreams, commit slips, produce their associations and make their communications deserves special attention. . . .
> The manner in which the patient talks, in which he greets the analyst or looks at him, the way he lies on the couch, the inflection of the voice, the degree of conventional politeness, all these things are valuable criteria for judging the latent resistances against the fundamental rule . . . [p. 45].

In more recent times, Felix Deutsch (1952), in his studies on what he termed analytic posturology, made careful observations of body movement in analysis and attempted a correlation between the patient's nonverbal behavior and the emerging themes in the analysis. Charting each change of position that occurred during an hour, Deutsch felt that he could predict from the appearance of certain postures the nature of the material that would be forthcoming. Flexion of an already crossed leg, for example, regularly heralded the appearance of oral fantasies. "In this postural configuration," he has written, "one can foresee the psychodynamics unmistakably presented, which, whenever it appears, makes the verbal expression which follow an affirmation of what it anticipated" (p. 207). It was also Deutsch's belief that all automatic postural movements represent, in some way, the search for a desired object from the past and a turning either toward or away from it.

During the past three decades the study of human communication by means of nonverbal behavior has become a highly sophisticated science. Taking advantage of modern film and videotape techniques, researchers such as Birdwhistell (1952) at the University of Pennsylvania and Scheflen (1963) at Albert Einstein have analyzed and annotated literally thousands of bodily movements in a wide variety of social situations. Their work has provided deeper understanding than was heretofore possible of the meaning of bodily movements both in individuals and groups.

As part of their research, they have studied kinesic communications in the psychotherapeutic situation. Whereas prior observations had focused primarily on the patient, these investigators stressed the importance in the treatment situation of understanding the nonverbal interactions of patient and therapist alike. Through the assumption of different postures such as crossing or uncrossing the legs, positioning of the head, as well as movements of the hands, the therapist could facilitate or impede the flow of material; and in his behavior he revealed, as well, attitudes toward the patient of which he himself was often unaware. Scheflen's (1963) investigations by means of film analyses also elucidated the typical patterns of movements which occur during the various phases of the psychotherapeutic hour. In this work he was able to demonstrate sequences of nonverbal behavior which occurred repetitively in each session and which were regularly associated with particular themes and affects. These movements, he believed, functioned as a reciprocal communication system to induce and regulate specific interactions in the therapeutic relationship.

In the psychoanalytic situation, the importance of the analyst's nonverbal behavior is well known. The manner in which he begins and ends a session; his posture, facial expressions, and tone as he greets or says goodbye to his patient, convey kinesic messages of which he may or may not himself be cognizant. In this connection the analyst's face is of particular importance. It is a common experience for the therapist, as he enters the waiting room, to observe a patient quickly scan his face for a clue as to his mood and feelings of the moment. E. H. Gombrich (1963), the art historian, writing on the psychological roots of pictorial representations, emphasizes the special place that facial features have in human awareness throughout life.

> We know that there are certain privileged motifs in our world to which we respond almost too easily. The human face may be outstanding among them. Whether by instinct or very early training we are certainly ever disposed to single out the expressive features of a face from the chaos of sensations that surrounds it, and to respond to its slightest variations with fear or joy. Our whole perceptual apparatus is somehow hypersensitized in this direction of physiognomic vision, and the merest hint suffices for us to create an expressive physiognomy that "looks" at us with surprising intensity [p. 6].

Significant communications are conveyed, too, by other aspects of the analyst's nonverbal behavior; the manner of his dress and bearing, his physical position vis-à-vis the patient, his office arrangements, his practice with regard to note taking, telephone calls, billing, and missed sessions; alterations of vocal pitch and tone during the hour, and, of course, the analytic attitude itself, which is so important an aspect of his communication.

There is, however, another aspect of the analyst's nonverbal behavior that has received relatively little emphasis in the literature: the bodily movements that accompany the act of listening. Certain of these movements, such as the tapping of a foot or motor restlessness may, through sound, be conveyed to the patient, and, in fact, act as conscious or unconscious communications. At other times the patient may detect from the slightest acoustical clues an otherwise unexpressed attitude or feeling on the part of the analyst. "I suspect some patients detect our attitudes intuitively," Greenson (1967) has noted "from minute changes in the rate and intensity of our breathing and from little bodily movements" (p. 388). For the most part, however, the analyst's nonverbal responses are not conveyed to the patient. They remain in the sphere of self-observation as the motor expression of his own shifting psychological state during the hour.

It cannot be claimed, of course, that all such behavior occurs in response to the patient's communications, any more than one can reasonably assert that every random thought the analyst has is produced in association to the analytic material. Changes in posture, as well as other bodily movements, may be motivated by a number of factors, including muscular fatigue and physical discomfort, long-established movement patterns that are characteristic for any individual, as well as stimuli that arise as the result of personal preoccupations and conflicts. Nevertheless, if it is true that the analyst, seeking to understand the patient's unconscious communications, is able to utilize the thoughts and fantasies that arise in his own mind to assist him in this process, it would seem justifiable to assume that another pathway for the expression of his unconscious mental activity, namely, that of motor discharge, can claim similar validity. Describing the relationship between psychological factors and body movement, Deutsch (1952) explains the situation this way: "if a psychic stimulus presses for a discharge, the functional organic process initiated by the stimulus—a muscular movement, for example, which leads to a postural rearrangement —continues and completes the psychological process" (p. 197). When the unconscious of the analyst is in tune with that of the patient—when in short he is listening well—certain aspects of his bodily movements, reflections of his own resonating mental processes, will occur in response to the patient's associations. Observation of his own nonverbal behavior may then be useful to the analyst in picking up cues to the unconscious meaning of the patient's communications and may in this way assist him in the process of interpretation.

I should like by means of a few brief clinical examples, to illustrate this use of the analyst's kinesic responses. During the course of an analytic hour a thirty-four-year-old businessman described a puzzling experience he had had the night before. He had been visiting a married couple who were close friends. While sitting in the living room he quite suddenly developed a pervasive feeling of anxiety together with palpitations, a sense of constriction in his chest, and a queasy feeling in the stomach.

This outbreak of anxiety was completely puzzling to him, for he had until that moment been feeling unusually well. During the hour he reviewed the events of the evening in an effort to identify the precipitating stimulus. As he did so, he recalled that soon after arriving at his friends' home he had been invited into the nursery to see their child, a five-month-old boy. While he was there the mother had diapered the infant, and it was then, the patient recalled, that he had first experienced a sense of uneasiness. He remembered a thought that had flashed across his mind at the time, namely, that the mother seemed to be pinning the diaper rather tightly and that, as a result, the child would surely be uncomfortable. As he related this story, the patient's hands, which had until then been folded across his chest, moved to the abdominal area. His right thumb was hooked around his belt and the fingers of that hand pointed toward the right lower quadrant.

As I listened to his narration, trying to comprehend the meaning of the events he was describing, I became conscious of the fact that, completely outside my awareness, I had grasped my own belt and had begun to make gently tugging movements as though it were too tight. At the same time I became aware of a feeling of some constriction around my waist. As both the loosening gesture and the accompanying feeling of tightness were highly unusual for me and there was no overt physical reason for me to be having such experiences, my attention was drawn to the possible significance of these phenomena. As I focused attention on them in light of the material I was hearing and the patient's own nonverbal behavior, the meaning of the patient's experience the evening before "arrived," as it were, in my mind. At the age of four the patient had developed an umbilical hernia, the cause of which was unknown. Instead of surgery, he had been treated by the method of binding his abdomen with tightly placed strips of adhesive. As a result, his abdominal area was often sore, irritated, and painful, and he experienced both a continual sense of physical restriction and limitation of his mobility as a consequence of his mother's anxious and protective attitude. The diapering of the child had been unconsciously associated with these experiences and had reactivated the profound castration anxiety connected with them. Interestingly, it was the changing of his own bandages that caused the most pain and created in him the greatest fear. Although this material had come up only once before in the analysis and was not in his conscious awareness as he related the precipitating event, it was by means of a bodily gesture that he made reference to it.

For my part, my own unconscious recognition of what lay behind the patient's experience of anxiety seemed to have taken at first a nonverbal form. Only as I was focusing attention on my spontaneous bodily movements did the interpretation occur to me as a thought. Once it did, and I communicated my understanding to the patient, there followed a flood of associations relating to the original physical experiences. Of course it is entirely possible that my associations alone would have led to the correct interpretation, but, at least in this instance, recognition of the analyst's kinesic behavior proved to be a useful cue.

In another situation the understanding of a visual image experienced by a patient on the couch, together with the slight alteration of consciousness that accompanied it, was facilitated by the observation of a spontaneous movement that I made during the process of listening to this material. The patient, a middle-aged man, arrived for his session one day with a heavy cold. With obvious misery he described the onset of his symptoms and his attempt to cope with them, his emergency use of aspirin and vitamin C tablets, the employment of nose drops and a humidifier, and finally, when his nasal passages remained clogged, the attempt to clean them out with the aid of a Q-Tip. In the course of describing these efforts, the patient began to experience a sense of light-headedness. He became dizzy, felt momentarily "separated" from his environment, and reported visualizing a thin steel instrument moving toward him. This was accompanied by a vague feeling of rising discomfort and the desire to turn his head to the left, which he did. The instrument could not be identified, but reminded him of the kind of tool a dentist uses to remove tartar from one's teeth. This account was delivered in a somewhat more nasal and high-pitched tone than was customary for the patient, a fact I had noted when he began to speak.

As I listened, I found myself touching my right ear, lightly fingering the lobe and then stroking the bone behind the ear. As I became aware of this activity, which, again, was not one of my more usual "listening movements," I focused attention on it. Then I realized that it was related to the experience the patient was describing. As a child of six, the patient had developed a nearly fatal mastoiditis. His illness had started with an upper respiratory illness and had rapidly progressed to involve the mastoids, requiring hospitalization and, ultimately, surgical intervention. The patient had been severely ill for some time, with the prognosis very much in doubt. The experience was fused with much preexisting separation and castration anxiety and left him with a deep-seated fear of physical illness. His recent cold, which involved the nasal passages, and to some extent the eustachian tubes, had touched off some of these anxieties. The alteration of consciousness associated with the illness was momentarily reproduced on the couch, a phenomenon that Stein (1965) has reported in the analyses of other patients who have had mastoiditis in childhood. My recognition of these connections, perhaps aided by the change in tone and pitch of the patient's voice, had initially taken the form of my touching my own ear. Interpretation of the patient's experience led to a clarification of the visual image. The patient remembered the painful follow-up treatment that was required after surgery: the doctor had used a thin steel instrument to probe and clean his auditory canal.

A third clinical example involved the use of a nonverbal cue to help in the understanding of certain transference aspects of a patient's behavior. The patient, a young woman in her third year of analysis, began a session one day in a sullen mood. In a tone that was at once a mixture of hurt, anger, and sadness, she spoke of the resentment she felt for a boyfriend who had been late for a date with her the night before. To make matters worse, instead of sleeping over, as she had expected, he gave the excuse of having an early morning appointment and somewhat abruptly had left her apartment. She did not elaborate on these thoughts, but, rather, remained silent for several minutes. She lay on her side in a huddled and protective position, arms folded across her chest, her knees flexed. Although the man in question was not someone with whom she was deeply involved, his behavior had unquestionably caused her great distress.

As I listened to her and observed her posture, I found myself rubbing my wedding ring with the thumb of my left hand. Although this gesture was not particularly unusual in itself—from time to time I found myself performing it when for one reason or another I was feeling lonely and missed my wife—the fact that there was no obvious personal motivation for this reaction at the time caused me to reflect upon it in terms of the emotions that the patient's mood and behavior had induced in me. Then I remembered certain relevant facts. The man about whom she had been speaking worked in the same field as her former husband, and his abrupt leaving had unquestionably reawakened feelings of sadness associated with the breakup of her marriage. More importantly, however, I recalled that in the previous session, which had occurred two days before, the patient had mentioned casually that she and a girl friend were thinking of going away for a brief vacation, and that she might have to miss several analytic appointments. Awaiting clarification of the meaning of this statement, I had said nothing in response, and the hour had ended without the topic coming up again. I had not been aware of the meaning to the patient of my having allowed the subject to pass without further exploration.

Now I realized that the patient's behavior was, in large measure, a transference reaction. When she was six years old, her father had become severely mentally ill and had been hospitalized for several months. Subsequently, her parents divorced, and, terrified of her father's paranoid outbursts, she refused to see him again. A year later he died, and she was stricken with feelings of remorse and guilt. She blamed herself for her behavior, but, unconsciously, was deeply resentful of both parents for allowing her to be permanently separated from her father. In her own marriage this pattern had been repeated. She married an emotionally disturbed man, continually criticized him for his erratic behavior, and became enraged when he left her.

My own behavior in failing to respond to her test statement

about missing several sessions had reactivated the feelings of anger, depression, and guilt associated with these previous experiences. Although these thoughts were not in my awareness at the moment, the touching of my wedding ring seemed, in retrospect, to be a way of my expressing an understanding of what the patient was communicating in her verbalizations and behavior; not only sadness at her loss, but the guilt and anger that she felt toward me as the abandoning father–husband she had rejected, and the displacement of these feelings onto the less emotionally cathected boyfriend.

It is as an aspect of his empathic responses that such bodily reactions of the analyst may best be understood. In one of the earliest attempts to define empathy, Theodore Lipps, writing of certain psychological responses to art in his *Raemesthetik* (1913) used the word *Einfuhlung* by which he meant to "feel" or "to read oneself into" another person or thing. To Lipps, insight involved the experience of viewing an object as if "opposite" to it, or standing beside it. In contrast, empathy was seen as a projection of oneself into the object with which one is identified. This early emphasis on that aspect of empathy which is intimately associated with feeling states and bodily reactions has been reiterated in various discussions of the empathic process. Fenichel (1926), in discussing the question of what needs to be added to identification to make it understanding empathy, suggests that unconscious communication by way of expressive movements may provide a clue. "The role of identification," he states, "might then be to bring about the taking over by the subject of the object's expressive movements, which in turn would awaken the corresponding psychic state in him" (pp. 104–105). Burlingham (1967), commenting on the phenomenon of empathy between mother and child, emphasizes the astonishing ability of the young child to pick up cues from the mother's facial expression, posture, and mood.

"The infant is," she writes, "above all a receiver of stimuli; from a certain age onward, he begins to assimilate what he received; i.e., he begins to observe, an activity which is, of course, not restricted to vision but spreads equally over the whole of the sense apparatus" (p. 765). She describes the infant's remarkable ability to sense the mother's mood from her facial expression and other bodily cues. He has in short a "capacity for empathy [that] may be advanced far beyond his other achievements" (p. 765). In his discussion of empathy, Schafer (1959) describes the process as one of "experiencing in some fashion the feelings of another person" (p. 347). It requires, he believes, "perceptual attention, or vigilance, to elusive clues, difficult to conceptualize, in motility, verbalization, affective expression and tempo" (p. 348). Halpern and Lesser (1960), discussing the critical importance of emotional communication between mother and child in the later development of the capacity for empathy, hypothesize a positive correlation between empathy and subliminal perception. They also suggest that the degree of perceptual receptivity may be related to the nature and quality of these nonverbal interactions.

It is clear, then, that the earliest feeling states between mother and child form the matrix from which ultimately evolves the more highly developed responses we describe as empathy in adults. Empathy in the analyst, as Schafer (1959) has pointed out, is a highly complex reaction, in which the momentary psychological state of another person is shared and comprehended. But what is shared or comprehended is not simply a feeling state, a perception, or a thought, but in fact is a "hierarchic organization of desires, feelings, thoughts, defenses, controls, superego pressures, capacities, self representations and representations of real and fantasied personal relationships" (p. 348).

The analyst's kinesic responses when he is in a state of empathic understanding reflect a bodily aspect of the empathic response that is related to the use of the body as a prime conveyor of affect between mother and child. Although, as Burlingham (1967) has pointed out, the sensitive and finely tuned capacity of the child to sense the mother's mood through facial expression and bodily movement is significantly dulled in later life, it seems possible that the analytic situation, in which the analyst's full faculties are geared toward empathic understanding and in which temporary ego regressions take place as an inherent part of the listening process, fosters the reawakening of what we might term *body empathy*. As part of the empathic response, there occurs not only freer access to memory, fantasy, and affective experiences as a consequence of the temporary regressions and loosening of ego and superego controls, but there is also in the analyst a keener awareness of somatic reactions, reflecting the increased cathexis of the body ego which accompanies the act of empathic listening. This temporary reinvestment of the body, which revives the latent sensitivity to kinesic cues that played so large a role in infancy and early childhood, then allows the analyst to react with bodily responses that reverberate with the unconscious communications of the patient. The revival of past inner experiences similar to those of the patient may then take the form of a bodily movement as well as a memory or an affective response.

In the first example cited above, it was clear that the analyst's own anxiety concerning bodily injury was revived by the patient's material. Because of the cathectic shifts toward increased awareness of somatic processes inherent in the attainment of an empathic attitude, together with some relaxation of ego defense and control, a direct bodily response was the initial reaction. This "body empathy," which can be considered a primal and nuclear aspect of the empathic experience, could then be utilized in the service of a cognitive and affective understanding of what the patient was attempting to communicate.

It is in the area of countertransference feelings, too, that an awareness of his kinesic responses can provide useful cues for the analyst. It is a common experience for the therapist who observes his bodily reactions to note from hour to hour changes in his posture, gait, and facial expression as he begins each session. For a patient who is working well and toward whom we have positive feelings, we may brighten our step or stand straighter or, unconsciously, adopt a more open posture of greeting. Toward one about whom we are less enthusiastic, who may at the moment be in a phase of intense resistance, who repeatedly acts out, or shows little talent as an analytic patient, we may literally adopt a different stance.

While the analyst seeks, in every case, to become cognizant of feelings in himself that may interfere with his analytic work, these may, as we know, become blocked off from consciousness and remain undetected for lengthy periods of time. Observation of his bodily reactions as they manifest themselves in posture, gesture, and movement enables him to enlarge the scope of his self-awareness and, at times, to gain access to attitudes and conflicts of which he is unaware.

Such was the case with my first analytic patient, an aggressive, hard-driving man whose fear of his passive, homosexual wishes made the analytic situation a continual threat to him. For months he could barely bring himself to lie down on the couch, and when he did, he placed both hands behind his head, elbows thrust back to ward off the attack he expected. Free association was all but out of the question, and it was a rare day when he brought in even the merest fragment of a dream. As a beginning analyst, I did not fully appreciate the intensity of the patient's anxiety, but found myself responding to the situation with feelings of frustration and despair. For my first case I had expected the ideal analytic patient, an attractive young woman whose psychological mindedness was matched only by her capacity for transference. Instead, I was faced with a man whose resistances seemed as unassailable as Everest, a patient whose scanty verbalizations resembled quotations from *The Wall Street Journal*, and whose incredibly taut musculature promised, at any moment, to catapult him precipitously from the room.

Faced with what I considered so little interpretable material, I became increasingly silent, and as I did so, the patient's hostility grew. Then, one day, I observed the two of us: the patient as rigid as a coiled spring, his elbows protruding like iron pickets, and I, folded into myself, my arms wrapped across my chest, maintaining a grim and stubborn silence. I realized, then, what was happening. I had been drawn into an unremitting battle of wills. Out of sheer frustration I had locked horns with the patient, and my silence was, in great measure, a retaliation. Consciously, I told myself there was nothing to say, but, in fact, my body posture spoke for me: I was not going to say anything. The analysis had deteriorated into a struggle over who would control it, and it was rapidly becoming a stand-off. Through observing myself in this way, I was better able to appreciate the importance of the anal–sadistic aspects of the patient's conflicts and could reorient myself to the analysis of his resistance and the anxieties they defended against.

At times, the analyst may discover in himself a pattern of bodily movement in response to specific kinds of material. With one patient, whenever he spoke of some painful adolescent experiences, I observed myself shifting my posture. Instead of observing his behavior on the couch, as I usually did, I found myself gazing at various objects in the room. At the same time I noticed that my shoulders and torso were angled away from him and that my right hand shielded one side of my face. Observing this, I became aware that the recital of his experiences had touched off painful affects in myself as the result of similar experiences of my own. In fact, my physical response to the material had been accompanied by a tendency to avoid a thorough exploration of it in the analysis.

I have found similar reactions in myself with regard to material concerning certain physical illnesses, particularly those that have played a significant role in my own life or in the lives of those close to me. The same has been true with regard to a patient's attitudes that I have found personally disturbing. In one instance I felt that I was sufficiently aware of my own reactions to a patient's anti-Semitism to believe that they were not interfering with the analytic work. The tenseness of my abdominal musculature whenever the topic came up, however, convinced me that they were continuing to play a role in my handling of the transference. Made anxious by the aggression inherent in these remarks and my angry responses to it, I had avoided bringing his anti-Semitism into the analysis as a topic for investigation.

In this connection it is interesting to consider what role the phenomenon Waelder (1960) has called *complementarization* may play in such reactions. By this term he meant that "behavior expressive of a drive tends to elicit in the object the complementary drive, a mirror image. Sadism, e.g., calls forth masochistic urges in the object and *vice versa*" (p. 107). It is interesting to entertain the possibility that such a complementary reaction, induced in the analyst by overt or covert aggression in the patient, for example, may have been warded off and unconsciously been expressed through a bodily response.

Thus far I have concentrated primarily on the manner in which the analyst's kinesic behavior may assist him in detecting previously unrecognized negative feelings for patients. It is by highlighting certain positive responses, too, that it may be useful. During the course of the analysis of a highly attractive young woman, I became aware of the unusual correctness of my posture as I greeted her. I made few spontaneous movements, and both my gait and posture conveyed a certain stiffness. I noticed, too, that the muscles of my arms and trunk were not relaxed as I sat in my chair, and that my tone conveyed a more formal quality than was true with other patients. Some self-analysis of these observations made clear to me what I had sensed in myself but had not sufficiently focused on; that I was responding to the patient's considerable charms by a defense of physical and emotional distance. My anxiety over my own positive feelings for her had led, not only to an exaggerated and rather sterile analytic stance, but to inadequate analysis of the patient's seductiveness both as a character trait and a resistance.

Observations of nonverbal responses in the analyst such as I have thus far described raise certain intriguing questions. Why is it, for example, that the analyst's comprehension initially takes a somatic form under some circumstances but not under others? How can we explain the fact that this route is more available to some analysts while others can make relatively little use of it? While a satisfactory elucidation of these problems must await further observation and research, certain tentative ideas may be put forth for consideration. In two of the cases discussed above, physical experiences of a traumatic nature played a central role. The patient with the umbilical hernia had suffered years of pain, together with the feeling of intense physical restriction due to the binding of his abdomen. The man with the mastoiditis had experienced a life-threatening illness that had profound reverberations on his character development and the nature of his symptom formation. The third patient, while not undergoing physical trauma of the same intensity, had in childhood been continually preoccupied with her body as a result of an obesity problem that was a source of profound conflict and shame. It seems possible, then, that the experience of being confronted consistently with material relating to intensely conflictual bodily experiences may serve to increase an analyst's own body awareness and facilitate this pathway as a route of comprehension.

There is no doubt, too, that the nature of the analyst's own bodily experience in childhood plays an important role in fostering such responses. While it seems self-evident that an analyst, while listening, utilizes his entire self in the process and that bodily movements are an integral and essential part of the "analyzing instrument," the degree to which bodily reactions are both available and useful to the analyst unquestionably differs from individual to individual. In some analysts who have had significant experiences of bodily illness or trauma, or who perhaps for other reasons of an innate or experiential kind have a highly cathected body ego, there may be an increased capacity to utilize bodily responses in their analytic work. In others, whose development along different lines may have led to increased investment in the visual or auditory spheres or in fantasy formation, or in individuals in whom defensive operations may be directed against awareness of bodily sensations, such experiences may play a lesser role in the analyst's use of himself. Further work in this field may clarify the various kinds of "analyzers" and the manner in which the differing perceptual styles of both analyst and patient may influence the nature of the analytic process.

6

The Use of the Self: The Analyst and the Analytic Instrument in the Clinical Situation

Central to my view of the analyst's role in the clinical situation and to many of the ideas contained in this chapter is the concept of the analyzing instrument. Associated most closely with the name of Otto Isakower (1963a,b), who elaborated on Freud's original metaphor, this conceptualization of the relationship between the minds of the two participants in the analytic situation is one of the more creative ideas that has been developed in psychoanalysis.

Freud's notion of the analyzing instrument was that of a telephone, with the patient's unconscious transmitting a message and the analyst's receiving it. Recommending in one of his technical papers that the analyst listen in an open-ended way, Freud (1912) observed that "he must turn his own unconscious like a receptive organ to the transmitting unconscious of the patient. He must adjust himself to the patient as a telephone receiver is adjusted to the transmitting microphone" (p. 115).

Taking as his starting point Freud's notion of a transmitting and receiving device, Isakower (1963a,b) developed it into a way of viewing not only the analyst's role in the treatment sit-

117

uation but the analytic process itself. In recent years, his ideas
have been explicated by Malcove (1975) and by Balter, Lothane,
and Spencer (1980). For Isakower, the analyzing instrument is,
in essence, a mind set existing in analyst and patient that fa-
cilitates the grasping of the latter's unconscious communications.

Isakower (1963a,b) presented his ideas at two faculty meetings of the New York Psychoanalytic Institute in October and
November of 1963. Minutes of those meetings record that he
described the analytic instrument as "a constellation of the
psychic apparatus in which its constituent structures are tuned
in a way that makes the apparatus optimally suited for functioning in a very specific manner." In its activated state, it is
"in rapport with its counterpart in the patient." He added, "One
might see it as a composite consisting of two complementary
halves." An essential feature, however, "is the unique and specific setting-in-relation to a near identical or analogous constellation in a second person. It represents an *ad hoc* assembly
for a special task and it is of a transitory nature."

Isakower made clear that when functioning optimally the
analyzing instrument is inaccessible to conscious observation.
Its characteristics can best be distinguished in retrospect when
its work is temporarily ended, "most opportunely, perhaps,
when that short phase of its intense functioning has occurred
just before the end of an analytic session."

At the second of the two faculty meetings, Isakower described the kind of subjective experience that, not uncommonly,
an analyst may have at the end of an hour when the analytic
instrument is in the process of being dismantled:

> The session is broken off. The patient is leaving the room. You,
> the analyst, are in the process of emerging out of the analytic
> situation, that near dream-like state of hovering attention. The
> patient is being separated from you and you are left alone. In
> this short moment of the severance of the "team" you are left
> in mid-air and you become aware of the denuded raw surface
> of your half of the analyzing instrument, the surface which is
> opposite the patient's half. This surface now becomes accessible
> to observation because its cathexis is not bound to the surface

of the patient's half of the apparatus. Now you, in a slow motion replica, can make observations. The slow motion comes from the induced process of re-integration of that part of you within yourself, a re-integration required by the withdrawal of the patient's half. There is a redistribution of cathexis and while this is going on you can, in fortunate instances, observe it. It can be observed because your observing function is no longer glued to its former object—the patient's half.

What Isakower himself observed in such circumstances was a variety of visual and auditory phenomena related to the material of the previous hour. Included were representations of the manifest content of the patient's verbalizations as well as representations of visual and auditory responses that occurred in the analyst.

It is clear that for Isakower the essence of the analyzing instrument is a particular state of mind experienced by both analyst and analysand. Central to this mental set is a variable degree of regression in both participants. This state of regression, which is a necessary condition in patient and analyst alike for understanding the unconscious communications of the other, is closely allied to the kind of ego regression that occurs in the artist during moments of creative activity. For Isakower, analysis was an art, and his mode of perception in the analytic hours was that of an artist.

The factors that foster regression in both members of the analyzing team and that allow for the development in them of the requisite mental states have been elucidated by Balter et al. (1980) in their article on the analyzing instrument. In analysand and analyst alike, they have identified three preconditions necessary for the effective functioning of the analyzing instrument. For the analysand, these include: (1) an increase in the attention he pays to his own physical perceptions; (2) suspension of his normally critical attitude toward the thoughts and perceptions that arise from within; and (3) the capacity and willingness to report verbally all that he is experiencing. For the analyst, these prerequisites involve: (1) the concentration of attention on the analysand's communications; (2) the concentration of attention on the analyst's own internal perceptions; and (3) the suspension of critical activity regarding these two objects of the analyst's attention.

When the requisite conditions are met in the analysand, the result is a state of ego regression that allows for the process of free association to develop. When they are fulfilled in the analyst, the complementary regression that takes place fosters the receptive state of mind that Freud (1912) termed "listening with evenly suspended attention" (p. 239). The capacity to give oneself over to regression is an essential element that allows analogous mental processes to take place in both participants. When the unconscious of patient and analyst are "set in relation" to each other, the analyzing instrument may be said to be operative.

For the contemporary psychoanalyst, Isakower's notion of the analyzing instrument is as evocative and useful a concept as it was when articulated in the 1960s, but it is even more valuable when reformulated in light of new knowledge gained since that time. For Isakower, as for Freud before him, the analyzing instrument was closely associated with verbal communication and with the auditory sphere. Although both were aware of the fact that communication in the analytic situation occurs through a number of modalities and both were sensitive to the nonverbal dimension, the notion of the analyzing instrument was conceived of as an apparatus constructed for the sending and receiving of verbal messages. For Isakower, these referred primarily to words, but they also included the sounds of an hour—the pitch, tone, and rhythms of speech—as well as its silences. Advances over the past decade in our understanding of the important role of nonverbal behavior in human communication and of the place of such communication in the transmittal and reception of unconscious messages in the analytic situation have allowed us to revise and expand Isakower's original model of the analytic instrument. Whereas initially it was conceived of as a system operating primarily through the verbal–auditory spheres, we may now regard it as a multichannel system containing components that register not only verbal and acoustic signals but also movement patterns, autonomic responses, and visual stimuli.

Every analyst is aware that important communications take

place on a nonverbal level during each analytic hour. Understanding the meaning of such communications has been relatively slow to develop in analysis, however, and their role in the expression of conflict and resistance, as an aspect of empathy and as a conduit for memory, is only now becoming more widely appreciated.

In my own analytic work, I pay particular attention to the kinds of postures, gestures, and movements that accompany the verbalizations of patient and analyst alike. In chapter 5, I have tried to demonstrate the way in which certain aspects of the analyst's nonverbal behavior may occur in response to the patient's communications. When he is listening well, the analyst automatically and unconsciously uses his body as a kind of seismograph that registers and reverberates with the steady stream of kinesic stimuli emanating from the patient. Awareness of his own bodily responses, as well as of the thoughts and images that accompany them, often provides the analyst with useful cues both to the nonverbal communications coming from the patient and to countertransference reactions of which he has been previously unaware. I would like, through a few brief clinical examples, to illustrate the way in which the analyst's use of himself as an instrument that registers not only the sounds of an hour, but also its sights and movement, may enhance his capacity to grasp the unconscious communications of his patients.

For me, the analytic hour begins before I rise to greet the patient. With the previous patient gone and the temporarily assembled analytic instrument now in the process of being dismantled, I turn my thoughts to the patient now waiting. Spontaneously, with as little restriction as possible, I allow an image of that patient to arise in my mind. At the same time, I try to become aware of my own inner experiences in doing so. Sometimes I find myself picturing the patient as I last saw him, and material from his previous hour may arise in my mind. Sometimes I picture him in a scene from his childhood or in a fictional scene that I have invented. I pay particular attention to the emotions I am experiencing as I conjure up images of the waiting patient. Often, these images and the feelings that accompany them tell me a great deal about the particular state of my countertransference feelings at the moment and the way in which those feelings resonate with the transference that has been developing. Sometimes the emotions that I am aware of in myself are consonant with the image I have of the patient. Thus, in the case of a woman whose recent hours have been filled with childhood memories of long hours spent alone and with a sense of despair in an empty apartment, I may find myself feeling sad and even protective as I imagine her in that situation.

Sometimes, though, the feelings that I am aware of seem to run counter to the image I have conjured up. In the case of a young man who had been complaining bitterly of indifference and mistreatment by his girl friend and members of his family and who, in my imagination, I had pictured being so treated, at times I found that my predominant emotion was one of irritation. The disparity between what I fantasize and what I experience emotionally is, to me, a useful clue to countertrans-ference responses that, while active, have been kept out of awareness. I believe this to be an important matter because I have found that, when present, such countertransference re-actions are inevitably communicated to the patient through posture, gesture, tone, or phrasing. The material of an hour or even entire segments of an analysis may be decisively influ-enced by them. Because they are often effectively defended against, however, such responses may, without self-scrutiny, go undetected.

As I approach the waiting room, I try to become aware of my posture, of my facial expression, and of the affect that I communicate in my greeting. Although I try to be reasonably consistent in the way I greet patients, end sessions, and bid them goodbye, subtle variations do occur in the course of any analysis. Such changes often reflect shifting countertransfer-ence responses and may exert a significant influence on the analytic work. Even slight alterations in the analyst's usual non-verbal communications can be detected with regularity in the material of the accompanying hours. Although awareness of such reactions in himself may require consistent and repeated self-scrutiny on the part of the analyst, such awareness is a necessary condition for understanding the myriad nonverbal communications between himself and the patient that accompany their verbalizations.

I make efforts to be aware of my inner experiences as I enter the waiting room, and I make an equal effort to observe the patient. Child analysts, and particularly those colleagues whose interests lie in infant research, have taught us the unique value of close and careful observations of children. The advances in both theory and practice derived from such observational studies have been widely recognized, but the value in adult analysis of comparably careful observation has not been fully appreciated. It is rare for case reports of analytic work to contain information on the patient's nonverbal behavior, its shifts and transformations in the course of analysis, and its relation to transference and countertransference phenomena.

Observation of a patient as one approaches him in the waiting room can yield a good deal of useful data. His posture, facial expression, and movements often reveal affects of which he himself is not aware. It is not unusual for the analyst to encounter a patient who, revealing through body language clear signs of depression, seeks to conceal his feelings upon seeing the analyst, and in the ensuing hour, displays strong resistance to the conscious recognition of his depressed affect. Also commonly encountered is the patient who reveals through a shift in his facial expression that one aspect or another of the analyst's appearance has registered strongly on him, but who avoids reference to this in his session. In these and similar circumstances, the analyst's observation of the patient as they encounter one another, and his judicious use of those observations, is an important, if sometimes neglected aspect of analytic technique.

Of equal importance is observation of the patient on the couch. Although as early as 1895 Freud pointed out the importance of posture, facial expression, and bodily movement as a vehicle for the transmission of messages in the therapeutic situation, these early observations were not further developed, and the phenomena of nonverbal communication remained, for many years, unintegrated into psychoanalytic theory or technique. Understanding this aspect of the patient's communications has continued to be a relatively neglected area. Despite evidence from the clinical situation (Deutsch, 1952) that has emphasized the consistent, and often predictable, relationship between a patient's verbalizations and his nonverbal behavior on the couch, it is not unusual in analytic work for such nonverbal behavior to be overlooked or to remain as isolated and dynamically nonintegrated observations on the part of the analyst.

Of particular interest is the fact that few analysts observe a patient's face while he is on the couch. With his chair positioned behind the patient, the contemporary analyst, like his counterpart of sixty years ago, is in no position to do so. Because facial expressions are so rich a source of communication in the analytic situation, the analyst may thus rob himself of a significant, even vital, source of data.

Dr. Annie Reich, an early supervisor of mine, pointed out to me the unique value of viewing as well as listening to the patient. Borrowing from some of the work of Wilhelm Reich and adding her own observations, she made consistent efforts to integrate the patient's movements, gestures, and facial expressions with his verbalizations. To do this, she pointed out, the analyst's chair had to be placed in a position where the patient could be seen in his entirety and not simply a glimpse of his head, as often occurred in the usual analytic setup. Dr. Reich's chair was placed essentially at a right angle to the couch at approximately the level of the patient's head. This allowed for a full view of the patient. After experimenting with various positionings of the chair, I have found that placing it at slightly less than a right angle to the couch allows me to remain out of view and yet be in a position to observe the patient's bodily movements and at least some of his facial expressions.

In Isakower's model, visualization of the patient is not mentioned as a source of data. Rather, visual experience in both patient and analyst is regarded as an aspect of the ego regression taking place in each. As he associates freely, the analysand may convey certain inner experiences relating both to past and present through visual imagery. The analyst, listening to this material as he listens to dreams, may visualize the images being described. In this way, many analysts not only dream along with the patient, but continually engage in a process of "seeing" along with him. Even when listening to nonvisual material, such analysts may find arising in themselves fantasies and memories that have a strong visual element. As Isakower suggests, when properly attuned, the analytic instrument often decodes messages by means of the visual as well as the auditory apparatus.

Omitted from Isakower's formulation is a consideration of how the process of visualization itself both contributes to and is an integral part of the analyzing instrument. Visualization in the analytic situation is analogous to the phenomenon in the auditory sphere that has been variously termed *evenly suspended* or *freely hovering attention.* Just as the analyst listens with equal attention to all of the patient's verbalizations and tries not to fix any particular aspect of the material in mind or make a conscious effort to concentrate on it, so he observes all of the patient's nonverbal behavior. Looking as he listens, he takes in and registers what he sees, but does not focus on any particular bodily movement or facial expression. The visual imagery that he registers makes contact via associative pathways with visual aspects of memory and stimulates the recall of memories that are linked with the patient's nonverbal communications. Often, it stimulates in the analyst kinesic behavior and autonomic responses that are reactions on an unconscious level to nonverbal messages. Thus, the analyst's visual perceptions join with his auditory perceptions to stimulate in him responses that draw on unconscious visual and auditory memory. In practice, both visual and auditory spheres play vital roles in the registration and processing of analytic data. Both are essential parts of the analytic instrument.

Another aspect of the analytic instrument that was underemphasized in Isakower's formulation was the autonomic system and the autonomic responses of both patient and analysand. While Isakower emphasized the analyst's self-observation and his awareness of his inner processes, his focus was on mental phenomena and particularly on the auditory and visual imagery that become available to him during the operation of that instrument. Analytic experience confirms that autonomic responses in both patient and analyst are regular, if often overlooked, accompaniments of the analytic hour. At times, the patient will be aware of and will report such phenomena. Descriptions of sweating, dryness of the mouth, facial flushing, tachycardia, feelings of coldness or warmth, or sexual arousal, although not commonplace, are not rare occurrences. Quite often, however, such phenomena either do not register in the patient's awareness or are not reported. In a similar way, autonomic responses in the analyst, although often providing important clues to the unconscious messages being transmitted by a patient as well as to countertransference reactions, are often overlooked as valuable analytic data.

I would like to cite material from several analytic hours to illustrate how an analyst's use of himself as an instrument that registers and resonates on multiple channels and through several sensory modalities can enhance his understanding of a patient's communications in the analytic situation.

Mr. A was a short, energetic, affable man whose anxiety over his aggressive and competitive impulses and his consequent fear of the analyst's retaliation led him to smile a good deal and indicate through body language that he was a compliant, nonthreatening individual. Whenever, in the transference, negative feelings toward the analyst were mobilized, the patient would become restless on the couch, begin a tapping motion with a foot, fall silent, and when able to speak, do so in a hesitant and disjointed manner.

Such feelings had been coming up in the analysis against strong resistance, and as I entered the waiting room at the beginning of one hour, I noticed Mr. A sitting upright in his chair, his body taut, and one foot already in motion. As I approached, he looked up, and in the instant before his usual smile covered it over, I noticed an expression on his face that seemed to convey a mixture of surprise and disapproval. In a flash it was gone, and as Mr. A rose and approached me, his smile seemed to broaden. As he passed me he glanced at my face, seeming to seek in it a clue to my feelings about him.

On the couch Mr. A assumed a familiar position, his body held stiffly, legs extended, and hands placed behind his head. In addition, however, I noticed that his elbows were positioned in such a way as to create a protective shield. As I observed him, I felt a tightening of my musculature. I was sitting rather stiffly and experiencing a tension in my body that was not usual for me. I was also aware that my heartbeat was rapid. A feeling of tension, in fact, dominated the room. There was an air of expectation as though something dramatic was going to happen. This electric quality was added to by Mr. A's silence. For several minutes he did not speak, but he began to move on the couch as the characteristic restless movements and foot tapping conveyed his irritation.

When he spoke, it was to relate a story of mistreatment at the hands of his girl friend. The theme was old and repetitive, the content a slight variation of incidents reported hundreds of times before. Mr. A's tone was flat, his narration lacking in strongly felt affect. As I listened, I found myself experiencing tedium, compounded by inner feelings of tension and irritation. The atmosphere continued to be charged.

After he had gone on for some time relating his story in a rather bland and controlled way, I took advantage of a moment's pause to direct his attention to the scene in the waiting room. I told him what I had observed in his facial expression and asked if he was aware of his own reaction. Suddenly, as if a reservoir had been tapped, Mr. A gave vent to a flood of feelings about my appearance. How, he wanted to know, did I come to dress the way I did? Who picked out my ties? He was startled by the boldness of the print I wore that day, which went with my sport jacket like oil and vinegar. My shirt did not match either, and my trousers needed a pressing. All in all, I looked like a Samuel Beckett character, fresh out of a dustbin. Mr. A then speculated on the woman who, in his imagination, was responsible for selecting my attire. He considered her inattentive and self-centered. She did not look out for me. She had let me deteriorate, and instead of presenting myself as I should be, a well-turned-out Madison Avenue doctor, I greeted my patients like a schmegge, like an analyst who slept on his own couch.

It was not difficult then for Mr. A to realize that he was experiencing me as the father of his adolescent years, the father whom he wanted so very much to be proud of but whose alcoholism led to a steady deterioration in his dress and behavior. For years, Mr. A had concealed his dismay and anger from his father, and rarely had he allowed himself to come in touch with his own feelings.

This pattern had been reactivated in the transference, and although repeatedly recognized, its understanding had remained intellectualized. Confrontation with a piece of his non-verbal behavior, which conveyed an involuntary reaction of disapproval and disgust, served as a wedge. It allowed Mr. A to experience more immediately his own spontaneous reactions and his defenses against them. And it was the monitoring of the analyst's own reactions within the analytic hour, as well as his observations of the patient, that aided him in recognizing the field of resistance that had begun to cover over Mr. A's spontaneous and important transference response.

A second case, that of Mr. L, bears some similarity to Mr. A's because an important reaction to the analyst was concealed in an analytic hour and could be detected through nonverbal clues. Like Mr. A, Mr. L tended to be friendly and outgoing. Unlike the former, however, what Mr. L defended strongly against was not his negative feelings toward the analyst but his love for him. Indirectly but persistently, Mr. L gave hints that he wanted signs of affection from the analyst. Often, this took the form of imagining that the analyst would bring him a gift, and in fact, he often treated the analyst's verbal interventions as though they were gifts.

Unlike Mr. A, Mr. L rarely permitted himself to be silent on the couch. Silence was equated with sadness and depression, affects that very much frightened him and that he vigorously defended himself against.

One day, however, Mr. L seemed more subdued than usual. Although he filled the hour with a stream of talk that related primarily to his weekend plans, there was in his speech a strained and forced quality. It was as though he was trying to be "up." Moreover, his posture on the couch was unusual for him. For most of the hour, he lay on his side with his legs curled under him. As he talked, he fingered the material on the couch, alternately rubbing it and pinching it between thumb and forefinger. He was speaking of the forthcoming weekend. He anticipated a full and pleasurable round of activities capped off by a dance at his country club. But he was sweating, and every now and then he burped as though he was suffering from a sudden case of indigestion. During the hour, while recounting the fact that one of his cars was in for repair and that he would be forced to take another, he began unconsciously to carry out some driving motions. At the same time a tear came to his eye and with a quick covering gesture that pretended to flick a piece of dust from a lash, he wiped it away.

As I listened to the material of the hour, I felt a heaviness within myself. An inexplicable feeling of sadness came over me. Memories of a similarly planned weekend in my youth that turned out to be a disappointment filtered into my consciousness. Despite the manifest content of Mr. L's thoughts, the mood in myself and in the room was heavy. Feelings of depression were in the air. When I noticed the tear in Mr. L's eye, I called his attention to the disparity between what he was saying and the feelings that he must have been experiencing. Then he revealed something that had happened just prior to the start of the hour.

I had arrived at my office in the family car, an old and weatherbeaten sedan that had seen better days. Being early for his appointment, Mr. L had been waiting on the corner about a hundred yards away and had seen me drive up. As he did so, he was aware of a sudden feeling of disappointment, but he put this reaction quickly out of mind. Now as I pointed out the emotions that seemed to be just beneath the surface, the feeling of disappointment surfaced again with great intensity.

Mr. L could not understand me driving so old and unfashionable a car. He felt very let down, almost tearful. Finally, a memory presented itself that clarified what was happening. Mr. L remembered the night of his high school senior prom and the promise his father had made that a newly purchased sports car would be available to him for the evening. He had conveyed this to his date, and both were looking forward to arriving at the prom in celebrity style. As it turned out, however, the dealer failed to have a new car ready as promised. It was with the keenest sense of betrayal and disappointment that, watching out the window, Mr. L saw his father drive up to their house, not in the Triumph that he had expected, but in the family's aging and battle-scarred station wagon.

This incident, long forgotten, contained within it the essence of Mr. L's relationship with his father, a relationship filled with yearning and disappointment. The memory that was recaptured opened the way to the exploration in analysis of that crucial relationship and its impact on Mr. L's identifications, symptoms, and object relations. It was primarily by means of his nonverbal behavior on the couch that Mr. L provided the clues to the transference reaction that opened the pathway to memory.

In another case, a critical experience of the past could also be recovered with the help of clues from the patient's body language. In this instance, however, the experience occurred not in adolescence but in the earliest months of life.

Mr. W was a tall, lean, and artistically gifted young man whose artistic career was very much hampered by his fear of failure. So great, in fact, was his anxiety over not succeeding and "failing flat on his face" but he was unable to enter a field for which by virtue of his training and natural abilities he was well suited.

Analysis revealed that one source of his difficulty lay in certain thought patterns laid down in the preoedipal years, particularly during the separation–individuation phase of development. Mr. W's mother was an anxious and fearful woman who had difficulty in allowing her young son to separate from her and to individuate in his own way. Through their close and intimate contact and the strong identification which it fostered, her fears became his own. This factor, as well as his anxiety over revealing his powerful sexual and aggressive impulses toward his mother, made him fearful of leaving her side. He experienced any assertive act as an aggressive one and any move toward independence as a threatened separation. Whenever Mr. W acted in an independent and self-sufficient manner, his behavior stirred up in him profound anxiety that was related to fantasies originating in the separation–individuation period. He imagined that he would be left all alone and in a helpless state. His mother would abandon him, and he would starve or perish. Unable to walk or move, he would be essentially paralyzed.

Although Mr. W's disturbed relationship with his mother

played a pivotal role in the development of his neurosis, it was not the only factor of importance. In fact, the degree of his anxiety and the extent to which it incapacitated him suggested to me that other, perhaps earlier, factors may have exerted important influences on him. Even if they existed, however, I had no idea what they might be.

While observing Mr. W during an analytic hour, I noticed something that I had seen before but which had not registered. While lying on the couch, Mr. W regularly kept his legs in the same position, stretched out perfectly straight with his ankles flexed and his feet always the same distance apart. As I observed this posture, a memory from my internship days arose in mind. I recalled working on the pediatric service and seeing a number of young children with deformities of the legs and hips whose limbs were placed in braces. I called Mr. W's attention to the positioning of his legs on the couch and asked him if anything about his posture came to mind.

Immediately he related a fact that he had long forgotten. Shortly after birth, his feet were noted to turn inwards as the result of a defect in his lower extremities, and for a year thereafter, he was placed in a leg brace nightly. His stance and walking were retarded, and the practicing subphase of the separation–individuation process was substantially delayed. In fact, his mother's anxiety over his well-being, combined with his own weakness of limbs, severely compromised Mr. W's ability to locomote independently. This, in turn, had profound effects on his further development, particularly on his ability to separate from his mother. Again, in this case, Mr. W's kinesic behavior provided an important clue to experiences that had their origin in the preverbal period and that had not surfaced through the channel of verbalization.

In the foregoing, I have cited instances in which the analyst's memories, as well as those of the patient, were valuable in understanding the latter's unconscious communications. Although not specifically identified by Isakower as part of the analytic instrument, the memory system is, in fact, essential to it. The importance of the patient's memories is well known. Perhaps less well recognized is the importance of the analyst's memories. Blum (1980) has pointed out that reconstruction of the patient's childhood is often accompanied by reconstruction of the analyst's childhood, and that these are independent, if overlapping, processes. In a similar way, the memories of the patient and those of the analyst arise independently but interweave and overlap. The analyst "knows" his patient not only through the process of being able, for brief periods, to identify with him, but through his own parallel life experiences. It is through his own memories and the affects connected with them that, in large measure, he understands his patient's inner experiences. This way of knowing constitutes an important, if sometimes overlooked, aspect of empathy. For the analyst to be truly empathic, his own memories must be available to him. This is one of the most important effects of the analyst's own analysis. It helps put him in touch with his own memories. When shifted into a mobile state, these memories are then free to rise up to meet those of the patient.

The following may serve as one more example of the analyst's use of his own memories. Mr. Y, a bright, energetic business executive who wished analysis because of persistent difficulties in his interpersonal relationships, was markedly anxious about using the couch. For almost a half-hour in his first session he remained seated, feeling confused and embarrassed by his inability to lie down. He made several efforts to do so, only to experience intense anxiety and be forced to resume a sitting position. Finally, on his fourth try, Mr. Y was able to ease himself into a recumbent position, although he maintained his head and shoulders well propped up with pillows. His anxiety had an intensity to it, as well as a childlike quality, that was familiar to me. But, listening to Mr. Y, I could not identify the source of this feeling of familiarity.

Then a memory arose in my mind, a memory of my being driven to the hospital at age four to have a tonsillectomy. Although, in all probability, what I remembered was a screen memory, the affect associated with it was undoubtedly related to frightening experiences that were characterized by a threat of bodily injury. The memory and feelings accompanying it were triggered by the material of the hour and particularly by Mr. Y's fear of lying down. This anxiety, which was clearly related to his fear of submitting passively to a doctor, had, through a momentary identification, triggered a memory of my own frightening surgical experience. That this memory from my childhood was meaningfully linked with Mr. Y's behavior became clear when, tentatively, he eased himself into a reclining position. Then I noticed two deep scars behind his ears, the result of a double mastoidectomy performed when he was six years old for a life-threatening illness.

As a final topic, I would like to take up another aspect of the analytic instrument: the analyst's communications to the patient. This is, of course, a vast topic to which I cannot do justice in this chapter. I comment, therefore, only on a particular facet of it.

In their teaching, Isakower, Arlow, and others have pointed out that when an analyst is listening well and his part of the analytic instrument is tuned in to the transmitting instrument of the patient, an accurate reading of the patient's unconscious communications is very likely to take place, with the result that a correct understanding of that message will "arrive" in the analyst's mind. This he communicates to the patient in the form of an interpretation. Thus, in this model, the analyst's interpretations are closely linked with the proper functioning of the analytic instrument.

What was not discussed in Isakower's initial remarks was the way that the analytic instrument operates to promote and regulate the metacommunications between patient and analyst. That this kind of communication exists as an important aspect of every analytic hour is a well-known, if infrequently studied, phenomenon. Close scrutiny of the verbal exchanges that occur within a given analytic hour will reveal not only overt messages conveyed by both participants, but covert messages as well. The manifest content of the communications is accompanied by a latent content that comments on, adds to, or modifies the manifest level. When his part of the analytic instrument is working well, the analyst will register with sensitivity the metacommunicational as well as the denotative aspects of the patient's communications. And his interventions will contain a latent message that reverberates with and responds to the latent messages inherent in the patient's verbalizations.

During one analytic hour, a fifty-five-year-old writer ex-

pressed great distress over a troublesome vaginal condition that
was causing her to lose sexual feeling. With anguish, she stated
her belief that she was like an eighty-year-old woman and was
doomed to a life of isolation and celibacy. Listening to her, the
analyst found himself picturing the patient's aged aunt. Some
years previously, this woman had developed a similar condition.

The patient's identification in fantasy with her aunt was
clear, and the analyst was able to interpret it. In doing so, he
was able to show the patient that it was, in fact, her fantasy of
being like her aunt that contributed to her sense of being old
and decrepit. But he contributed something else as well. In
response to the patient's fright and anguish, the analyst's voice
took on a calm and reassuring tone. Through his manner and
phrasing, as well as through the decisive quality of his voice, he
was conveying another message. What he was communicating
was something like this:

> I hear what you are saying. You are afraid that because of your
> problem I will find you ugly and unattractive. You are worried
> that I will see you as an old and shriveled woman. In fact, you
> are not that way. A large part of your fright stems from the
> fantasy that you have developed that you are like your aunt and
> that her fate will be yours. I know this is a fantasy and I do not
> share it. I see you as you are and do not believe, as you do, that
> your current problem makes you a less attractive woman.

There is little doubt that this kind of message, the metacommunicational one, plays a significant role in every therapy.
As yet its place in theory and technique has not been fully
elucidated. But there is little question that every correct interpretation is correct on more than one level. Grasping the essence of what the patient is attempting to convey, the analyst
responds with a verbal interpretation indicating that he understands the message. But through his inflection, his tone, his
timing, his phrasing, and particularly through the affect that
he conveys, the analyst responds to another message, to the
covert communication which, often enough, contains within it
a comment on the interaction between patient and analyst.
When the analytic instrument is operating on only one channel

and fails to register the patient's metacommunications, the analyst's "correct" interpretation may elicit little response because it is, in fact, only partially correct. But when the analytic instrument is well tuned and is able to register on several channels at once, the analyst's intervention will reflect his intuitive grasp of the multiple levels of meaning of the patient's communications. It is then that the patient has the experience of feeling truly understood. And it is at such times that his response to the analyst's interpretation will, in all likelihood, contain the confirming affects and associations that have come to be associated with its correctness.

IV

*Countertransference, Insight, and
Self-Analysis*

7

On Countertransference Enactments

A colleague of some renown who, though large in reputation, was extremely small of stature, received a telephone call from a man who wanted a consultation. The appointment was made, and at the arranged time the new patient arrived. About to enter the waiting room to greet him, the analyst suddenly stopped at the threshold and, momentarily, stood transfixed. There in front of him was a Paul Bunyan of a figure, fully six feet, eight inches in height, weighing perhaps 260 pounds, and wearing cowboy boots and a ten-gallon hat. For several more seconds the analyst looked at him in silence. Then, with a shrug of his shoulders and a resigned gesture, he motioned toward his office. "Come on in, anyway," he said.

This opening phase carried with it worlds of meaning for both analyst and patient. It highlights the well-known, though sometimes overlooked fact, that from the very outset of treatment, transferences are activated in the analyst as well as in the patient. Whether overt or disguised, dramatic or barely perceptible, the analyst's transferences may exert a significant influence, not only on his perceptions and understanding, but on the particular form and manner in which the patient's transferences emerge. Conveyed in tone and gesture as well as in words, these reactions may be expressed in ways more subtle than obvious—in the barest of nods, the most minimal of smiles, the scarcely audible grunt, the slightest variation in words of greeting or of farewell.

The analyst's countertransference reactions, however, may be expressed in ways that are even more covert, as aspects of his well-accepted methods and procedures. I am using the term *countertransference* here, as I do throughout this volume, to refer to influences on the analyst's understanding and technique that stem both from his transferences and from his emotional responses to the patient's transferences. When they take this form, countertransference reactions are intricately intertwined with and embedded within customary, and often unexamined, analytic techniques and the attitudes and values that inform them.

The way in which we listen, our silences and neutrality, the emphasis we place on transference phenomena and interpretation of the transference, our ideas concerning working through, termination, and what constitutes a "correct" interpretation—these and many other facets of our daily clinical work may, and not infrequently do, contain concealed countertransference elements.

It is on this aspect of countertransference that I shall focus in this chapter because it seems to me that our understanding of the phenomena of countertransference can be enhanced by consideration of some of its subtler as well as its more obvious expressions.

It is the latter aspects, the noisier and often dramatic forms that, for the most part, have received attention in the literature. Illustrative in this regard are some of the statements made by Annie Reich (1966) who remarks that "countertransference pushes the analyst to act out in a positive or negative way." The affects stirred up in him, she says, "carry the full charge of repressed impulses suddenly bursting out from the depth. Thus they lead to real action, to over-strong emotion or to the opposite, to rigid defenses or blank spots" (p. 352). She describes the not uncommon situation in which the analytic material touches on some specific problem of the analyst, precipitating in him an inappropriately strong response. "In all relevant situations," she states, "the intensity of conflict interferes with understanding. Sublimation fails. Real action, over-strong emotion, misunderstanding, blocking, etc., occur. Where minimal amounts of energy should lead to thought, that is to trial action, real action occurs" (p. 355).

Such responses on the part of the analyst are, of course, not rare. Much that we call countertransference behavior can accurately be described in these terms. Because reactions of this kind impinge directly on the analytic work and constitute obvious sources of difficulty, it is understandable that when, in the 1950s, the problem of countertransference began to attract the attention of analysts, such phenomena became the focus of interest. Even today the idea of countertransference, for many colleagues, is synonymous with overt actions and with an identifiable piece of acting out on the part of the analyst.

Typical of the kind of material that one hears at case conferences—when the issue of countertransference is mentioned at all—is the revelation made recently by a colleague well known for his candor.

"By mistake I ended one session three minutes early," he reported, "and I became aware then of how intensely frustrated this patient was making me. In fact, I was in a fury. She reminded me of the stepsister I could never get along with. She is the same kind of controlling, manipulative woman. After I realized my error, I did a piece of self-analysis which has helped me avoid a repetition of this problem." "Now," he added with a grin, "I usually begin sessions a couple of minutes late."

While such reports are unquestionably valuable, they refer to only one aspect of countertransference—that characterized by overt and rather obvious actions on the part of the analyst. In this regard they may be compared to a view of acting out that includes in such behavior only gross motor actions. This perspective, as Boesky (1982) has pointed out, constitutes a limited way of conceptualizing the highly complex and diverse behaviors that come under the heading of acting out. For some patients acting out will be expressed not in motion, but in immobility; not in words, but in silence. For others acting out may be conveyed in subtle vocal qualities—in the pitch, tone, and rhythms of speech as well as in syntax and phrasing. Boesky has used the term *actualization* for phenomena of this kind, so as to distinguish them from the more obvious kinds of motor actions that are commonly associated with the term *acting out.*

A similar distinction may be made with regard to counter-transference phenomena. Oftentimes it is not his overt actions, including even troublesome lapses of control, that are the source of the analyst's greatest countertransference problems, but the covert, scarcely visible, yet persistent reactions that pervade his manner of listening and responding.

This idea is not new. To the contrary, in recent years a number of authors, writing from quite different perspectives, have focused on the manifold, and often subtle, ways in which countertransference reactions may influence the analytic process. Langs (1975), emphasizing the importance of the frame-work and boundaries of the therapeutic setting, points out that the way in which these ground rules are managed implicitly conveys to the patient a great deal about the analyst's intra-psychic state.

In another vein, Arlow (1987) discussed indicators of coun-tertransference reactions. These include not only blind spots with regard to specific material and parapraxes concerning such matters as billing and appointments, but certain reactions of the analyst that occur outside the consultation room. Among these are recurrent thoughts about the patient, often accom-panied by feelings of depression or other mood changes, a repetitive need to talk about the sessions, and the appearance of the patient in the manifest content of the analyst's dreams.

Stein (1981) has stressed the importance in analytic work of analyzing the positive, or so-called unobjectionable part of the transference. Not uncommonly, he points out, hidden be-hind this transference picture, there are powerful competitive and negative feelings as well as idealization of the analyst. Un-critical acceptance of the old analytic maxim that the positive transference should not be interpreted unless it becomes a re-sistance may contain a well-rationalized countertransference reaction. Oftentimes it is the aim of such reactions both to sustain the hidden gratifications afforded the analyst by the patient's positive view of him and to avoid confrontation of the aggression that lies behind the surface attitude.

Focusing on the patient–analyst interactions that comprise

the essence of analytic work, Sandler (1976) has pointed out that in analysis each party seeks to impose on the other an intrapsychic object relationship. Responding to the patient with spontaneous actions, affects, and associations, the analyst employs a "free-floating responsiveness" that complements his "free-floating attention." While invaluable in providing cues to nonverbally transmitted communications from the patient and the analyst's response to them, these reactions may also contain significant countertransference elements. Unless these are grasped by the analyst, he may find himself simply accepting the role imposed on him by the patient and joining him in a piece of mutual acting out.

Writing from a Kohutian perspective, Wolf (1979) has noted the regular occurrence in analysis of minicountertransferences. These are inevitable failures of empathy and understanding on the part of the analyst based on momentary countertransference reactions. While such reactions are the source of temporary disruptions in the established analytic process, in Wolf's view they also provide an opportunity for patient and analyst to gain insight into the precise nature of these disruptions and their transference meanings.

MacDougall (1979) has pointed out that the use of ordinary analytic technique with patients who have suffered traumatic experiences in the preverbal period and for whom silence and abstinence are experienced as fresh traumas not infrequently contains countertransference elements. She writes:

> Like all other human beings we as analysts have difficulty in hearing or perceiving what does not fit into our preestablished codes. Our own unresolved transference feelings here play a role since the garnering of analytic knowledge has been accomplished and [is] deeply impregnated with transference affect and thus tends to carry an inbuilt resistance of its own, making it difficult for us to hear all that is being transmitted. We tend to resent the patient who does not progress in accordance with our expectations or who reacts to our efforts to understand as though they were hostile attacks upon him. These problems added to our personal weaknesses, provide us with a delicate task [p. 301].

In what follows I shall also discuss the question of analytic technique and the way in which countertransference elements may be concealed within our standard, well-accepted, and quite correct procedures. In citing case examples, however, my focus will not be on the severely traumatized patient or the more disturbed one, but on patients whose symptoms and character problems make psychoanalysis carried out in an unmodified way clearly the treatment of choice.

Some years ago, after I had begun analytic work with a man of considerable artistic talent and ingenuity, I discovered in myself an unusual phenomenon. I noticed that despite having listened to Mr. K for better than four months, I had not missed a word he had spoken. This, I must confess, was for me a situation worth reflecting on for I was aware of a tendency, when I was tired, conflicted, or anxious, for my attention to drift in the direction of my own associations rather than those of the patient. This had not happened with Mr. K, and I was on the verge of considering myself cured when I gave some thought to the way I had been listening to him. Then I realized that in listening so alertly, so carefully, and with such rapt attention, I had done nothing more than trade one symptom for another. My listening had taken on a special quality that I now recognized as familiar. It contained something akin to awe, and I realized that although I had missed nothing, neither had I offered much in the way of interpretation.

I became aware, too, of a frequently recurring theme in my visual associations to Mr. K. This involved the depiction of an orator or public speaker holding forth before an entranced audience. It did not take much more detective work for me to understand what had been happening. I had been listening to Mr. K as, for years, I had listened to my father holding forth at the dinner table, expounding his personal view of world history. Long after dessert was served, I would sit transfixed listening to him spin tales of biblical times and of the *tsouris* experienced by Rabbi Joshua, later known by the name of Jesus. It was his show, and if I spoke at all it was simply to ask for more details—the equivalent of my interventions years later with my patient.

Mr. K's talent for story-telling and his transference wish for me to play the role of appreciative audience had transported me back four decades. I was listening as I had listened as a boy of ten—silently, intently, half-mesmerized. Only later did I realize that the particular way in which I listened was serving an old and familiar purpose—to keep from my awareness the negative and competitive feelings I was experiencing toward the performer on stage.

Like the rather extended silences that, in this case, I found myself slipping into, silence in the analyst not uncommonly contains elements of countertransference. Familiar to all of us are the silences that reflect anger, boredom, depression, and fatigue. Familiar too are the silences of confusion, of retaliation, and of momentary identification. Less well recognized as a potential conveyer of countertransference feelings is the kind of silence that, as analysts, we strive to achieve as part of our analytic instrument—the silence of empathic understanding. Precisely because this attitude is so important to us, so much emphasized, and so valuable in our work, countertransference elements that on occasion may be concealed within it are easily overlooked.

This was brought home to me in the course of analytic work with a middle-aged professional woman. During one session in particular I became aware in myself of unusually strong feelings of empathy. In that hour I was able to see what Mrs. A saw, experience what she experienced, feel what she felt. It was with considerable surprise, after the patient had left the office, that I noted in myself some irritation with her and the thought that what she had told me was only one side of a complex story. This reaction caused me to reflect on the material of our hour and, with the patient out of the room, once again to associate to it. I then realized that the scene Mrs. A had depicted was entirely familiar to me and that in my adolescence I had played one of the central characters. Distraught over an argument with her husband, Mrs. A had been unable to sleep. She waited up until her teenage son had come in from an evening out, and then talked to him at some length of her distress. He had listened and been understanding as I had been when, under similar circumstances, my mother had confided in me her hurt and anger over my father's behavior.

As I listened to Mrs. A and imagined the scene she was

depicting I had, unconsciously, become again the son at the kitchen table listening to and sharing his mother's upset. I had become the good listener, the empathic listener, but also the listener who had to conceal from himself some feelings of resentment at what he was hearing. It was only after Mrs. A was gone that I, like the adolescent who, when alone, can experience certain emotions that do not surface in a parent's presence, became aware that my responses during the hour were only one side of a complex countertransference reaction. The other side, the resentment I felt over Mrs. A's presenting herself as the helpless victim and her husband as the brutish aggressor, had been defended against as similar emotions had been defended against years before: by the upsurge of the strongest feelings of empathy.

For many colleagues the experiences in childhood and adolescence of being an empathic listener to parents or other family members has played a role of importance in their choice of vocation. It is not a rare occurrence for the memories of these experiences to be evoked in the analytic situation. Then silently, outside of awareness, the analyst's usually valuable empathic responses may contain enactments of those memories—enactments which, subtly, can alter and distort his perceptions and understanding.

Neutrality, too, may become invested with countertransference reactions. The analytic idea of neutrality is a highly complex one. It involves not only a way of listening that receives with impartiality material deriving from each of the psychic agencies and a technical approach that eschews the resolution of conflict through influence in favor of interpretation, but it implies in the analyst a state of receptivity that can accomplish these goals. The proper use of neutrality as a technical measure requires a considerable degree of inner "neutrality"; that is, a state of mind in which ego functions necessary for analytic work are not impaired by conflict. The relation between these two forces of neutrality, its outer one which is an integral aspect of analytic technique and the inner one which defines one of the psychological conditions for the employment of that technique, has not been focused on in discussions of the issue of neutrality. Tensions and disharmonies between these two aspects of the anlayst's neutrality frequently underlie its countertransference distortions.

Such a situation developed during the analysis of a young attorney. This was a man of outward charm and inner rage. So well concealed was his anger that he appeared to all the world to be a man of the utmost graciousness and wit. To his qualities of keen intelligence and sophistication, was added a persuasive tongue, so that Mr. C was known for his ability to attract clients. This talent he utilized in the analysis in playful, witty, and seemingly good-humored efforts to get me to render judgments on one or another of the fanciful—and invariably self-defeating—schemes and projects in which he was forever engaged.

In the face of Mr. C's charm and persuasiveness, I remained admirably neutral—or so I thought. Repeatedly, if not doggedly, I identified and interpreted his central inner conflicts, his obvious oedipal rivalry, and his unconscious guilt and preoedipal attachments—all with no effect whatever on him. Not for many months was I able to confront Mr. C directly either with the destructive impact of his behavior on his personal and professional life or with his aggression in the analytic situation. The reason for this was simple. Aggression in Mr. C, though deep and pervasive, was so well concealed, so covertly expressed, that for some time I was not consciously aware either of its presence or of the strong counteraggression it was stimulating in me. In a vague and not easily definable way, I felt uncomfortable with him, and I began, therefore, to pay attention to my autonomic responses during sessions. With regularity, I found my heartbeat to be rapid, my mouth dry, and my guts tense and knotted. It became increasingly clear to me that these were signs of concealed anger occurring in response to the covert anger directed at me.

Because of this state of affairs, I was unable to attain a properly "neutral" (that is, relatively conflict-free) inner receptivity. Since I was not consciously aware of this situation, but perceived it intuitively, I unconsciously overemphasized the outer aspect of neutrality, its technical side. I became not only a neutral analyst, but a determinedly neutral one. Afraid in the face of Mr. C's persuasiveness—and the aggression that lay behind it—to lose my stance of neutrality, I lost what Sandler has termed the analyst's *free-floating responsiveness*. In this case that meant the ability to confront Mr. C more directly with his behavior both within and outside the analytic situation.

Reflection on my responses to Mr. C led me to a memory that helped clarify some of my countertransference reactions. As a youngster I had great admiration for an after-school sports group leader who, for a time, became for me a father surrogate. Bright, witty, and ingenious, he was also something of a provocateur with his charges. In ways that were both humorous and vexing, he would tease the boys about aspects of their dress or behavior. Increasingly I became angry at this leader, but because he was emotionally important to me I concealed my feelings both from him and myself. It was not until after I left the group that I realized how large a role aggression on both sides had played in our relationship. No doubt Mr. C's behavior in the analytic situation, which in many respects was similar to that of the group leader and other important figures of my childhood, aroused in me a familiar pattern of response. This response, with its emphasis on attempting to quiet an inner disturbance through greater emphasis on outer neutrality, led to its inappropriate use.

Central to the question of working through, all analysts would agree, is the matter of repetition. It is the repetition of interpretations, first in one situation, then in another, that permits a patient to take the necessary steps from insight to the resolution of conflicts. Scrutiny of the analyst's use of repetitions, however, and the patient's response to them may reveal an interaction between patient and therapist that is quite different from that taking place in the usually conceived process of working through. Not uncommonly, a familiar scenario has developed. The analyst offers an interpretation which in one way or another is resisted. He interprets again, and once again the patient's resistance rises up to meet the intervention. Consciously aware of the need for repetition to foster working through, the analyst once more repeats his interpretation—only this time more insistently. Again the patient offers resistance—only this time more stubbornly. I need not go on to complete the picture. Within the framework of what appears to be a necessary, if painstaking, process of repetition and the gradual working through of resistance, a formidable, if unconscious, battle has been joined. As a result of the arousal of infantile conflicts in both parties, the process of repetition becomes a hammer blow against an iron door. The result, unless this transference–countertransference interaction can be identified and effectively interpreted, is the kind of stalemate that often characterizes such struggles in childhood.

Even in situations in which the process of working through takes place gradually, the interaction between patient and analyst may bear the hallmarks of similar parent–child relationships. The analyst interprets and the patient accepts perhaps a fraction of his offering. Further interpretations may lead to the acceptance of additional fractions. No doubt this is what is meant by fractional discharge. Under favorable circumstances this situation may continue until the patient's mouth has opened wide enough for the analyst to slip in a few spoonfuls of his special nourishment.

Much has been written in the analytic literature on the process of termination and the complex emotional responses it evokes in analyst and patient alike. Less discussed has been the issue of the decision to terminate and how this decision is arrived at. Frequently the idea of terminating is first broached by the patient. For some, this decision is reached when particular goals have been met, motivation to continue has slackened, or a plateau has occurred in the analysis. For others the idea of terminating has clear transference meanings and is related on the one hand to feelings of rejection, anger, disappointment, or frustration or, on the other, to anxiety over victory and success. Such situations are well known and require no elaboration here. What has not been studied with equal intensity are those situations in which the issue of termination arises as the result of covert, often unconsciously transmitted cues that pass between the participants in the analytic situation. These cues are manifestations of subtle and easily overlooked, but critically important, transference-countertransference interactions. The following examples may clarify the kind of situation I have in mind.

For some years I had been working with Mr. R, a middle-aged businessman whose deliberate and weighty verbal style was exceeded only by the ponderousness of his thought processes. He was not an easy man to listen to or to analyze, and at various times in the treatment I had the thought that in the face of his rock-ribbed obsessional defenses my interventions were little more than small-arms fire careening off a fortified concrete bunker. For more than nine years I had persisted, partly out of stubbornness, partly out of pride, but also because I detected each year grindingly slow but tangible progress in the patient's self-understanding and in the mitigation of troublesome symptoms.

About halfway into the tenth year of treatment, Mr. R suddenly brought up the idea of termination. He had been thinking, he said, and he believed that he had gone about as far as he could in his analysis. Although certain problems remained, he was much improved. Since, so far as he could tell, things were pretty much at a standstill, he doubted if he could expect many more gains by continuing.

I was surprised by this turn of events. To begin with, Mr. R was not a man who usually took the initiative in making decisions. Passivity was deeply rooted in his character, and I had long been convinced that when it came time for termination, I would have to raise the issue. Furthermore, there was nothing in the recent material that suggested Mr. R had been thinking about termination. It is true that the analysis was proceeding with the speed of a hippo moving upstream and in the past few weeks the resistances had been unusually tenacious, but this situation had existed before and I had not been thinking about termination. Or had I? I began to wonder.

I now gave much thought to the idea of ending and it seemed to me that Mr. R was probably right. In all likelihood we had gone as far as we could. There was no question that in many ways Mr. R was better; as for the rest, analysis had at least given him some tools to work with. I was on the verge of saying just that to my patient and setting a mutually acceptable termination date when something gave me pause. The rather abrupt way in which termination arose and my ready agreement with Mr. R made me uneasy. I decided to wait a bit and to review the material of the week prior to Mr. R's raising the question.

As I did so I remembered one session in which I had been particularly frustrated. On the basis of what seemed to me to be clear-cut material, I had made an interpretation connecting certain aspects of Mr. R's behavior in the transference to ways in which his mother related to him. Not only did the patient refute the interpretation out of hand with a barrage of sarcastic rejoinders, but in that session he could accept nothing else I offered. I recalled feeling tense and angry. In the face of his assault, I had lapsed into silence. I recalled also that in that hour, and in a subsequent one, I had been aware of experiencing a fleeting visual memory that involved my former analyst. This memory centered on a case conference at our institute which I had attended and at which my former analyst was a discussant. Although when it arose I was aware that such a memory must constitute a meaningful response to the analytic material, I could make nothing of it and so let it pass.

Now I returned to that memory and let myself think freely about it. What came to mind was something I had forgotten. In connection with the case presented at the conference, a patient who had been in analysis for quite a number of years, my former analyst had made the remark, "If you have not broken through after nine years of analysis, perhaps you had better rethink the value of continuing." My memory of that meeting was clearly a shorthand reference to that statement. In the face of Mr. R's stubborn and frustrating resistances I was, in effect, telling myself, "Your own analyst would not continue in such a situation. He would advise you to quit. Perhaps you had better listen!"

How I managed to communicate to Mr. R my feeling that we were at an impasse and that there was no point in going on is in itself an intriguing question. I had said nothing to Mr. R about ending and consciously was not thinking in those terms. What I realized in reviewing the situation, though, was that in response to the powerful resistances I had recently encountered, despair had set in and I had begun to withdraw. I spoke less, and when I did my tone was somewhat muted. I was aware, too, that fatigue, if not exasperation, had crept into my voice.

Always sensitive to the slightest hint of rejection and by nature a counterpuncher, Mr. R had reacted to these clues in characteristic fashion. He struck back by being the first to propose termination and, by that means, sought to reject me before I had a chance to send him away.

The analysis did not end at that point, but went on for another two years during which Mr. R made more progress than he had in the previous nine. However, we had come within a hair's breadth of terminating the treatment. Had we done so, the decision to end would have seemed, on the surface, entirely reasonable. It would have been initiated by a patient who had been in analysis for nine years, who had made substantial progress in a number of areas, but whose treatment had now reached a plateau. It would have been agreed to by his hard-working analyst who had taken him a fair distance and who now recognized on clinical grounds that further progress was unlikely. That a countertransference factor was, in fact, the determining one might well have gone unrecognized. How often, one wonders, does the decision to terminate come about in a similar manner?

Of primary importance in our technique is the matter of transference interpretation. The current well-accepted view that such interpretations are the only mutative ones has led in some instances to a way of listening that may be called listening *for* the transference. While such a focus in listening may be most valuable in detecting what Gill (1982) has termed the experience of the relationship, it may also prove problematic. Not only may the analyst's listening processes be restricted and, in the extreme case, deformed by so narrow a focus, but the analyst's less than subtle reactions to transference material may lead to its more abundant appearance. It may happen, too, that there is formed between patient and therapist a defensive collusion that has as its unconscious purpose the exploitation of the transference so as to avoid the emergence of other anxiety-laden material.

Such was the case with Mrs. G, a clever and sophisticated woman who oriented herself to others by picking up in them the slightest behavioral and verbal cues. During a difficult time in her life, when her husband had become acutely ill, she brought in material that contained within it detectable, though quite concealed, references to her analyst. Though it took a hawklike alertness to the barest hints of transference to dig out these nuggets, I did so and was rather pleased at being able to interpret certain transference feelings that had not surfaced previously. Only after this period had passed and Mrs. G's husband had recovered, did I become aware of how patient and analyst had utilized this transference material. Terrified that her husband would die and unable in the analysis to face this possibility, Mrs. G had, unconsciously, made use of her knowledge that I invariably reacted with interest to transference material by feeding me bits and pieces of it as a decoy. For my part, Mr. G's life-threatening illness had reactivated some painful memories concerning personal losses which I, too, was eager to suppress. By joining with my patient in a particular kind of detective game called "locate the transference," I had colluded with her in doing just that. At this time in the analysis the central issue was not the subtleties of the transference, as important as these were, but Mrs. G's inability to face the reality of death—a reality that her analyst was also quite willing to avoid.

Finally, I wish to say a few words about the issue of correct interpretations. Although one of our primary goals as analysts is to offer interpretations that are correct, the extent to which our interventions are, in fact, accurate is not always easy to assess. The commonly held view that a correct interpretation will regularly elicit in the patient material that confirms it requires some rethinking in light of contradictory clinical evidence.

Every analyst has had the experience of making interpretations which, while later proven correct, are initially met with responses of silence, of incredulity, of anger, of denial, of awe, of protest, of depression, or, in some cases, reactions characterized by an increase of symptoms. This state of affairs suggests that we may need to inquire further as to what constitutes a correct interpretation. On what level of meaning is its correctness to be judged? Is it solely the cognitive–denotative level, the overt meaning of the analyst's intervention and the resonance of his words with the preconscious of the patient? Or must we include also the metacommunicational level, the covert message hidden behind and within the analyst's words? If this is the case, how do these two levels relate to one another and to the "correctness" of an interpretation? Can an interpretation be correct on one level and not on another? If so, will a patient experience the intervention as correct or must both levels resonate with the analogous ones in himself in order for him to have the inner experience of an interpretation being true? Clearly these are complex and relatively unexplored areas that will require further investigation. For the moment, however, I must limit myself to the briefest discussion of a patient's negative response to a "correct" interpretation.

When I first began to see her, Mrs. L was a woman in her late thirties who, since the age of four, had sought reparations for the sudden loss of her mother. Full of rage, she had clung to and tortured three husbands before taking on her analyst. In all these relationships she threatened repeatedly to leave the men in her life but never did so. Instead it was they who, weary and battle-scarred, threw in the towel.

Her threats to end the analysis were no less frequent. Quite regularly, after excoriating me for not getting her out of her present unhappy marital situation, she threatened to get rid of me too. Although for the most part I was able to maintain my equanimity in the face of Mrs. L's attacks, on occasion I found it difficult to do so. During one session in which, once again, she threatened to leave treatment. I offered an interpretation aimed at bringing to the fore one of the genetic determinants of the repetitive pattern in which she was engaged.

She was treating me, I said, the way she treated her husband, her husbands before him and, in childhood, her feared and hated stepmother. Although she had told me many times that she was leaving treatment, in fact she seemed very frightened to do so. She acted as though I were the only analyst in the city and in this attitude she was responding to me as though, in fact, I were her stepmother. With her mother gone, she could never follow through on her ever-present plan to leave her stepmother as this woman had become the only mother she had.

The patient's response lingers in memory. She became tearful and agitated, accused me of wanting to get rid of her, and felt totally hopeless. She sank into a depression that lasted for several weeks and, for some months thereafter, was wary of any interpretation I might offer.

The cause of Mrs. L's reaction was quite clear. She had understood her analyst's message correctly. The manifest interpretation was probably correct enough, but these were not the words that reached her. It was my true meaning. Responding with anger to her sustained provocations, I had reacted like her stepmother and her husbands; they had invited her to leave. Because this countertransference reaction was so unacceptable to me, so contrary to a helpful intervention, I had blocked it from conscious awareness. It found its way out not in the formally correct overt interpretation, but in the covert one that served as a vehicle for the expression of my countertransference feelings.

Reactions such as Mrs. L's raise interesting questions about patients' negative responses to interpretations. No doubt some of these responses constitute aspects of the classical syndrome of the negative therapeutic reaction in which the issue of unconscious guilt often plays a central role. Others may derive from quite different sources. Among these are negative responses that represent accurate and intuitive readings of the analyst's hidden communications. In such instances we have to be alert to the possibility that aspects of the very interpretive process itself may imperceptibly have become an enactment. It is just such subtle and well-concealed enactments on the part of the analyst that, in many cases, continue the greatest source of countertransference difficulty.

In summary, I have wished in this chapter to call attention not to the more obvious forms of countertransference that have been commented on by previous writers on the subject, but to its subtler ones. Often well camouflaged within the framework of traditional, time-tested techniques, this aspect of countertransference may attach itself to our way of listening and thinking about patients, to our efforts at interpretation, to the process of working through, or to the complex issue of termination. Less recognizable than its more boisterous counterpart and in some respects less tangible, this side of the problem of countertransference is no less important. For it is precisely those subtle, often scarcely visible countertransference reactions, so easily rationalized as parts of our standard operating procedures and so easily overlooked, that may in the end have the greatest impact on our analytic work.

8

Countertransference Resistance and the Process of Self-Analysis

Among those advances in analytic technique which have taken place in recent years, few have been more important to our clinical work than the gains made in our understanding of the subtle expression of transference, resistance, and countertransference which not infrequently lie concealed behind the surface aspects of the analytic material. Increasingly analysts have come to recognize not only the covert, often scarcely visible manifestations of these forces in the analytic hour but the dynamic interplay that regularly occurs between them. The well-accepted notion that the cornerstone of modern psychoanalytic technique consists in the analysis of resistances, and particularly of transference resistances, has been augmented by our greater awareness of the analyst's countertransference contributions to the development of transference and resistance.

In light of the increasing sophistication with which clinicians regularly identify and interpret transference– countertransference interactions and the value placed both on doing so and on recognizing their relation to the ever-present factor of resistance, it is noteworthy that the phenomenon of countertransference resistance has been so little explored. In fact, the entire question of the analyst's resistances and their con-

157

tribution to the analytic process has received comparatively little attention.

This neglect has historical roots and underlines the psychological barriers that analysts have had to overcome traditionally in the process of deepening our understanding of countertransference. For some four decades, from 1910 when Freud first identified the phenomenon until the 1950s when Heimann (1950) and Little (1951) drew attention to it as an important vehicle for understanding unconscious communications in the analytic hour, the topic of countertransference was rarely mentioned in the literature. Analysts were reluctant to deal with it, at least in print. No doubt it took decades of clinical experience for the full range and complexity of countertransference reactions, as well as their potential value, to be appreciated, but this was not the only factor of importance in their omission from the literature. Resistance also played a role. The practitioners of this new science were not yet ready to follow Freud's lead, to examine in depth their own countertransference experiences, or to share such experiences with others.

When, in time, the combination of decreased resistance and growing clinical sophistication made possible more open discussion of countertransference issues, there was a tendency among early writers on the subject to focus on its overt, clearly visible forms. In her well-known articles, Reich (1951, 1960, 1966) emphasized these aspects of the problem and it is not surprising that she viewed countertransference from a single vantage point; as an impediment to effective analytic work that must be overcome.

For some time this view became the accepted position among most classically trained American analysts. It remained for an Argentinian of the Kleinian school to bring to the subject a broader and far more complex perspective. Heinrich Racker (1968) broke new ground both by describing in rich detail a variety of oedipal and preoedipal countertransference responses and by drawing attention to the complex interrelationships that exist between transference and countertransference.

Still, it took several more decades for authors such as Sandler (1976), MacDougall (1980), McLaughlin (1981), Gardner

(1983), and Poland (1986) to tap the rich vein opened by the study of countertransference phenomena and to underline the fact that the psychoanalytic process, by its very nature, is an interactive one that involves the constant interplay of two psychologies.

Even today, however, resistances among colleagues to more than casual self-scrutiny in the analytic hour and to recognition of the way that their behavior, verbal and otherwise, influences the emerging material remains a formidable problem.

Silverman (1987) has pointed out that the notion of the perfectly analyzed analyst, though long recognized as a myth, dies hard. We have had a need to believe in it just as we have had a need to believe that the training analysis has the power to immunize against troublesome countertransference reactions. Commenting on this misconception, Glover (1927) put the matter succinctly.

> Granted that the analyst's own specific inferiorities, his unconscious sexual anxieties and guilt over frustrated hostility have been effectively reduced in the training analysis, and that therefore he should be free from the tendency to take umbrage or to counterattack, we must nevertheless admit that the transference situation produces real and unavoidable stimulations and must be met as a current source of tension [p. 91].

Nowhere has our inherent resistance to close self-examination been more evident than in the reluctance of analysts to confront the phenomenon of resistance in ourselves as it operates in the analytic situation. As contrasted with the familiar and expectable forms of countertransference which are often openly expressed, understandable through introspection and frequently ego alien, the analyst's resistances may operate silently, almost invisibly, and be so imbedded in character and style that they remain quite acceptable to the ego.

In some respects the situation may be compared to the challenge presented by the analysis of the ego as contrasted with that of the drives. Freud was well aware of the fact that the former was the incomparably more difficult task. Whether manifested in transference or countertransference, the claims of the drives make themselves known in ways that are more or less obvious. The ego, on the other hand, may utilize for purposes of defense certain functions such as perception, memory, motility, thinking, and speech in ways that make recognition of its defensive aims a formidable task. So it is with certain aspects of the analyst's resistances which may be so intertwined with his usual defensive operations and so cleverly concealed behind layers of more accessible countertransference responses that for long periods of time their influence may go undetected.

Only a few authors have commented on the question of the analyst's resistances with more than passing interest. Racker (1958) has spoken of the phenomenon of counterresistance and its relationship to interpretation. He points out that counterresistance in the analyst arises as a consequence of his unconscious identification with the patient's resistances. Sharing such resistances for reasons which relate to conflicts of his own, the analyst offers interpretations which are necessarily incomplete. It is through recognition of the incompleteness of his interpretations that he becomes aware of his counterresistance and its impact on his understanding.

Glover (1927) has also described the phenomenon of counterresistance. For him the term is all but synonymous with the analyst's negative countertransferences whose rich variety he catalogues in his discussion of these phenomena. Like Racker, however, Glover also speaks specifically of certain resistances which arise in the analyst in response to the patient's resistances. Such reactions, he believes, play a central role in the analytic process.

"Allowing for differences in character, temperament and symptom type between the analyst and his patient," he writes, "the counterresistances of the analyst in any given situation are similar and equal in intensity to the resistances of the patient in that situation" (p. 92). Glover also notes that the analysis of oedipal material in both its positive and negative forms may evoke in the analyst resistances that are related to the unconscious arousal in him of both heterosexual and homosexual impulses. In drawing attention to some of the forces that may underlie and feed the analyst's resistances, Glover has anticipated the kinds of issues with which I will also be concerned.

In line with the thinking of Racker and Glover, Arlow (1987) points out that oftentimes analysts identify with patients' defenses as well as their impulses and fantasies and unconsciously employ similar maneuvers. Blum (1987) makes a similar observation and stresses the frequency with which counter-identification occurs as a part of the analyst's countertransference response.

In his paper on the psychology of the analyst at work, Spruiell (1984) mentions another facet of the analyst's resistance; that which is directed against recognition of his countertransference responses. This is a commonly encountered situation and one whose effect on the analytic process is of unquestioned importance. It is, however, the other side of this coin that I wish to focus on in this chapter, namely, the analyst's unconscious use of his countertransference reactions to screen from his awareness the existence of resistances within himself. Such resistances, often operating as silent forces within the analytic situation, may have a far-reaching effect on its outcome. I will illustrate this phenomenon with two clinical examples.

Some years ago I had the puzzling experience of working with a bright, attractive, and talented young woman, well motivated for analysis, to whom I could not listen. Or, to put it more exactly, to whom I could listen well and attentively for only parts of her hour. With embarrassing regularity I would find in the course of sessions with her that my mind would wander to personal concerns. Sometimes I would find myself daydreaming of recent events. At others, it was snatches of memory that distracted me. Most often these involved momentary triumphs of adolescence; my driving in the winning run in a championship baseball game (a memory preserved in proof condition) or my managing to wangle a date with the neighborhood beauty who, because of her fondness for hamburgers, we named Miss White Tower.

Although I would have been relieved to discover that these seemingly private and disconnected musings were in fact camouflaged associations to the material of the hours, I could rarely convince myself that this was so. Later, as it turned out, I came to understand that at least some of these memories did have relevance to the analytic situation and that oftentimes they con-

stituted a shorthand way of expressing particular countertransference feelings. At the time, however, I could discover no such
bridges.

Needless to say, this was an embarrassing situation and a
distressing one. At the start of each session I would resolve to
give Ms. F my full and sustained attention. Insofar as it was
consciously possible to do so, I set myself to listen carefully in
the analyst's proverbially evenly hovering manner and to be on
guard against the slightest departure from this task. All would
go well for a spell. Sometimes my attentiveness would remain
undisturbed for thirty or forty minutes, sometimes for the full
hour. On occasion several hours would pass with no loss of
attention and during one period, feeling as though I had set
a new personal record, I put together a string of more than a
dozen sessions in which I connected well with my patient.

More often than not, however, the familiar problem would
reassert itself and I found myself missing words and sentences
here and there. Sometimes if a dream was involved I could
correct the situation by asking Ms. F to repeat a particular
segment. At other times, however, I was too embarrassed and
too fearful of revealing my lapse to say anything and so let the
matter pass.

What was particularly troubling about my problem was that
self-analysis, or the efforts I had thus far made at it, had yielded
few insights into its sources. I had been aware all along that
certain features of Ms. F's speech, the slow and deliberate quality of her delivery combined with a descriptive style that proceeded in ways more circuitous than direct, evoked feelings of
impatience in me; but thus far I had not been able to deepen
my understanding of this reaction.

Now I returned to it, and in a more sustained and persistent
manner allowed my mind to play over my responses. What I
first came into contact with was that the reaction of mild annoyance of which I was conscious was, in fact, not so mild. I
realized that I was more than a little put off by Ms. F's indirect,
meandering style which chugged along an endless track but
seemed never to reach its destination.

The daughter of well-respected, socially prominent parents
who drank heavily and spent their evenings engaged in mutual

carping and recriminations often followed by obvious and noisy sessions of lovemaking, Ms. F had a series of unsuccessful love affairs which were characterized by a tendency to provoke quarrels followed by efforts to repair the relationship through seductive, teasing behavior. She was, however, better at teasing and at being flirtatious than she was in bed. There she was regularly frigid, often suffered from vaginismus and secretly disliked sex. Like her mother, who was a well-known hostess and knew how to be alluring to men, Ms. F could be witty and engaging. Like her mother, however, she told interminable stories whose main purpose seemed to be to enthrall the listener. There was in both mother and daughter well-concealed resentment toward men which took the form of engaging their interest, holding them with a nonstop narrative while using posture and bodily movements to provoke and tease, and then frustrating them through a sudden withdrawal of interest. This pattern was repeated in analysis, but in more subtle ways. Ms. F would often begin sessions with an account of a dream or of emotions experienced in a previous hour in a thoughtful and reflective way. The development of useful insights seemed within reach, but then, after this promising beginning, Ms. F's associations would run aground. Her thoughts would veer off in another direction. She would launch into a description of some outside event, spinning out her tale like an endless ball of yarn. So lengthy was her story and so seemingly aimless the narrative that not infrequently I would find myself bemused, frustrated, and, I now realized, more than a little angry. More often than I had recognized I felt that I was being tantalized by being led on a trip that promised much in the way of enriched understanding but which ultimately became a blind detour leading to nowhere. Why I should have had to minimize my reaction to Ms. F's behavior in analysis and conceal its strength behind a laundered version of the truth now became the focus of my interest. As I reflected on the matter, I recalled certain scenes from my youth. These involved memories of my father holding forth at the dinner table with lengthy explanations of history that rewrote the textbooks. Weary and angry at being unable to stem this narrative floodtide, my siblings, sooner or later, would disappear. I, however, would remain the loyal, if exhausted, listener. Although my mind would inevitably wander to concerns of my own, I would feel guilty about such lapses and never let on that I was anything but fully attentive. Clearly it was important for me then to maintain a positive image of my father as a fascinating story-teller and for him to believe that in me he had an appreciative audience. For complex reasons, the negative side of my feelings about these virtuoso performances, and about the performer, had, at that time, to be kept out of my awareness.

Was not this situation similar to the one, that years later, I had fallen into with Ms. F? Like my father, this patient was someone whom I admired but whom I also found exasperating. This familiar situation had automatically triggered in me an old, well-established defensive reaction. Instead of experiencing clear-cut anger and frustration at someone who was, in fact, being frustrating, I was aware only of feelings of mild annoyance that did not disrupt my positive feelings for Ms. F. I had been caught up, it seemed, in a true piece of countertransference.

Having now accomplished what I thought to be a useful piece of self-analysis, I looked forward to much improvement in my ability to listen to Ms. F. It was with great disappointment, then, that I realized with each passing hour that not much had changed. I still found it difficult to remain fully attentive to Ms. F and I still had to struggle against a tendency for my mind to wander.

This was not supposed to happen. Once the roots of a countertransference reaction were explored and contact made with its original sources, was the problem not supposed to dissolve? Certainly the literature was replete with examples of just such experiences. In fact I could not recall coming across a report, including articles of my own, in which a self-analytic effort had not been instrumental in breaking a log jam.

I was discouraged but there seemed no alternative other than a return to the drawing board. Once again I took up the task of self-analysis in the hope of learning something new. This time I attempted to alert myself not only to the subtleties of the communications that passed between Ms. F. and myself but especially to the metacommunications, to the concealed messages that were contained behind and within the overt exchanges. This level of interaction involved not only spoken words but their accompaniments in nonverbal behavior.

Until then I had paid no special attention to the shifts and changes in Ms. F's posture on the couch. Now I watched her closely. As I did so, I became aware of the effect that her movements were having on me. For portions of the hour, and sometimes for all of it, Ms. F would lie quietly, her legs crossed at the ankle, her hands either resting on her abdomen or touching her forehead or hair. At certain times during most hours, however, she would shift position. She would uncross her legs, flex her knees slowly and teasingly, place her hands behind her head and rotate her body a half-turn in my direction. (I sat to her left at approximately a 45° angle.) These movements would be accompanied by a noticeable change in the rhythms of her speech. Ms. F's slow and deliberate manner of speaking became even slower. The words seemed to be pulled out of a barrel of molasses and Ms. F's drawl, already prominent, became a caricature of a Tennessee Williams heroine. At the same time, she would often allude to something about my person, perhaps my jacket, tie, or haircut in a way that was at once complimentary, mildly sardonic, and inviting. Not bad for a fellow who does not know Barney's from Armani she would seem to say, but a woman like me could teach you a lot more. Then, just as my interest would be piqued by these remarks, Ms. F would shift the topic, return to a stultifying account of a recent event, and leave me and my wardrobe behind.

To this shift I would find myself reacting with increasing irritation and with what I now recognized as a wish to tune out. Clearly Ms. F's style, meandering, indirect, often repetitive, was trying to listen to. I had long recognized that, unconsciously, her delivery served both offensive and defensive ends. It concealed and obfuscated, but it also provoked. Ms. F had more than her share of competitiveness with and hostility toward men and one of the chief aims of her speech pattern, in form and content, was to induce feelings of frustration and anger in her analyst.

This she accomplished, but that the roots of my responses to Ms. F lay not only in the difficulties I was experiencing in listening to and in understanding her, but also stemmed from a deeper and more troubling source, did not become clear to me for some time. When it did, it was a fragment of memory, a totally unexpected piece of memory, that provided the first clue.

On one occasion when the above-mentioned scenario was unfolding and Ms. F was shifting positions and slipping into the familiar molasses speech pattern, I found myself recalling a scene that had taken place about a quarter century earlier. This memory involved a seminar on psychoanalysis and literature in which, as a resident, I participated. The novel we were reading at the time was *Crime and Punishment* and all at once I remembered an interpretation that the seminar leader had offered. Raskolnikov, he inferred, must have had a possessive, insensitive, and highly seductive mother who, consciously or not, stimulated his erotic feelings and then frustrated him. The rage that built up in the helpless boy was enormous. When, years later, under conditions of stress and deprivation he is faced once again with a provocative old woman who unconsciously represents the frustrating mother of his youth, he kills her.

Why so distant a memory, and such a strange one, had surfaced at this time was a mystery not difficult to solve. It was my shorthand way of acknowledging something that preconsciously I understood but had blocked from conscious awareness; that a seduction was taking place before my eyes, and that I was responding to it. In body language as well as vocal patterns, in tone and gesture, posture and movement, Ms. F was acting in ways that were both inviting and frustrating. Like Raskolnikov, I was responding with rage to the mixed signals I was receiving and to the frustration I was experiencing. Aspects of Ms. F's history and certain of her associations had suggested that, unconsciously, she harbored a beating fantasy that at times was enacted in disguised ways. Although I had long suspected that such a fantasy might be providing the motor power for Ms. F's masochistic provocation of authority figures, its covert operation in the analytic situation, and my response to it, was a dynamic that I had failed to recognize.

The reason for this now occurred to me. In my youth I

had been enmeshed in a relationship with a relative that had contained undertones of covert seductiveness and had, as a consequence, experienced much confusion, anger, and guilt. Now I recalled those days and feelings of chaotic confusion rose once again to torment me. They were not comfortable feelings, and observing Ms. F now I recognized that they were readily stimulated by the resonance between her concealed seductive behavior and my former experiences. Like her mother, Ms. F, as a teenager, often teased and provoked her father into angry outbursts which sometimes took the form of striking her. In this way she simultaneously expressed her resentment at his withdrawal and preoccupation with alcohol, her disguised wish for exciting physical contact with him, and her need to provoke retribution for these sinful wishes.

It became clear to me that unconsciously Ms. F wanted me to become enraged with her in the same way and, by acting out this rage in word or deed, gratify her regressively distorted wishes for sexual satisfaction and punishment. Since the anger I felt was unacceptable and threatening to me, as it had been in the original situation of childhood, I did as I had done before. As a youngster I had failed to recognize the seduction that was taking place, emphasized the hostile and competitive elements in the situation, and substituted mild feelings of annoyance for the deeper and more threatening currents of rage that were stirring within me. I also did something else. I focused my attention on the difficulties and frustration that I was experiencing with my father in order not to see that it was with certain women in the family that I was experiencing even greater conflict. My self-analytic efforts had followed a similar path. The initial way station was the memory I'd had of my father holding forth at the dinner table and the complex of feelings that his nightly lectures evoked in me. While these memories were pertinent to my countertransference reactions and illuminated one root of the problems I was having with Ms. F, their appearance in consciousness as the first relevant memories to surface also served a defensive purpose. Behind them, less accessible and covered over by these comparatively benign recollections, were memories of a more troubling kind.

By all rights this should have been the end of the story.

Having uncovered this deeper source of countertransference
difficulty and having been in touch once again with memories
of certain painful experiences of childhood, I should have been
able to listen to Ms. F with the joyful attentiveness of a man
suddenly cured of deafness. That this did not happen constituted for me a fresh disappointment, a puzzlement and a blow
to my rapidly ebbing confidence in the effectiveness of my self-
analytic efforts. Not that the work I had done was without
effect. My capacity to listen to Ms. F was considerably improved.
I followed the winding trail of her associations more faithfully
and with greater staying power. It was also true, however, that
when my patient shifted into her slow-motion scenario, I still
found the going rough. After a short time restlessness set in
and I would become distracted.

The end of the tale is, as all such clinical vignettes are, a
happy one. I was able, finally, to overcome most of the problem
I was having with Ms. F and to have to contend only with a
degree of boredom, irritation, and restlessness that was man-
ageable and did not interfere with sustained and attentive listening. Because I have been (as my father's son) long-winded
in recounting these events, I will not report in detail the final
chapter of this story. I will merely mention that there was another, even more conflictual, layer to my countertransference
problem and that putting myself in touch with this dimension
of the problem seemed to help a good deal. Like the earlier
insight that I had obtained, this piece of understanding touched
on a sexual matter and reached awareness on the wings of a
memory. This memory, also like its predecessor, related to residency days and centered on a brash and cheeky fellow resident
whose secret pleasure it was to shock people. One day after
interviewing a young and attractive schizophrenic woman who
had just been admitted to the ward, Dr. G approached me and
inquired casually if I ever got an erection while interviewing
attractive female patients. Startled and made anxious by his
boldness, I, of course, denied any such experience. He, on the
other hand, freely admitted to having such reactions which he
claimed to be able to use as a diagnostic tool.

This memory conveyed a clear message. Ms. F's movements
on the couch, seductive as I found them to be, had threatened

to produce in me the very reaction that my outspoken friend had described. Sensing this through slight physiologic cues that must have registered preconsciously, I automatically defended myself against the development of such a response. The primary defensive maneuver I used was one not uncommonly employed in such situations: distractability augmented by motor restlessness. My mind wandered from the immediate situation and from the threatening interaction that was taking place between patient and analyst. In this respect, I was behaving rather like the adolescent who finds himself aroused in an inappropriate social situation. Anxiously he turns his imagination to something else, perhaps baseball. Then thoughts of fornication may be replaced by fantasies of hitting a grand slam, or driving in the winning run.

The anger that I had experienced, with its clear countertransference roots in particular childhood experiences, also functioned as a resistance to awareness of the concrete sexual response to Ms. F that threatened; a response that could have been both humiliating and disruptive. It took time and the overcoming of considerable resistance in myself for my efforts at self-analysis to come into touch with this dimension of the problem, just as it took time and persistence to recognize that my annoyance with Ms. F and my distractability had their roots not only in experiences with my father, but in others involving female relatives and caretakers. What I am describing, then, is layers of countertransference reactions, each having its own source, each being important in its own right, but with one level of countertransference used to screen and protect against recognition of others that are unconsciously perceived as more anxiety-provoking.

Clearly such complexity and denseness of countertransference does not occur in every instance of such reactions, or even in a majority of cases. Many countertransference reactions have a simpler unidimensional structure with a single clear root and it is these, almost exclusively, that one finds reported in the literature. Others, however, are multidimensional, containing at their deeper levels affects connected to childhood fantasies and experiences that are sufficiently painful or troubling to the analyst that he may need to defend against them by focusing attention on other, less disruptive countertransference responses.

My second example will not be a lengthy one. I cite it to illustrate the way that countertransference responses, and the self-analysis of them, may be unconsciously used by the analyst to help keep in repression long forgotten memories stemming not only from infancy, but from later childhood and adolescence.

My experiences with Mr. V were, in many respects, the opposite to those I described in the case of Ms. F. Although it is true that during a consultation session I forgot to unlock the door for one of his early morning appointments, thus revealing early on more than a little discomfort in seeing him, I was able to listen to him well. Unlike Ms. F, Mr. V held my attention completely. In fact what alerted me to the likelihood that a subtle countertransference reaction was being enacted in my work with him was the quality of my listening. Much has been written about shifts in the analyst's levels of attention and consciousness, almost always in the direction of sleep or, as I have just reported, distractability. Little has been said about the opposite side of this coin, vigilance in the analyst. This was such a case. As I listened to Mr. V, I felt on the alert, subtly on guard. I sat straight up in my chair and often found that my musculature was tense. I listened carefully, and missed nothing, but there was something rigid, and unrelaxed in my listening. I did not fantasize much and I did not allow my mind to play over the material. I was rather like a computer taking in and registering data but producing thoughts and formulations, not daydreams.

As I reflected on this situation I realized that I had been there before, that there was someone else to whom I had reacted in a very similar way. Actually there was more than one person, but the first memory to present itself to my consciousness, and thereby to screen out others, involved a boyhood chum that I had not thought about in forty years.

Boris was a strange fellow. A refugee from Nazi Europe, he combined in one individual the resourcefulness of Gide's Lafcadio, the guile of Felix Kroll, confidence man, and the wide-eyed appeal of Oliver Twist. He was both man and boy, innocent and sophisticate, friend and foe. Boris' charm lay both in his talent as a teller of tall tales and in his unabashed delight in playing the rogue. From him I learned the most evil practices including the ploy of placing a penny on the Broadway trolley tracks, retrieving it after it had been run over and properly squashed, and using the now flattened coin as a slug to make nickel telephone calls.

Not all was fun with Boris, however. He had a dark side, and when crossed displayed flashes of violence so intense that even the Irish toughs in the neighborhood backed off. It was rumored that Boris was Jewish by birth and that under the threat of persecution he had converted to Catholicism. No one knew the truth and Boris would not say. There were things that one simply did not ask him. Once I heard that he was a gambler, that he bet huge stakes on stickball games in the Bronx, and that he hung around with the Mafioso-types who masterminded the college basketball scandals. I kept this information strictly to myself for I knew that if I even hinted at having heard such things I ran risks that made being in a dark room with Peter Lorre seem like a parlor game.

Mr. V was like that. He, too, had charm and liked to fill the analytic hours with accounts of exploits that were meant to amuse and entertain. But, as was true of Boris, there was something about him that was menacing. He, too, had secrets and, like his earlier counterpart, made clear that these were not to be touched.

One such secret involved his father who had gotten into trouble with the law when Mr. V was a teenager. In the family this was a shameful episode that was never talked about. When, years later, Mr. V was in a position to do so, he surreptitiously destroyed the official files on his father's case. He wanted to obliterate every trace of the incident. I suspected that Mr. V's obvious identification with his father concealed illicit impulses of his own that he wished to destroy, but what these might relate to I could only surmise.

The first real clue to what might lie behind the wall of stone that Mr. V threw up around him came through my growing awareness that the reactions I was having to this patient, ones mixed in equal measure of admiration, awe and intimidation, had their roots not only in my friendship with Boris, but in an earlier relationship as well.

As I listened to Mr. V, images of my friend became mixed with memories of a person whom I had also long forgotten but who had about him an even more forbidding quality. This was Gus, the leader of an after-school sports group which, as a youngster, I had attended. Gus was a hero of the First World War, or claimed to be, and a rough and tumble character. As a coach he was a stern taskmaster, the Vince Lombardi of Central Park, and if one missed a block or tackle he unleashed a vocabulary worthy of a spit and polish top sergeant. What frightened me most about Gus, though, were the underground rumors that he was a homosexual. It was said that over the years he had selected certain boys to approach, seduced them, and turned them gay. This was a terrifying thought and although I craved his approval, it was with a feeling of dread that I noticed that he had taken a shine to me.

These memories surfaced, I believe, in connection with small cues transmitted between Mr. V and myself, cues that spoke to a growing bond between us and to Mr. V's yearning for and fear of a loving relationship with a man. Central to this fear were certain events of childhood in which his older brother had cajoled and strong-armed my patient into acts of mutual masturbation. Mr. V had never overcome the shame he felt in connection with this experience, had tried to obliterate it from memory, and was very much on guard against any reawakening of the frightening and stimulating feelings that it had aroused. This guardedness took the form of an aggressiveness and a readiness to attack which lay just millimeters beneath the surface. I sensed this, felt the violence in Mr. V's personality, and was wary of him. It was this concealed, but palpable violence that, from our first contact, I felt in Mr. V and that had caused me, unconsciously, to want to distance myself from him.

What I also sensed, however, was the yearning for contact, the frustrated homosexual love that was also there, and these yearnings stimulated memories of the days with Gus when similar conflicts had been aroused in me. Because such memories and the conflicts connected with them had the potential to arouse discomfort, I unconsciously protected myself against their emergence by recalling an individual who appeared later in my life, who shared with Mr. V qualities of outward charm and inner rage, but who stirred in me no homoerotic feelings.

As was true of Ms. F, there existed in Mr. V still another dimension to his conflicts and one that had important effects on his analyst. This had to do with deep-seated feelings of defectiveness with which Mr. V struggled and which he sought tenaciously to conceal from himself and others. In fact, Mr. V was born with a minor abdominal defect which was magnified by the treatment he received for it. For several years his abdomen was wrapped in bandages whose nightly application, and especially their removal, caused him much pain. He was treated as a delicate and vulnerable child for whom normal physical activity constituted a threat. As a consequence, Mr. V developed a sense of himself as weak, helpless, and fragile. His self-image was further impaired by the unconscious association he made between his secret wound and the female genitals and by the fantasy that he developed, when surgery was finally performed at the height of the oedipal period, that he had been violently assaulted and his already impaired body irreparably damaged.

It was Mr. V's profoundly defective sense of self, a complex set of ideas related to an arrested body image, to self-castrative wishes, and to unconscious fantasies of being a girl, that constituted his deepest secret. Clearly the homosexual episode in latency and the yearnings it stimulated were connected with these conflicts, but it was less the homosexuality itself than the threatening self-representation it seemed to confirm that Mr. V had at all costs to defend against.

For my part, these concerns resonated with experiences and fantasies of my own that in childhood had been the source of much anxiety. The life-threatening illnesses in my youth that both my father and brother had suffered and the feelings of dread and helplessness I experienced at those times, feelings no doubt compounded by unconscious wishes to rid myself of these rivals, added to the already pronounced fears of death and bodily injury that characterized my early years. At the age of three I had undergone surgery without the slightest understanding of what was happening and some of the fantasies I elaborated in connection with that experience were not so very different from the imaginings that so disturbed Mr. V.

I had no wish to stir these troubled waters, and yet if I was to work effectively with Mr. V and to reach the sources of his distorted self-image there was no way that I could remain safely in the shallows. Blum (1980) has pointed out that as we analyze ever more deeply, reconstruction of aspects of the analyst's life inevitably takes place alongside that of the patient's. Not infrequently, troubling aspects of our own lives, often related to disruptive experiences and fantasies of childhood and adolescence effectively buried before and after our personal analysis, threaten to reemerge as we confront correspondingly painful material in the lives of our patients. It is natural that we would wish to avoid such unfriendly poltergeists and prefer to deal with ghosts of a more palatable sort. All too often the unconscious obliges us and presents first to memory a cast of characters and selected events that, though meaningfully related to the interactions of the analytic hour, also manage, through their noisy entrance, to take center stage and keep their more mischievous counterparts stewing in the wings.

Disturbing though my experiences with my old coach, Gus, were, the memories of that relationship did not touch the core of my childhood anxieties, rooted as they were in frightening physical experiences, in the way that material concerning Mr. V's bodily anxieties and his sense of personal defect did. At base his fears were about castration and annihilation as mine were and I did not welcome the return of such specters. It was less unsettling to remember Boris, and even old Gus. After all, the issues raised by these revenants were ancient ones, belonging to another time and another place, while those mobilized by Mr. V's childhood anxieties had greater currency. Although they had been reduced by my analysis, they still maintained a silent presence in the background, a presence that, with the passage of years, had begun to cast a thin shadow on my consciousness. Working with Mr. V had stimulated these primitive fears and, by raising to awareness memories connected with fears of a lesser order, I had attempted to defend myself against their reemergence.

The fact that countertransferences may be used in the service of resistance has implications for the process of self-analysis and it is to this subject that, finally, I wish to turn. The use of self-analysis by colleagues is a variable and highly personal matter. Some like Kramer (1959), Myerson (1960), and Beiser (1984) have reported its use to help resolve troubling personal situations that have arisen either in connection with their clinical work or independent of it. Rare is the individual like Kenneth Calder (1980) who makes self-analytic work a daily routine. Most, it seems, employ it intermittently when the need is felt, using the method of controlled associations, that is to say, deliberate efforts to associate to some aspect of thought or experience, free associations caught on the fly, or some combination of the two. It is not, however, the use of self-analysis to solve personal problems, valuable as this process is, with which I am now concerned, but rather its use in the analytic situation.

Not uncommon are instances in which the analyst's understanding of a patient has been enhanced by the self-analysis of a dream, fantasy, slip, or piece of countertransference. Gardner (1983) has given us a particularly elegant account of his experiences in this regard and Silverman (1987) has also demonstrated impressively how progress in certain cases is dependent on fresh insights gained through self-analysis. Baum (1977) and Arlow (1987) have pointed out that a supervisor is often in a position to help a younger colleague identify countertransference problems and, by encouraging introspection in the analyst, assist him in making the necessary corrections.

Such reports underline the importance of self-analysis in clinical work and are valuable in providing demonstrations of its use. Few accounts in the literature, however, describe the struggle that often accompanies self-analytic efforts. They tend rather to follow a pattern with which we have become familiar. When faced with troubling countertransference reactions or sometimes just in the course of his daily work, the analyst becomes aware of something in himself, a memory, attitude, dream, or symptomatic act, that he recognizes as occurring in response to communications from the patient. He undertakes a piece of self-analysis, comes to understand the roots of his reaction, and, armed with this new knowledge, is now able to work more effectively with his patient. Rarely reported are instances in which attempts at self-analysis have encountered formidable obstacles, have proven disappointing, or have failed altogether. While much self-analysis is no doubt successful and is carried out without undue difficulty, not uncommonly the process meets with strong inner opposition. The analyst's initial insights, often accepted as the key to troublesome countertransference responses and utilized as such, may, in fact, function in part as a decoy. While they may unlock one level of understanding, they may also leave others, often the critical ones, untouched. In his early writings on the subject, Freud (1910) recognized both the problem of resistances in the analyst and the need through an ever-searching process of self-analysis to overcome them: "We have noticed that no psychoanalyst goes further than his own complexes and internal resistances permit," he has written, "and we consequently require that he shall begin his activity with a self-analysis and continually carry it deeper while he is making his observations on his patients" (p. 145).

Although it is common for many analysts to regard self-analysis in the clinical situation, as in the personal one, as an intermittent process to be undertaken only when an indication arises, this attitude overlooks the importance of ongoing self-analysis in the process of analyzing. My own view is that self-analysis in the sense of the analyst's awareness of his own experiences, including bodily movements, physiologic reactions, and visual images, as well as thoughts and fantasies, is an essential aspect of his technique. While he may not, and probably should not, concentrate on these reactions in any active, deliberate way any more than he listens in a highly focused manner for particular material, the analyst must be aware both of their presence and of the fact that they are influencing his response to the patient. To borrow third-hand the metaphor that Sandler (1976) borrowed from Freud, the analyst operates not only with free-floating attention and free-floating responsiveness but also with free-floating awareness of his bodily and mental experiences. This means that as it operates, the analytic instrument includes a sensor that picks up the sounds, movements, and inner stirrings of the analyst himself. This data is fed into the stream of information that flows continuously between patient and therapist. When a piece of countertransference behavior erupts or a signal is given by means of unusually strong affects, physiological responses, or the emergence of particular fantasies that one threatens to do so, his attention becomes directed to the data being transmitted from that sensor. Then, aided by this information, the analyst switches into a more active self-analytic stance and seeks to explore the sources of these responses.

Employing a mixture of techniques, including dream and daydream analysis, free and controlled associations, reflection, and increased awareness of his nonverbal reactions, the analyst attempts to catch hold of subtle, though important, cues arising from his unconscious. He is aware, however, that the interior pathway along which he journeys contains a series of snares and traps that take the form of attractive and inviting resting places. Like a deep-sea diver exploring a sunken ship laden with valuables, he knows that he may, upon reaching the foredeck, come across a number of intriguing items. Recognizing their worth, the experienced analyst nonetheless takes them for the curios they are; he knows that to find the treasure he is seeking he must continue his descent to still deeper levels.

9

The Analyst and the Patient's Object World: Notes on an Aspect of Countertransference

In this chapter I shall discuss certain aspects of the analyst's emotional reactions, not directly to his patients, but to objects in the patient's world. Our usual conceptualizations of *countertransference*, whether the term is defined narrowly as those responses induced in the analyst as a consequence of the patient's transferences, or more broadly as the emotional reactions evoked in him by the totality of the patient, emphasize the dyad of patient and analyst and contain, implicitly, the idea that countertransference reactions occur solely in response to the patient. While it may be assumed by inference that our ideas of countertransference include the analyst's emotional reactions to all the material brought by the patient, including that pertaining to the objects in his world, the particular question of what effect the analyst's mental representations of the patient's objects may have on his analytic work has received comparatively little attention in the literature on countertransference.

Although as early as 1910 Freud commented on "the 'countertransference,' which arises in [the physician] as a result of the patient's influence on his unconscious feelings" (p. 144) and counseled the analyst to begin his activity with self-analysis, it

179

was not until some forty years later that analysts began, in a more systematic way, to investigate the phenomenon of countertransference.

Heimann (1950) regarded the analyst's emotional responses to his patient as one of the most important tools for his work, and the analyst's countertransference reactions as instruments of research into the patient's unconscious. Since, for her, the emotions induced in the analyst by his work with the patient reflect aspects of the latter's unconscious, she regarded countertransference phenomena as essentially creations of the patient which reflected parts of his own personality.

Little (1951) emphasized the central position countertransference plays in analytic work, particularly with seriously disturbed patients. She noted that patients often become aware of real feelings in the analyst even before the analyst is fully aware of them. This sensitivity on the part of the patient, properly used by the analyst, may alert him to countertransference responses that had been outside of his own awareness. Counseling the analyst not only to gain as much awareness as possible of his own emotional responses, but to allow in himself a freedom to respond with strong emotions, particularly to severely disturbed patients, Little also recommended, under particular circumstances, that the analyst share with the patient certain of his countertransference reactions.

As noted earlier in her series of thought-provoking papers, Reich (1951, 1960, 1966) takes issue with the notion that countertransference can be used as a therapeutic tool. In her view, countertransference reactions indicate difficulties in the analyst's capacity to listen and to understand. While temporary or trial identifications with patients can be useful processes, countertransference as such is, in her opinion, not helpful. Extremely valuable, however, is the analyst's ability to acknowledge and to overcome it.

Winnicott (1949) sought to distinguish the idiosyncratic from the therapeutically useful in countertransference and attempted to separate out reactions in the analyst that occur as a consequence of the existence in him of well-established conflicts, character problems, or personality traits, from truly objective countertransference reactions. These latter reactions, which include feelings of hate as well as of love, he regarded as responses to the actual personality and behavior of the patient. Stating that "a main task of the analyst is to maintain objectivity" (p. 196), he also believed that for certain patients the evocation of hate in the analyst is part of a maturational process. Under such circumstances the analyst's awareness of his feelings of hatred and of the objective basis for such feelings can be utilized to provide the kind of emotional feedback that, for certain patients, is a necessary part of the therapeutic process.

While these authors, in a variety of ways, broadened and deepened the concept of countertransference and clarified its potential usefulness in the analytic situation, their attention was focused almost exclusively on the responses evoked in the analyst by the particular conflicts and personality traits of the patient and by the transferences he develops. Before 1950, only one author, Helene Deutsch (1926), commented on the possible impact the analyst's reactions to objects in the patient's world might have on the analytic work. She noted that situations may arise in which the analyst identifies with a patient's infantile objects and obtains such strong gratification from this identification that he experiences great difficulty in relinquishing it. Such reactions on the part of the analyst, she believed, have the effect of impeding the free development of the transference.

Beres and Arlow (1974) cited a clinical example in which the analyst had an empathic response not only to his patient, but to a rather pathetic-sounding girl friend of the patient's toward whom he had acted provocatively. The analyst's feelings of empathy, experienced first toward the girl friend and then toward the patient, provided him with a clue to certain unconscious conflicts that lay behind his patient's behavior. Bernstein and Glenn (1978) have observed that child analysts may develop strong emotional reactions not only to their patients, but to their patients' parents and other family members. It was Racker (1968), however, who undertook the most comprehensive investigation of the complex interplay between these two phenomena. Following Heimann, he thought of countertransference as comprising all of the emotional responses stirred up in the analyst by his contact with the patient. "It is [in the analyst] this

fusion of present and past, the continuous and intimate connection of reality and fantasy, of external and internal, conscious and unconscious, that demands a concept embracing the
totality of the analyst's psychological response" (p. 133), he has
written. Although this definition of countertransference is perhaps overly broad and fails to distinguish between those neurotic responses of the analyst that are played out in relation to
a variety of individuals and those more specific reactions evoked
by particular patients, it is one that perhaps for lack of more
precise terminology has come into common usage. For this reason I also employ this comprehensive definition of countertransference in this chapter.

   I would include as countertransference phenomena not
only emotional responses in the analyst deriving from his interactions with the patient, but also those emotional reactions
that color and influence his perceptions of the patient, whatever
their source. The analyst's responses to his patient may be influenced in important ways not only by his perceptions of the
patient, the particular transferences that develop, and the objects in the patient's life that, for the analyst, become part of
the imaginative world in which he places each patient, but also
by his perceptions of individuals who are known to both the
patient and himself. His perceptions of events and experiences
they may share can also significantly affect the therapist's attitude toward and understanding of his patient.

   Writing from a point of view that has been influenced by
Kleinian thought, Racker makes a distinction between complementary and concordant identifications in countertransference
reactions. Complementary identifications, by which Racker
means identifications of the analyst's ego with the patient's internal objects, are produced because the patient treats the analyst as a projected internal object and the analyst consequently
identifies with this object. It is this process, Racker states, that
is meant when, in common usage, we employ the term *countertransference*.

   Concordant identifications refer to the processes whereby
the analyst identifies a part of his personality (e.g., superego
pressures, libidinal or aggressive drives, or aspects of his ego)
with a corresponding part of the patient. By virtue of this pro-

cess, certain psychological experiences that arise in the analyst reflect and reproduce the psychological experiences of the patient. Racker (1958) had used this idea to discuss the phenomenon of counterresistance in the analyst. It was his view that the analyst's resistances, which oppose the making of certain interpretations, correspond to and illuminate particular resistances occurring in the patient with which the analyst has unconsciously identified. Such resistances in the analyst provide him not only with a clue to the existence of similar resistances in the patient, but indicate that the interpretation being opposed is incomplete. A deeper understanding of both the patient's resistances and the conflicts that give rise to them would lead the analyst to a more comprehensive and more accurate interpretation.

Racker (1968) also makes a distinction between direct and indirect countertransference. Direct countertransference refers to responses in the analyst induced by the patient himself; indirect countertransference refers to the analyst's emotional reactions to others (such as supervisors or colleagues) that influence his perceptions of and reactions to his patient. For example, a young candidate, anxious about a difficult case, might project his superego anxiety onto his supervisor or teacher. His fear of their critical reactions, then, would influence his approach to and understanding of the patient. At the same time, through a process that Racker terms *subtransference*, a certain amount of the analyst's superego anxiety might be projected onto the patient. The analyst, feeling himself to be doing poorly with the case, might react with hostility to his patient, whom he would experience as being highly critical of him. Racker's comment on the way in which transference and direct countertransference responses interact with indirect countertransference reactions that develop as a consequence of the analyst's relations with particular objects in his world was the first recognition of these complex phenomena.

Racker was aware, too, of the impact that objects in the patient's world may have on the analyst and his understanding of a case. Although he recognized that, for the analyst, both the patient and his objects may be unconsciously associated with an imago of the preoedipal mother and be responded to as such, in his discussion of this issue he focused primarily on oedipal countertransference reactions. In these responses, the male analyst, reacting to the positive oedipal transference of a female patient, experiences in fantasy his patient's husband as an oedipal rival. If the negative complex plays a role of importance in his own psychology, the analyst may wish for the love and approval of the male in the triangle who unconsciously represents the father.

While such reactions unquestionably occur, and their recognition helps enhance our appreciation of the fact that oedipal countertransference responses may be experienced by the analyst not only in terms of the patient alone, but may involve fantasies about significant objects in his world, they constitute only a small fraction of the emotional responses aroused in the analyst as a consequence of the mental representations he forms of the patient's objects.

Each patient brings to the consulting room a world of people, and, in the course of his working day, an analyst will find himself hearing about and responding—often with strong emotions—to a host of individuals: chauvinist husbands, rebellious wives, long-winded uncles, stingy bosses, prankish children, indulgent grandparents, joyous lovers, loyal friends, dull-witted colleagues—in short to a cast of characters worthy of a Chekhovian drama. Frequently the patients' portraits of these individuals contain aspects of themselves—and perceptions of their analysts. Analysis of the projections, defensive distortions, displacements of unacceptable affects, impulses, and character traits, as well as the transference displacements contained within those object representations, comprises an essential part of the analytic work.

The way, however, in which the analyst responds to material about his patient's objects depends not only on his understanding of the patient and the transference developments at any given time, but also on the impulses, affects, fantasies, and defenses evoked in him in response to the mental representations he has formed of those objects. These representations exist apart from, although they may at times supplement and augment, countertransference reactions that develop in response to the patient's transferences. The latter reactions arise when particular transferences touch on and awaken dormant conflicts in the analyst. The representations the analyst forms of objects in the patient's world, which can be an equally potent force in influencing his reactions to the patient, are even more complex. They are derived from several sources: from factual reports about the objects and the patient's conflicted and distorted perceptions of them, to both of which the analyst brings his own ideas, judgments, fantasies, and values; from split, divided, and displaced transferences and the analyst's response to these; from the analyst's self and object representations, past and present, which are stimulated by the material concerning the patient's objects and which become fused with his fantasies about them; and from the analyst's direct countertransference responses which regularly color, and not infrequently distort, his perception of the objects in the patient's life.

It not infrequently happens that emotional reactions stimulated in the analyst by material concerning a friend or relative of the patient manifest themselves in him as a feeling or fantasy, not directly about the patient, but about that figure in his world. This situation became apparent at a clinical conference in which an analyst found himself describing the young son of one of his patients with unusual warmth and admiration. Clearly he had developed the image of a bright, energetic, thoroughly likable youngster, and this came through in his presentation. Some reflection on this response made clear to him that the image he had formed of this child was associated in his imagination both with an idealized picture of himself as an adolescent and an idealized view of his own son. What then became evident was that the patient had, in the analysis, presented a similar idealized view of his son and himself as a parent in order to avoid experiencing the guilt that recognition of his competitive and resentful feelings toward the boy would evoke.

The analyst, for his own reasons, had joined him in this idealization. His son, who was in a state of emotional turmoil at the time, was the same age as the patient's child, and the analyst was struggling with many ambivalent feelings about his youngster. He was critical of himself for having these feelings and was struggling to keep at bay the notion of himself as a failure as a parent. To have allowed himself to become more cognizant of his patient's underlying conflicts and his powerful feelings of guilt with regard to his son, and to have confronted him with these, would have brought to the fore the similar feelings in himself he was attempting to stave off. On a deeper level, it would have evoked critical feelings toward his own parents who, like his patient, had contented themselves with an idealized picture of him and had not wished to recognize the distress he had experienced as a child. He was able to avoid all of this by accepting the patient's idealization of his son.

Often the analyst's reactions to the patient's objects are not recognized as countertransference phenomena. One analyst, quite well attuned to his own complex and shifting feelings toward a young male patient, described the patient's father, who had failed to support him following a divorce, as a "no-goodnik" and a "phony whose pie-in-the-sky schemes had made everyone else suffer." When this reaction was pointed out to him, he recognized immediately that certain residues of feeling, derived from his own family circumstances, had unconsciously influenced his attitude toward the patient and his father.

At a seminar in which I was presenting the case of an adolescent girl, there was general agreement among the participants that the patient's mother was a horror. Each presentation which involved material about the mother invariably elicited from the group adjectives such as "hostile," "jealous," "selfish," and "destructive." One of the seminar members, carried away at one session by a report of the mother's unsympathetic attitude toward her daughter, was moved to declare with much feeling that "this woman has been responsible for destroying this child." I myself disliked the mother quite thoroughly—until, under threat by the parents to end the treatment, I agreed to meet her. The picture I had of her was of an ambitious, self-centered, pretentious, and inflexible woman whose considerable personality problems and unreflective attitudes had contributed substantially to the development of pathology in my patient. It turned out that I was not entirely wrong in this view. But what I had not bargained for, and what, in retrospect, I realized I had not been open to hearing in the material, was that the mother was far more intelligent, sensitive, insightful, and embattled than I had imagined. The patient's intensely positive transference and my emotional reactions to it, added to by conflicts and preset attitudes of my own and reinforced by the remarks of the seminar members, had combined to create a situation in which I had been unable to filter out the inconsistencies and distortions in the patient's account of her mother (or to hear the occasional more positive comments about her) in order to gain a more realistic view of this woman.

Such situations are not rare in analytic work. The analyst's unconscious identification with his patient and his consequent adoption of the patient's view of his objects may, of course, contribute to their development, as may direct or displaced countertransference reactions that go undetected. Of equal importance in such reactions, however, is the capacity of the patient's representations of his objects to stimulate in the analyst the reemergence of affectively charged self and object representations which become linked with his representations of the patient's objects.

Freud, although he was well aware of the importance of countertransference responses in analytic work, did not single out for attention the particular aspect of such responses that pertain to the patient's objects. Reading his case histories, however, makes clear that Freud's own emotional reactions to objects in his patients' lives was often strong—and strongly stated. Speaking of Dora's mother, he writes (1905), "From the accounts given me by the girl and her father I was led to imagine her as an uncultivated woman and above all as a foolish one, who had concentrated all her interests upon domestic affairs" (p. 20). And, at another point, he remarks that her "peculiarities made the house unbearable for everyone" (p. 26).

Although it is not possible to know what influence Freud's deprecatory attitude toward her mother may have had on his work with Dora, it is perhaps not unreasonable to assume that it had some effect on his capacity to listen objectively to material about her. One may wonder, too, whether Freud's reaction, based perhaps on certain personal values, as well as on objective facts, made it difficult for him to appreciate early on the importance of Dora's unconscious yearnings for maternal affection. The contribution countertransference reactions made to the course of Dora's analysis was not discussed in the case history, but would seem to have been a factor of importance in its ultimate outcome. Certain of these responses related not only to Dora herself, but to her parents and to Herr K and his wife, toward each of whom Freud had developed very definite feelings. One may reasonably speculate that the emotions stirred up in him toward these crucially important figures in Dora's life must have colored and influenced the way he perceived the complex interactions between them.

Some of the numerous meanings a patient's objects may hold for the analyst, as well as the multiplicity of factors that go into the creation of the mental representations that he forms of them, can, perhaps, be illustrated by some of my responses in the course of analytic work with a young business executive. The repeated tendencies of the patient, a man in his early thirties, toward neurotic entanglements with his employer, together with persistent dissatisfaction with his work situation, provided the chief motives for his seeking analysis.

Early on in the treatment, I noticed that the hours devoted to descriptions of the boss and the patient's ongoing problems with him held a certain kind of fascination for me. The prototype of the powerful business tycoon, Mr. B, as he was known throughout the industry, was, in fact, a man of unusual talents. At once shrewd, witty, daring, and abrasive, he possessed the kind of charisma that stirred in those around him unusually strong feelings of love and hate. With little formal education, he had, through immense drive, remarkable foresight, and plain good luck, built a firm whose influence was such as to touch princes and heads of state.

For my part, I joined those who found Mr. B an intriguing figure, part Machiavelli, part Barnum, and I looked forward each day to hearing the latest account of the moves and countermoves that characterized his operating style. Although I was aware that, as part of the developing transference and as a wish to avoid certain conflicts of a troubling nature, the patient was playing the entertainer and was deriving considerable gratification from recounting his adventures with Mr. B, I realized that my reactions to the boss were not, in their entirety, related either to these transference manifestations or to my direct countertransference responses to the patient. And, although I was aware of the impact Mr. B was having on my imagination, the way in which my image of him linked with other object images, both past and present, and influenced my reactions to the patient did not become clear until two events brought those realities home to me.

The first occurred after the patient had been in treatment for just seven months. Certain shifts and realignments taking place within his company at that time made it appear as though he would be transferred to another city and his analysis would have to be interrupted. The patient was an extremely likable fellow, and I was not surprised by my feelings of sadness and loss at the thought of ending my work with him. What I was not prepared for was my sense of loss at the idea of hearing no more of Mr. B and the fascinating world around him—a world I had come to share with the patient and that, in ways that I had not been aware of, had taken on importance for me as well as for him.

The second incident occurred approximately a year after the threat to the analysis was removed by the transfer, at the eleventh hour, of a colleague of the patient's. At that time Mr. B was striken with a sudden heart attack. Severely ill, but attempting still to give dictation to his secretary during her ten-minute visit to the coronary care unit, he did something quite unusual. He heeded the advice of family and friends and turned over to the patient and another associate a major share of the responsibility for the management of the firm.

On the day he learned of his promotion, the patient came to his hour in a state of excitement not unmixed with apprehension. For years he had yearned to attain a position of power and influence in the company, and for years he had been frustrated. Now his dream was coming true and he was both exhilarated and frightened. As I listened, I noticed a puzzling reaction in myself. Although I had an understanding of what the patient was experiencing, I became aware that I was not tuned into or empathic with his feelings. Rather, I felt some annoyance with him. Subsequent reflection made clear to me that this troubling reaction was, in large measure, connected with Mr. B. Although I had not been fully aware of it, I had, in fact, been angry at the patient for seeming to forget him, for concentrating solely on himself and his own good fortune while his mentor, the man who had taught him so much, lay ill, perhaps dying, in the hospital. Prompted by this realization, which came on top of a growing awareness that material about Mr. B had a special resonance for me, I determined to examine as closely as possible the emotional responses stirred up in me by hearing about this charismatic figure. Utilizing whatever powers of self-analysis I could muster, I attempted to trace the roots of those responses through associations, dreams, fantasies, and emotional reactions within the analytic hours themselves.

What I uncovered is neither surprising nor unique. On the contrary, it became clear that what had taken place was a reaction to the most familiar of emotional situations. It is, however, precisely for that reason that it seems worth reporting, for it is not only his subtle and elusive responses to the patient's objects that the analyst may overlook, but even the most obvious ones.

Some time before the analysis with this patient began, my father had developed an incapacitating illness. My conscious reaction to this event was a mixture of sadness, anger, and loss. Less consciously, and detectable only in dreams and fantasies, there was another reaction, which might best be described as one of guilty satisfaction that it was me to whom the other family members looked for advice, guidance, and leadership. It was this reaction, activated in response to the patient's expressions of satisfaction at having gained power as a consequence of Mr. B's illness, that I could not accept in myself and that gave rise to a critical feeling toward my patient.

I became aware of how certain early childhood images of my father had become fused with those I had formed of Mr. B. Far from being a successful entrepreneur in reality, my father was, nonetheless, to me a man of magic. I became aware, too, that residues of certain transferences toward my former analyst had become interwoven with the ideas I had formed of Mr. B. Based on certain realities, but clearly related to childhood views of my father, these idealized transferences contained the image of a strong, physically powerful, magnetic person. The death of my former analyst, which had occurred just a few

months after I began work with the patient, no doubt reactivated and gave fresh intensity to these old images which, like
the earlier idealizations of my father, had not been completely
eradicated. By fastening themselves onto the image of a new
object, Mr. B, they gained renewed life.

There were also views of myself hidden in the picture I
had of Mr. B—although clearly ones born of fantasy. As a child
I had reacted to the fear I felt when I overheard my father on
the telephone raging at some employee, by joining him in
imagination as commander of the troops, chief operating officer, and ruler of a vast army of salesmen. It was not difficult
then, years later, to respond to my patient's transference fantasies of me as an authoritarian father with a reawakening of
some of these old images, to identify with the powerful Mr. B,
and to react through this identification with feelings of resentment at the patient's neglect of him.

I have mentioned thus far only those aspects of my countertransference reactions to the patient that occurred in response to his transference to me as a powerful father. This
transference, in fact, played an important role in the patient's
treatment, as he had, for years, wanted nothing more than to
gain his father's favor—a wish that was reactivated both in his
relations with Mr. B and in the analytic situation. It was, however, not the only transference of importance. The patient had
a much admired older brother to whom he felt inferior and
whose accomplishments he sought to emulate. Often, in the
transference, he experienced me as the superior, gifted, and
envied brother. More hidden, but equally important, were his
feelings of rivalry with me, as well as secret feelings of supe-
riority of his own.

For my part, I have, in fact, a younger brother whose respect and admiration I have greatly valued. It was all too easy,
therefore, for me to accept the transference as the older, respected brother and to join with the patient in overlooking the
feelings of envy and rivalry that existed between us. It was not
until I had gained greater understanding of my reactions to
Mr. B that this aspect of the countertransference was clarified.

I became aware, as I reflected on the multiple meanings
of my countertransference responses to the patient's advance-

ment in his firm, that it contained feelings of envy and jealousy. The patient was on his way to achieving a long-cherished goal—one that promised great personal and financial success—and I envied him his good fortune. Moreover, he had become the chosen brother, clearly Mr. B's favorite, and this fact activated feelings in me that I had long forgotten—wishes to be my father's favorite and for him to pass on to me the chief's mantle.

In recent years there has been increased interest in object relations theory and its clinical applications. While the role of objects has, from the time of its origin, been central to the theory and practice of psychoanalysis, this interest has been reflected in efforts to explicate more precisely the role of internalized objects in human development (Kernberg, 1976, 1980). It has been stimulated, also, by new knowledge, derived largely from studies of children and borderline patients. In their writings about the clinical situation, object relations theorists have focused on the patient's internalized objects and the way in which these internalizations have affected his psychological development, his conflicts, his symptoms, and the nature of the transference. Racker is one of the few authors who has paid attention to the analyst's internal objects and the way that they may affect both his countertransference responses and his technique. Racker's focus, however, is primarily on the interplay of object representations as they occur between analyst and patient. He places relatively less emphasis on the interplay in the analyst between memory and fantasy and between self and object representations as these are stimulated in the psychoanalytic situation.

As a counterpart to the patient's use of free association, the analyst's listening state of mind allows for the emergence in him not only of spontaneous associations, but of fantasies and memories that are closely linked to past and present self and object representations. Affects originally associated with these self and object images are often activated in this way. Unpleasant or painful affects may stimulate in the analyst defensive operations aimed at eliminating them or reducing their intensity. Thus, the evocation in the analyst of self and object linked memories creates in him a dynamic state in which certain reawakened affects, wishes, and superego responses give rise to the employment of those defensive operations originally used against them. When an imbalance in this dynamic process occurs, either from the side of defense or from the side of the resurgent forces, the stage is set for the appearance of overt countertransference reactions.

Such reactions, when they occur directly in response to the patient, are all too familiar to us. When the forces of defense have become particularly strong, and the analyst, unaware of their effect on him, is unable to counter them, a situation akin to resistance in the patient develops, and the analyst may find himself distracted, becoming drowsy, or in other ways not attending to the patient. Anxiety-provoking affects, along with reactivated wishes and superego responses of a threatening nature, which are not automatically contained by the defensive processes but which cannot be correctly identified or utilized in the service of self-reflection, may lead to misunderstanding of the patient's communication and to inappropriate responses on the part of the analyst.

Less familiar is the way in which affects and wishes played out in relation to his representation of the patient's objects may become, for the analyst, a vehicle for the conveyance of countertransference responses. For example, affects aroused in him by the evocation of emotionally important object representations may be discharged toward the patient's objects with far greater ease, and with less awareness on the part of the analyst, than would be the case if they were directed toward the patient himself. In the case of the adolescent girl whom I was treating, both the patient and the image I had of her mother had the capacity to evoke in me negative reactions based, in part, on the reawakening of rivalries and resentments associated with objects in my childhood. But I could more easily accept and discharge aggression toward the mother than toward the patient. Somehow emotions evoked by the patient's objects, even quite intense emotions, do not register as readily as countertransference responses. In that way, important affects and strivings aroused in the analyst may, outside of his full awareness, find a pathway for discharge and escape useful understanding and effective control.

It is clear, then, that the patient's objects serve a number of functions for the analyst; and not the least of these is to help protect against the recognition of direct countertransference responses. Affects and impulses felt toward the patient that give rise to conflict in the analyst's mind may be partially or totally displaced by experiencing them in relation to objects in the patient's world. While the tendency to do this is perhaps greater in the case of strongly negative affects, positive feelings and particularly sexual responses may unconsciously evoke this defensive reaction.

When the patient stimulates marked ambivalence in the analyst as a consequence of associations that he makes between the patient and certain ambivalently cathected objects of his own, splitting of the countertransference may occur. In such instances it is most likely that an object in the patient's life will become the target of one side of the analyst's ambivalence and the patient the other. This situation occurs with some frequency in the analysis of severely disturbed patients in whom aggressive conflicts and the expression of aggression play a central role, and in whom splitting of the transference in the treatment situation is an important defensive maneuver. When unacceptable or conflicted self representations are stimulated in the analyst by the patient and the transferences that develop, an analogous process of splitting of aspects of his projected self-image between the patient and figures in his life may also occur.

Since our usual way of conceptualizing countertransference responses is in the dyadic mode, it may escape the analyst's awareness that at times what is being stirred up in his imagination by the totality of the patient and his world is a complex interrelationship between himself, the patient, and various of the patient's objects. Racker touched on this when he described the way in which reawakened oedipal conflicts in the analyst may be played out in fantasy vis-à-vis the patient and the patient's spouse. Reactivated feelings toward siblings, parents, and other family members, as well as childhood memories and fantasies concerning family interactions, may find hidden expression in the analyst's perceptions of relationships within his patient's family.

In a clinical situation of which I became aware, a young

colleague was treating a married man who, in the course of his analysis, entered into an affair with his secretary. The patient would talk alternately about his wife and mistress, and the analyst found himself developing intense feelings toward each. The mistress, who was antagonistic to the analysis, he regarded as shallow, aggressive, and conniving; the wife, who supported it, he thought of as loyal, intelligent, and kindhearted. And although there was no clear reason for him to think so, he had the persistent expectation that his patient would leave his wife.

It took some time for him to recognize the correspondence in his own family life which lay behind these reactions. As a boy of sixteen he had developed the idea that his father, at whose store he had an after-school job, was romantically attached to an attractive young bookkeeper whom he regularly insisted on driving home after work. Mutual feelings of dislike quickly arose between the boy and this young woman and he often imagined, with deep sorrow and with the image of his mother alone and in a state of despair, his father running off with her. Only years later did he come to understand the aspect of his reactions to his father's behavior that had to do with competition with him. It was this situation, long forgotten but reactivated in memory by his patient's affair, that gave rise to the analyst's emotional reactions to both women; reactions that, until he was able to understand their origins, had a significant impact on his understanding of the case.

In a similar way, family myths and secrets, as well as various aspects of the family romance of the analyst, may be reactivated in his imagination by material concerning the patient and his family. Early on in the analysis of a young man whom I was treating, he reported discovering during latency that, for a number of years before he went on to a successful business career, his father had been a police officer. Although for some time thereafter little mention was made of this fact, I became convinced that it was a matter of greater significance to the patient than he himself knew. Although, as it turned out, there was some evidence from dreams to substantiate this hunch, I came to realize that it was not, in its entirety, based on clinical intuition. Rather, it related to a fantasy I had developed during my own latency years. My father, raised in Canada, would often

entertain his children with tales of adventure and daring involving the Canadian Royal Mounties. To a seven-year-old,
however, he was no mere story-teller; he was, in fact, a member
of that elite corps on a secret mission to New York, and I was
certain that his exploits in cracking a spy ring, led by the Nazi
superintendent of our building who allowed no ball-playing in
front of the house, would ultimately win for him recognition
as a national war hero.

The imaginations, expectations, and preset attitudes that
may develop in the analyst as a consequence of such reactivated
fantasies may influence, not only specific reactions to the material related to them, but his understanding of central conflicts
in his patient.

The process of reconstruction, too, may be significantly
influenced by the analyst's perceptions of his patient's objects.
Greenacre (1975), Blum (1980), and others have, in recent
work, pointed out the value of reconstructing not only the intrapsychic meaning of a patient's experiences, but the external
reality as well. As part of this external reality, the figures of the
patient's childhood play a central role. While it is crucial for the
development of insight for the patient to understand the way
in which he perceived these individuals and the way in which
his own conflicts may have distorted that perception, it is equally
important for both analyst and patient to arrive at some understanding of their actual qualities. While the unfolding of the
transference provides vital information about the nature of the
patient's objects, the analyst, in the course of listening to a great
deal of material about them, also draws his own portraits of the
persons who populated his patient's childhood world. To the
extent that the analyst's view of these figures in the landscape
are, outside of his awareness, influenced by self and object
images of his own and by his childhood memories, his reconstructions will be contaminated by personal elements. Blum
(1980) makes the point that "reconstruction of the analyst's
childhood and reconstruction of the patient's childhood are
quite separate, if at times reciprocal, processes" (p. 49). They
can remain separate, however, only if the analyst has sufficient
awareness of how his own world of objects may influence and
color his perception of objects in the patient's world. This

awareness is also necessary for the process of reconstruction to assist the analyst in assessing the impact on his work of his countertransference reactions. Blum has pointed out that understanding the genetic antecedents of the patient's transference neurosis will help in disentangling and evaluating possible unfavorable effects of the countertransference. This valuable process can go on only if the analyst's reconstructive efforts are not themselves influenced by unanalyzed countertransference factors.

As a final note, I shall discuss a particular problem in the analyst's relation to his patient's objects. This situation occurs when, either through personal acquaintance or as a consequence of information learned about him from other sources, such an object is known to the analyst. This is not an unusual situation and in fact, it was an important, if neglected, aspect of the Dora case.

Some years before Freud began his analytic work with Dora, he had treated her father for a long-standing nervous condition that he correctly diagnosed as syphilis. That Freud had strong, and decidedly ambivalent, feelings about his former patient is clear from the description of him contained in the case history. Noting that he was an individual of unusual "activity and talents," Freud also described him as possessing shrewdness and perspicacity. He concurred, however, with Dora's description of her father as insincere, with a strain of falseness in his character, and as someone who only thought of his own enjoyment. "He was one of those men," Freud (1905) wrote, "who knew how to evade a dilemma by falsifying their judgment upon one of the conflicting alternatives" (p. 34).

As in the case of Dora's mother, the effect of Freud's feelings about the father on his treatment of the girl is not known to us. That his critical attitude must have been a factor of some importance in the analysis, however, seems clear. Freud thought Dora had much in common with her father. One cannot help wondering to what extent the link he made between his young patient and the man whom he had personally treated for a venereal disease and whom he regarded as devious and untrustworthy, influenced his attitude toward her, conscious or otherwise. One wonders, too, whether Freud's disapproval of

his former patient as a narcissistic and rather self-serving individual made more difficult the recognition and appreciation
of the developing father transference.

    It is well accepted today that in situations in which an object
is known to both patient and analyst, the therapist's prior feelings and attitudes toward that object, including biases of various
kinds, may have a profound impact on the analytic work.
Awareness of the part of the analyst of such responses in himself
is useful but, when limited to this level of understanding, may,
paradoxically, prove deceptive. By concentrating his self-awareness on those feelings and attitudes toward the patient's object
that have been stimulated in him by personal contact with or
knowledge of that object, the analyst may be lulled into the
conviction that his conscious awareness of such reactions will
protect against untoward countertransference responses. He
may overlook affects and fantasies arising outside of consciousness, stimulated by the link between the object known to him
and internalized self and object representations. It is possible
for the analyst, by focusing on his more consciously available
reactions, to effectively screen from his own awareness those
deeper and more concealed countertransference responses
whose expression in the treatment situation may provide a
measure of instinctual or narcissistic gratification.

    This situation arose in the course of my work with a most
difficult and provocative young woman whose displays of
aggression within the analytic sessions and unremitting acting
out outside it caused me to regard her as a borderline patient.
Doubts about the accuracy of my diagnosis were raised in my
mind when, in one session, the patient gave an unusually perceptive, insightful, and appreciative account of a complex paper
presented at a scientific meeting the night before by a colleague
and friend of mine. This colleague was a controversial figure
whose work invariably aroused much criticism from the establishment in his field. He had always impressed me, however,
as a man of unusual originality and creativity whose ideas, if
anything, were somewhat ahead of his time. I was aware that
my fondness for my friend had colored my attitude toward my
patient so that her appreciation of him seemed a sign not only
of good judgment, but of improving mental health. When, how-

ever, these more optimistic feelings about the patient persisted, and I began to see in her possibilities of growth and maturation that I had not seen before, I became curious about what other factors in myself may have contributed to this change of attitude.

For some time my efforts to unravel this mystery yielded few clues. One day, several hours after attempting to no avail to rethink the problem, a memory presented itself to me that dated back more than forty years. What I remembered centered on Gus, an influential figure of my childhood (mentioned in earlier chapters), and the leader of an after-school sports group to which I belonged as a youngster. An eccentric and controversial individual whose salty language and brusque manners managed to alienate a good many parents, including my own, he nevertheless had played for me a role of central importance in those years, and it was with a deep sense of loss that I learned my parents had decided to withdraw me from the group. All my protests failed, and I was resigned to life in a state of abject misery, when help came from an unexpected source.

Visiting us at the time was a cousin of mine, a young woman who, because of her outspoken and rather flamboyant manner, I had always regarded as a bit eccentric. Hearing about my plight, she immediately grasped the importance to me of my relationship with the group leader and she mounted a brilliant, articulate, and ultimately successful campaign to get my parents to change their minds. After that I saw nothing eccentric about my cousin. To me she was the prettiest, the most intelligent, the most vivacious of my relatives.

Clearly it was the unconscious connection I had made between my patient, who had in essence defended an embattled friend, and this champion of my early years that was at the root of my altered perceptions in this case. Associations of this kind, that link objects in the present with the memory of self and object representations arising in childhood or adolescence, may go unrecognized by the analyst in his effort to guard against the intrusion of conscious biases about an object known to the patient and himself. While awareness of his conscious attitudes and feelings toward such objects can serve a useful function for the analyst, too complacent an attitude regarding the protective value of such self-awareness may make difficult his recognition of the link between the image of the object known to both patient and analyst and the reawakened self and object images of the analyst's childhood, a link that, in fact, constitutes the deepest source of countertransference difficulties.

10

Secrets, Alliances, and Family Fictions: Some Psychoanalytic Observations

It is not rare in the course of clinical work for a psychoanalyst to learn from a patient of the existence of a family secret that has played a role of particular importance in his childhood. Associated with such secrets in many instances are secretive alliances between the involved family members as well as pacts, conscious or otherwise, that serve to regulate the extent to which communication about the secret is permissible. Some secrets, of course, concern facts that must be concealed. Others, however, pertain, not to facts, but to fiction, and constitute family myths that may have a profound impact on the psychological economy of individual family members.

It was the Dora case, as well as other clinical experiences, that drew Freud's attention to the significance of such phenomena. It was, in fact, Dora's history, in which secret collusions and family intrigue played so large a part, that Freud had in mind when, in 1905, he wrote, "We are obliged to pay as much attention in our case histories to the purely human and social circumstances of our patients as to the somatic data and the symptoms of the disorder. Above all, our interest will be directed towards their family circumstances" (p. 18).

Since that time, and most particularly in recent years when such innovative studies as the simultaneous analysis of parents and children have been undertaken, analysts have sought to refine their understanding of the role of the family in child development. One aspect of that problem encountered with some frequency in the clinical situation but little elaborated in the literature, either from the point of view of theory or practice, concerns the relationship of individual to family secrets and the impact of secrets and secretive alliances within a family on individual psychology.

The patient who first called my attention to the importance of these issues was a young woman, barely out of adolescence, who sought analysis for feelings of depression. While still a teenager, she had begun an analysis in the city in which she then lived, but this was terminated after less than two years when her analyst, an older man, relocated to another part of the country. Early on in our sessions, I had the impression that the patient retained many unspoken and unresolved feelings about her former analyst, but when this was subsequently raised as a possibility, she minimized his importance to her. He was, she said, something of an ass: dogmatic, conceited, and a moralist to boot. She had been helped in the early months of treatment, she acknowledged, but its value had soon worn thin, and by the time her analyst announced his change of plans, she was ready to quit anyway.

For some months this seemed to dispose of the matter, as the patient plunged with impressive dedication into her new analytic experience. The few references she made to her former analyst were to disparage him in comparison to me. Whereas he was opinionated, I was more open-minded and flexible; moreover, his training was inferior to mine. He had graduated from an unorthodox institute and his approach was eclectic, whereas I had had my training at the Source. Besides, she had learned more in the few months of the present analysis than she had in the nearly two years of her previous treatment. All of this I was tempted to agree with, except for the fact that the patient seemed too vehement about it, too keen on convincing me. I began to listen for hints as to the meaning of the way she spoke about her analysts—old and new.

It took the better part of a year for the true picture to emerge, but when it did, it was a very different one from the view originally presented. Far from being indifferent to her former analyst or to his leaving her, the patient was, in fact, quite romantically attached to him and experienced his departure as a profound hurt that only gradually gave way to rage. At several points in the analysis, especially when her feelings of depression returned, she longed to see him and thought seriously of finding his telephone number and calling him long-distance. He was, she imagined, divorced now and living a lonely and forlorn existence. When she learned that he was coming to New York to attend a convention, she had the strongest impulse to go to his hotel and to surprise him by ringing up from the lobby. Although apprehensive of what his response might be, she fantasied that his true feelings would emerge and that he would greet her with a joyous hug.

All of this the patient had kept to herself. Such thoughts, she explained, simply never arose in her mind while she was on the couch, nor did the criticism of me as a doltish follower of the party line that occurred to her outside the hours.

The patient's feelings about her former analyst, and my inadequacies in comparison, were, it became clear, a secret that she had to keep from me, a secret that quite literally seemed to disappear from her mind in my presence. And, behind this "transference secret" was another secret, one that since early childhood had exerted the most profound influence on her imagination and that both colored and dominated much of her fantasy life.

When she was six years old, the patient's parents divorced, and when she was eight, her father, who had seen her irregularly in that interval, moved to the West Coast and essentially disappeared from her life. Her mother's attitude toward the father was unremittingly hostile and contemptuous. He was, she would say, a selfish and irresponsible man who thought only of himself and his own well-being. They were, she would often say to her daughter, well rid of him.

Several years later the mother remarried, and her attitude toward her new husband was as admiring and complimentary as it was scornful toward the old. Just as the mother seemed to tolerate nothing good said about the patient's father, she allowed no criticism of the stepfather who, in addition to earning a handsome living, was the soul of generosity.

Under these circumstances, many of the patient's feelings and fantasies about her father, and her stepfather as well, were driven underground and became a secret. It did not take long for her to get the mother's message; she was to have nothing favorable to say about her father or even, she was convinced, to have any kind thoughts about him.

The secret feelings that the patient concealed, and that she herself found quite disturbing, involved not only the two men, but her mother as well. On the surface the youngster was compliant and uncritical. Privately she was furious at her mother, was deeply resentful of her attitude toward the father, and blamed her for driving him away.

Behind this attitude lay two memories, themselves secret, that fused with the more conscious secret about the father and, in fact, formed a deeper, and more deeply repressed, part of it. These memories, which took much analytic work to recover, occurred about the time of the parents' separation; one some months before, and the other soon after it.

The first memory concerned the child's unexpectedly coming upon Paul, a neighbor, who was later to become her stepfather, alone with her mother in their apartment. She had, on that occasion, sustained a sprained wrist in an after-school group that she attended and had been sent home early. There she found Paul, who, her mother explained, had dropped in to make a phone call. Later that night, at bedtime, the mother said to the child that it would be a good idea for Paul's visit to be their secret, as her daddy did not like anyone using their telephone and he would be angry if he found out. Under these circumstances, the secret was kept and, in fact, this family secret was never again mentioned by the patient, her mother, or the stepfather. After some time it seemed to pass from consciousness and was buried under the more available secret thoughts about the father.

The same fate, in essence, befell the second secret, which concerned the mother's reaction to the father's moving out. In the course of the analysis, the patient recalled hearing her mother crying at night, talking at length on the telephone, pleading for the father to come back. In the child's presence, however, she put on a different face. She attempted to appear carefree and unconcerned, and, when the youngster asked about it directly, denied missing her husband at all. This message, too, came through to the child. Her mother's sadness was not to be mentioned. She needed to conceal such feelings, and her daughter was to have no awareness of them either. It did not take long before the patient heard, repeatedly, a version of the marriage and the divorce appropriate to the emotions the mother wished to convey. This official explanation, which soon gained the status of a family myth, became, for her own defensive reasons, the youngster's view of the truth as well; and the frightening memories of hearing her mother in distress and crying at night faded from conscious awareness.

When she was fourteen, however, the patient learned the truth from her grandmother. Something of a dreamer, her father was nonetheless a devoted husband who put up with a great deal of contempt from his wife. When she actually became involved with another man and he learned about it, he packed his things and left. It was then that the mother had second thoughts. Suddenly she found assets in him that she had not seen before. She wanted him back, but he would not return. He was through for good. All this the patient accepted without question. She had no doubt that it was true. Somehow, she had known it all along.

The grandmother's revelations, however, had a stimulating effect on her. It was then that her fantasies and imaginings about her father grew in intensity. Secretly, she thought about him all the time, imagined him living alone and being lonely, and fantasized being reunited with him. No doubt the very great increase, both in intensity and frequency, of these fantasies, was, in part, attributable to the onset of adolescence with its greatly increased strength of the libidinal drive and the reawakening of oedipal yearnings. But there was another factor as well; a contributing cause that was not clarified until the patient was well into her second analysis, and this constituted the patient's most shameful secret.

Her stepfather, it seemed, had made a sexual overture to

her a few months before the grandmother's revelations. The casual teasing and touching that had been, for years, a part of their relationship had given way, on this occasion, to seductive fondling. Aroused and confused, the patient had allowed her stepfather to caress her genitals, and she, in turn, had felt his erect penis through his trousers. This experience, it became clear, was an expression of the revived oedipal strivings and an identification with the mother. But it represented, as well, a living out of a fantasized and elaborated version of the secret liaison, which, as a child, the patient had discovered and which had remained as an unspoken and untouchable family secret.

The sexual episode with her stepfather, however, produced in the patient the greatest fear and humiliation, and she tried to put it out of her mind and to pretend that it had not happened. By focusing her thoughts and imagination so intensely on her father, she unconsciously aided that process. It is my father three thousand miles away whom I love and wish to be with, she was saying, not my threatening stepfather. Focusing on her father, then, not only defended against the dangerous temptation of the current situation, but helped to reduce her guilt over what had happened. It helped, also, to conceal her anger at both men; at her father for abandoning her and at her stepfather for taking advantage of her vulnerability.

The meanings, then, of the patient's secret in analysis became clearer. Her feelings for her first analyst, whom she imagined I deeply resented, had to be hidden from me as her love of her father was hidden from her mother and stepfather. In her behavior, too, she seemed to be reenacting another family secret. It was the mother's hidden wish for her husband to return that the patient had become aware of, but had to forget. And, although her secretive behavior in analysis derived both from the oedipal secret that was so dangerous as well as from memories of her mother's behavior, it must have been contributed to in some degree by something that I communicated to the patient. For, as I examined my own responses, I was aware of some competitive feelings toward her former analyst and a desire to show that I was, in fact, the better man. Thus I, like her mother, had somehow signaled that it was the new man in her life who was to be admired, and the old forgotten. It became clear, too, that the patient's secret wishes not only expressed a deep attachment to her therapist, but also concealed her anger at him for leaving her. In this way she was able to preserve him, as she had tried to preserve her father, as a positive figure, despite the outward posture of indifference.

But the secret did something else as well. It helped protect the patient against erotic transference feelings that were emerging in the analysis with me. Preoccupied with such feelings and terribly frightened that they might escape her control, she focused her thoughts on her former analyst just as, before, she had utilized thoughts of her father to help fend off dangerous feelings about the man in the immediate present.

It was clear, too, that behind this secret lay the secrets of the patient's childhood, those crucially important and multilayered secrets that contained within them the core of the patient's neurotic conflicts. It was the exploration of the transference secret that opened the way to recovery of the others that lay behind them and that demonstrated how such secrets can be used as screen experiences. Somewhat analogous to the vividness of detail found in certain screen memories, these secrets, especially when they include a strong visual component, may contain within them memories of unusual clarity. The secret itself, in fact, may press with great intensity on the patient's awareness and claim an inordinate amount of his attention. This intensity, although it may reflect the hidden presence within the secret of drive derivatives pressing for discharge, also has a defensive, protective function. It helps keep out of awareness the deeper layers of the secret; layers that may contain either other secrets that have been long repressed, or memories and strivings of a highly conflictual nature.

Kestenberg (1972) discusses the formation of screen memories and emphasizes the contribution of parents to the structuring of them. It is between the ages of three and four, she states, that memory fragments are organized and gain meaning, although in later phases they become further elaborated by the then-prevailing ideational content. As the young child "organizes his nonverbal memories under the guidance of his parents who supply the words and structure, he is bound to delete or distort what his parents themselves deny or repress" (p. 109).

"And when a child remembers something his parents need to forget," she adds at another point, "he frequently loses access to a verbal communication of the memory and acts out in a way particularly resistive to analysis" (pp. 110–111).

In the same paper, Kestenberg also takes up the influence of parents on remembering and forgetting. Noting that certain patients in analysis are unable to accept a reconstruction or an emerging memory unless they get "permission" from the parents, she has observed that such memories often contradict important aspects of what they have been told about themselves. Unlike the personal myth described by Kris (1956) which, as a defensive alteration and elaboration of memory, serves to screen out highly conflictual experiences and fantasies, these memories are, in fact, correct. While, at first, patients may believe them to be fantasies, or even dreams, later they come to realize that what they have recalled is true and that their parents, to protect an image of themselves that comes closer to their ego ideals than the facts allow, have, in fact, misinformed them.

Some of these issues, as well as others of considerable theoretical interest, were illustrated by another patient, a middle-aged woman whose seeming amnesia for her childhood and much of her adolescence was so extensive as to prove a formidable obstacle in the early phase of her analysis. Work with her soon revealed that this inability to remember was not only a particular difficulty of hers, but was, in fact, a characteristic shared by every member of her family.

The manifest reason for this was apparent enough. During the war, the family had undergone considerable privation and suffering and had managed, by the slimmest of margins, to escape extermination at the hands of the Nazis. To this trauma the parents reacted by an attempt to eradicate all memories of that time. This need to forget, which was shared by both parents and which, on the surface, related to these wartime experiences, nevertheless contained within it individual motivations which stemmed from quite different sources.

The father had been orphaned when very young and had many bitter memories of his childhood. He had coped with these, in part, by weaving a romanticized and quite clearly fictionalized version of his life history. Within the family, it was understood that the father's distortion of the truth was important to him and was not to be challenged.

The mother, in turn, had lost a sister in childhood, her own mother while she was pregnant with the patient, and an infant son shortly after his birth several years before that. For some time she had suffered from depressive episodes, but she would never speak about these or any other experiences of a personal nature. She tried, as she had done with the war experiences, to blot them out of her mind.

As for the patient, she, too, followed the defensive pattern of her parents and attempted to deal with her conflicts by the use of massive repression. Her own need to forget related in part to a traumatic separation that she suffered during the war as well as to many painful and humiliating experiences that she endured as a refugee child in America. Hidden behind these experiences, however, lay the patient's need to conceal from herself both her intense aggression toward the mother and the existence of powerful sadomasochistic sexual fantasies that, arising in early adolescence, caused her the greatest shame.

There was, however, another secret in the family that was never spoken about; a secret so painful to the mother that she exerted, through her handling of it, a powerful influence on the patient to forget. This influence, it became clear, reinforced and dovetailed with the patient's own need to keep memories associated with the secret from her awareness.

It was through a piece of acting out and a screen memory that the facts could be pieced together. The first clue was provided by a quite inappropriate affair that the patient entered into when she was a married woman in her late twenties. This conduct was very much at odds with other aspects of her character, and, looking back on this time, the patient was puzzled about the motivation for her behavior. The details of this piece of acting out, as they were clarified, provided an initial insight into its origins. The patient had had an affair with a colleague, and as she spoke about this, she recalled that, when she was between the ages of four and five, her mother had taken her on regular visits to the apartment of a photographer. It was possible, ultimately, to deduce from a number of clues that the mother had had an afair with this man and that, about this time, she had become seriously depressed. The patient's own affair, occurring at a time of depression, represented an unconscious identification with her mother and with the mother's behavior in attempting to cope with her own depressed feelings.

During this period of work, the patient reported a screen memory, placed at about age five, in which she is in the family apartment with her father. He puts on her coat and takes her to her aunt's house to visit the mother who is living there. The mother comes down some stairs and gives her a dish of ice cream. Further reconstructive work showed, ultimately, that this memory distorted certain facts, incorporated elements of a lie that the patient had been told by the parents about her mother's depression, and aided the repression of the family secret.

The truth was that, following the breaking off of the mother's affair, she became suicidally depressed and was hospitalized for a period for six months. The patient was told that she had gone to her sister's house to help take care of her, because her aunt was ill. In fact, the aunt had been ill for some years with a chronic disease, and the mother did, from time to time, spend several days at her home. There were many clues, however, apparent even to the child, that the story she had been told was not true. Gradually she came to understand that her mother was at some kind of hospital, but that she was not to know this or speak of it. Her memory, it seemed, incorporated the story of her mother being at the aunt's house and fused it with memories from other periods when she had actually been there. It also made reference to her being alone with her father, a situation that gave rise to many secret feelings, and, in addition, concealed the deprivation and anger that the patient experienced at being abandoned under the pleasant memory of being given a dish of ice cream.

Although the patient was quite convinced that the reconstructions arrived at in her analysis were valid, she could not fully accept or work meaningfully with them until they had been verified by her mother. When she sought this verification, an interesting thing occurred. Rather than responding with the denial that was characteristic of her, the mother, after only a short period of hesitation, confirmed the truth of these events and elaborated on them. Moreover, she indicated that she was glad that the truth had come out. For years she had worried that she had harmed the patient by her affair and by lying to her about where she had been during the period of her depression. Concerned about her image in her daughter's eyes, she had not been able to tell her the truth. Now, confronted by what the patient had uncovered in her analysis, she could do so.

These, and other cases like them, raise some interesting questions about the influence of secrets and secretive alliances within a family on the developing personality. This is a highly complex problem involving a great many variables unique to each child in each particular situation. Here I shall touch only on certain general aspects of that influence.

The function of memory was, in both the cases I described, significantly affected by the existence of secrets and collusions within the families, the second patient in a quite pervasive manner, the first in a more limited and spotty but still significant way. In her discussion of this issue, Kestenberg has emphasized the influence on memory of the parents' need for a child not to remember certain events. This, of course, plays an important role in the problem as it touches on the child's most basic fears of object loss and of loss of love. Equally important, however, in its influence on memory and other ego functions, is the effect that family secrets and collusions may have on stimulating the libidinal and aggressive drives.

Certain secrets, especially those that relate to a parent's romantic and sexual life and that come into awareness during the oedipal and early latency period, can have as strong an impact on the imagination and on sexual fantasies as actual sexual stimulation or the witnessing of sexual activity. Not only are voyeuristic impulses, primal-scene fantasies or memories, and oedipal wishes stimulated by awareness of the parent's secret activity, but a stamp of reality is given to the notion of an illicit, secretive relationship. Nor is it only in the case of secrets of a sexual kind that the child's sexual fantasies may be stimulated. The child inevitably experiences family secrets in terms of his own secrets, which, in part, include secret sexual wishes and masturbatory practices.

In addition, the very existence of secrets and collusions within a family often intensifies the child's aggressive conflicts. When he senses the existence of a secret that has not been revealed to him, the youngster's fantasies and concomitant anxiety may be strongly stimulated, as are his feelings of frustration at being excluded. If, on the other hand, he becomes a partner to the secret, the injunction to keep silent and the anxieties engendered by that command create a heavy burden that frequently stimulates resentment. Moreover, feelings of guilt may be deeply intensified by the creation of a secret bond with one of the parents, as are the child's conflicts over his loyalty to each.

In the face of this increased pressure from the drives, as well as the stimulated fantasy life to which the secret in the family has given rise, certain children will respond with an augmentation and extension of the protective mechanisms of repression, suppression, and denial, so that the function of memory is significantly affected. In such instances, the forgotten secrets act as one category of repressed memories, but one that, because of the intensity and condensation of the drive derivatives associated with them, require a corresponding intensity of the repressing forces to keep them from conscious awareness. It is partly for this reason, too, that the tendency to act out such secrets is so strong.

In other individuals, however, the existence of the secret or a secretive alliance is accepted by the ego as a vehicle for the expression of the stimulated drives. Rather than repressing the secret, these patients, in a sense, can never forget it. It takes on for them an intense and haunting quality which is due, not only to the concealed presence within the secret of the drive derivatives, but to the fact, as we have seen, that the secret often serves a screening function as well.

There is another factor, however, that may invest thoughts about the secret with a special intensity and persistence. The word *secret* is derived from the same root as "secretions," and because of the secretive nature of the intimate bodily processes, the idea of a secret oftentimes is associated, unconsciously, with the private secretions of the body. In this way secrets are closely linked in the mind with issues of control and power. When the child learns of a parental or family secret that is being withheld from him, it often can light up old issues of control of the body, and particularly of sphincter control, and is experienced as an act of aggression. On the other hand, when he is enjoined to keep a secret, familiar resentments over having to control himself may emerge in the child, as well as a gratifying sense of power over the parents.

Thus, the issue of conscious withholding, which is so important in the maintenance of family secrets and collusions and which occurs regularly as a factor in the analysis of patients with this history, inevitably calls into play reactivated aggressive and sadistic impulses. These, as one might expect, may have an intensifying effect on certain aspects of superego development and on the internalization of the increased aggression. The individual who cannot forget a secret may, then, from this perspective, be expressing these impulses in precisely this phenomenon. Enjoined by the parent to forget the secret, he is doing precisely the opposite.

In addition to memory, other functions of the ego may be affected by the existence of a secret in the family. There may be considerable disparity between various perceptual experiences, so that what a child observes, for instance, may be denied outright by a parent. This state of affairs may involve various modalities of perception and, depending on the age and psychological status of the child, the extent of the confusion engendered by such experiences, and the difficulty of their integration, they may have the effect of weakening both the sense of reality and certain aspects of the synthetic function of the ego. It is not unusual for individuals in whose development family secrets have played an important role to experience difficulty in trusting their own perceptions. Their judgment, too, which is partially based on perception, is continually brought into question. While, clearly, such problems are overdetermined, the role that such secrets have played in creating confusion in the child's mind and affecting these several aspects of ego functioning cannot be ignored.

It is not surprising, then, that problems of learning are so often associated with the existence of some family secret. Not only is the issue of knowing the forbidden involved, but the various ego functions so important in learning may have been affected in the manner described. Moreover, the increase in libidinal and aggressive drives may have made their neutralization more difficult and additionally affected autonomous ego functioning. The child's inability to learn and, in fact, his failure to remember what he has learned, can also be unconscious expressions of hostility toward parents and serve as a kind of mockery of the injunction to forget.

Superego development, too, may be significantly affected by the existence of secretive phenomena within families. The effect on superego functioning, in fact, can be manifested in a variety of ways, but for the purposes of this discussion, I shall cite only one.

Both patients I described demonstrated a quality in this sphere that can, perhaps, be termed a certain kind of inconsistency of the superego. Both suffered from very profound feelings of guilt which could, in part, be traced to their participation, both in reality and fantasy, in their mothers' secret lives. The stimulation to their sexual and oedipal fantasies was intense, but also strong was guilt over their secretive collusions and in response to the considerable feelings of hostility that developed toward the mothers. Alongside these feelings of guilt, however, went a tolerance for deceit and subterfuge in particular areas, especially with regard to their romantic lives. The first patient was given to telling rather dramatic lies about her popularity with men, and when it came to gaining the favor of a man, she had no hesitation about betraying a friendship and acting in a dishonest and underhanded way. The second patient, known for her impeccably moral behavior in other respects, nevertheless had no compunction about becoming involved in several inappropriate affairs during her marriage and about treating her husband in a strikingly callous and even cruel way.

How can one understand such contradictions? One factor among the many involved seems to relate to the deception, collusion, and intrigue with which both patients were intimately associated during the phase of superego formation. Such exposure had on that development, it appeared, a paradoxical influence. On the one hand, it contributed to an intensification of guilt. On the other, it seemed, partly as the result of identifications with the mothers whose deceits were experienced in large measure as aggressions, to foster a tolerance for deception and lying in a relatively isolated sphere. The fact that, in each patient, a portion of the ego ideal involved the idea of a secretive and illicit sexual relationship contributed to the split in superego functioning and perhaps to the immunity from feelings of guilt in this particular area. I have observed a similar dissociative quality in superego functioning in several other patients in whom family secrets and collusions have played a significant part, but whether this phenomenon can be found with regularity in such cases is a matter for further investigation.

Thus far I have discussed certain problems in individual development that may occur as a consequence of the exposure of a child to family secrets. It should be pointed out, however, that personal secrets and perhaps, to some extent, secrets within a family, are ubiquitous phenomena and may have a stimulating effect on various aspects of development. Just as the toddler's use of the word *no* and, at certain phases of his growth, his negativity, may be utilized in the service of the separation and individuation process, so those aspects of the child's thought and behavior that are uniquely private and exist as his personal secrets may promote both individuation and a growing sense of personal identity. In fact, in those pathological instances in which a child is allowed no secrets and in which there is an invasive attitude on the part of the mother, one may anticipate difficulties both in the child's ability to separate from her and in his capacity to maintain distinct and separate ego boundaries.

The impact that a parent's secret, either confided to or discovered by a child, may have on this aspect of his psychological growth depends of course on its nature and the quality of the parent–child relationship, as well as on the age of the child and individual features of his development. Of interest, however, is the fact that, in both patients cited, separation from their mothers presented a problem of enormous difficulty. Each, however, responded to this problem in quite a different way.

The first patient developed a defiant and rebellious attitude together with an exaggerated posture of independence that served to cover over, with the thinnest of veneers, her unresolved dependency longings. The second woman simply never separated from her mother. Although she married and had children of her own, her deepest tie was to her mother and she never lived more than a few blocks from her. At the start of the analysis, in fact, mother and daughter had apartments one floor apart in the same building.

Family secrets, like other mysteries that may exist in the child's world, may exert a powerful stimulus both on intellectual development and on his curiosity and imagination. In later life a number of pursuits, and particularly creative activity, may be influenced by a continuing need to rework and to resolve conflicts surrounding the family secret. In literature, the theme of a family secret whose concealment and ultimate revelation plays a central role in the lives of the fictional characters has been an important one in both classical and contemporary works and finds particular expression, of course, in the drama of Oedipus himself.

In more recent times, one might cite, among many others, certain novels of Henry James and of Ford Madox Ford as being centrally concerned with the existence of secrets. Ford's most famous work, *The Good Soldier*, may serve as an example. The story opens with Dowell, the narrator, reflecting in an incredulous manner on his opacity in not having been aware of a secret that, for over nine years, had existed in front of his nose. The secret was simply this: during that period his wife had been having an affair with his best friend and, moreover, for some time before that she had been carrying on with a rather brutish fellow who visited her with some regularity.

As the book chronicles the development of these relationships, it becomes abundantly clear that Dowell has a powerful need not to know about these secrets. His state of mind highlights the defensive purpose that such self-imposed ignorance may serve, for, by means of it, he both participates vicariously in the expression of certain forbidden impulses and, at the same time, reinforces their repression. These impulses involve not only the sexuality which he so assiduously avoids, but, perhaps more important and more central to Ford's theme, a powerful and untamed aggressive urge, which, fused with sadism, helps bring about the ultimate destruction of the only two people for whom he has ever been able to feel love.

I want, as a final note, to describe another situation that arose in the course of the second patient's analysis and that demonstrated how a secret shared between patient and analyst can sometimes have a significant impact on the analytic work. While this patient was in treatment, I suffered a painful personal loss. By virtue of professional and other connections, a certain number of my patients knew about this situation. Some would bring it up spontaneously; in the case of others, I had to ferret out their concealed feelings about it. For me this was not, emotionally, an easy task, and I found that if a patient knew nothing of my personal situation, I was relieved.

In the case of this particular patient, however, the issue was unclear. She had enough contacts in the field to possibly have heard something, but I was not certain that she had—or that is what I chose to believe. In fact, the patient gave a number of hints that she knew the truth, but when I did not pick these up she did not pursue them. She was, in fact, waiting for permission from me to reveal what she knew. I, on the other hand, was not keen on dealing with this painful issue with still another patient, and, by not following up on the clues she was providing, I was, in fact, communicating as much. Thus, a conspiracy developed that served important dynamic needs in both patient and analyst.

It was only after I had come to a better resolution of this problem in myself that I was able to hear what the patient was saying and to open up the issue with her. It then became clear that her need to keep secret what she knew was, in part, a transference reaction. As a young child she learned from a relative that she nearly had a brother, but that he died soon after birth. Her mother, however, never spoke of this event, but her eyes often teared up when the fact of her having only one child was mentioned. Wanting to speak of what she had heard, the patient from time to time gave hints that she knew about this secret, but the mother never responded to these clues. When on one occasion she approached her father to verify the facts, he acknowledged the truth of the event but cautioned her not to speak of this tragedy to the mother. The patient was thus reenacting with me the situation she was in for so many years with her mother.

She took my failure to pick up on the hints she offered as a sign that I could not cope with discussing this painful issue, and she imagined, as she had about her mother, that if she broached it without my permission, I would react, out of my hurt, with massive rage. Thus, until I gave her a sign that she could reveal the secret, she kept her very intense feelings about the situation and the memories it evoked unspoken and inaccessible to analysis.

It occurred to me that perhaps this was not an isolated situation; that more often than we may be aware of, secrets of one kind or another exist between patient and analyst. Issues may arise which stir up mutual anxiety and may, consciously or otherwise, be avoided by both. Situations may also develop in which information gleaned by either patient or analyst about the other may not, for one reason or another, be fully aired in the analysis. In a training situation, certain information learned by the analyst about his candidate–patient can, at times, fall into this category. On the other hand, observations that a patient has made about his analyst in areas in which he senses a narcissistic vulnerability may, as the result of a tacit understanding that develops between them, remain unspoken.

A patient whom I saw in consultation reported that he had noticed, for some months, signs of failing health in his previous analyst. He had been unable to bring up this sensitive issue nor, despite growing signs of his incapacity, had the therapist. The issue did not surface until, arriving for his hour one day, the patient found his analyst so ill that he was unable to function. This forced an end to the analysis in what was clearly an untherapeutic way. Awareness of the role that secrets and unconscious collusions can play in the analytic situation, as well as outside of it, may alert us, then, to important issues in the treatment that, because of a mutual need for avoidance, may have previously gone undetected. The analysis of such secrets may open the way to a deeper understanding of those secrets in the patient's life that contain within them conflicts of the most fundamental importance.

11

Concluding Remarks

It is not unusual for its critics to label psychoanalysis a static field. Compared to other sciences, they contend, progress in analysis has been meager. Not only do analysts practice essentially as they did two decades ago, but the voluminous psychoanalytic literature contains precious little that is new or innovative. Rooted in the contributions of Freud, it consists essentially of commentaries on, emendations to, and variations on the great themes he articulated in his seminal works.

Those who hold this view have not read the literature they criticize, or if they have read it, have failed to appreciate the enormous changes taking place in our field. The last two decades have been times of challenge to well-accepted ideas; of reevaluation of theory and technique, of the development of important and original concepts, and of the critical revision of others. Controversial ideas concerning object relations theory, self psychology, borderline states, depression, psychosis, and the therapeutic action of psychoanalysis have stirred debate, stimulated thinking, occasioned much reexamination of long-held beliefs, and have constituted powerful incentives for growth and change.

The aspect of psychoanalysis with which this volume has been concerned, communication in the analytic situation, has long been of interest to psychoanalysts. Freud recognized the

importance in analysis of communication between the unconscious of patient and analyst and the way of listening that he
recommended, one of evenly hovering attention, was designed
to enhance the analyst's capacity to receive such communications. Freud's original ideas concerning the way that messages
are sent and received in analysis, were not further elaborated,
however, and although during the past several decades a number of papers have appeared in the literature which touch on
this dimension of analytic work, it was not until recent years
that it has been more thoroughly explored. Especially valuable
have been the contributions of James McLaughlin (1975, 1981,
1988), Robert Gardner (1983), and Warren Poland (1986,
1988). In their writings these colleagues have illustrated how,
as he works, the inner experiences of the analyst spring from,
resonate with, and elucidate the inner world of the patient. The
originality and courage displayed by these colleagues, who have
been willing to share in print certain illuminating personal experiences occurring in the course of analytic hours, has been
unique. Perhaps more than any other recent contributors in
this area, their work has given us valuable insights into the
psychology of the analyst as he goes about the business of analyzing.

The efforts of these and other authors have made a good
beginning in the exploration of an area of psychoanalysis that
has not as yet been sufficiently well studied. Many of the reasons
for its comparative neglect have been touched on by Warren
Poland in his introduction. From the time that analysts of the
interpersonal school began publishing their ideas, classical analysis was wary of their approach. On guard against efforts to
alter and dilute its essential character, classical analysis found
little of value in a theory that emphasized the role of objects in
human motivation and development to the exclusion of the
drives. Arriving at a time when analysis was still trying to establish itself in this country, when it was under siege from many
quarters, and when repeated efforts were made by its detractors
to deny the importance of infantile sexuality and of the unconscious, the attitude of analysts trained in the Freudian tradition was to view the interpersonalists as one of their adversaries.
As a result, the intrapsychic world of the patient, regarded as

the proper and sole province of analysis, was set over against the interpersonal. Data arising from the former was considered analytic; that deriving from the latter not truly so. Moreover, those practitioners who espoused the interpersonal view were regarded as purveyors of an ersatz brand of psychoanalysis; one that, while usurping its name and certain of its trappings, omitted its essence.

In this atmosphere, appreciation, and especially creative exploration, of the interactional aspect of the analytic situation was slow to develop. The antagonism that developed toward the interpersonalists, with its accompanying tendency to regard material on the transactional level as superficial and not worthy of serious study, slowed recognition of the importance of the analyst's contribution to the development of transference and to the character and fate of the analytic process.

Gradually, however, this perspective has gained the interest of a number of colleagues who, recognizing that the analyst is never simply a blank screen on whom the patient projects his conflicts, began to study the myriad ways in which aspects of the psychology of the analyst impinge on, interact with, and help shape the analytic material.

Historically, the influence of both the British object relations and Kleinian schools, as well as increased clinical experience, paved the way for this shift in emphasis. These theoretical approaches, both of which emphasized the centrality in human psychology of the child's earliest object relations, also stressed the importance in analysis of the interaction of patient and analyst. Much attention in each was paid to the interweaving fantasies, displacements, and projections of both participants in the analytic situation, and the understanding of such phenomena as reflected in the patient's material was regarded as a primary task of analytic technique. Also important as influences in this development were the writings of Heinrich Racker (1968), whose comprehensive study of countertransference demonstrated both the complexity of the phenomenon and its impact on the analytic process. Hans Loewald's original papers (1972, 1978), linking the concepts of drive and object, both helped bring object relations theory into the mainstream of analytic thinking and provided the theoretical underpinnings for the point of view that regards the interaction of patient and analyst as contributing to the shape and form of the transference.

The current interest in the contributions that the psychology of the analyst makes to the analytic process is reflected in the recent surge of papers and books on the subject of countertransference. For many years analysts had little to say on this subject. Now it has become a fruitful area for analytic investigation, a development which was stimulated by the acceptance of a view of countertransference which regards it, not only as a potential impediment to the analyst's understanding, but as a complex mental phenomenon whose exploration can tell us much about the ongoing analytic process.

The changes in thinking about transactional phenomena that have taken place over the last decade have led a number of colleagues to view that aspect of psychoanalysis in ways that are substantially different from those of their predecessors in both the classical and interpersonal schools. They do not regard it as deriving from an alternative view of human development in which the role of the drives is brought into question. Nor do they consider interpretive work at the interpersonal level to constitute the core of the analytic process. Rather, they see the interactions between patient and analyst as a pathway for the expression of unconscious processes in each and as a vehicle for the understanding, not only of the overt aspects of the transference–countertransference interplay, but of its covert dimensions which contain the metacommunicational messages that play so important a role in the analytic process. Transference is not viewed as a one-way street consisting solely of projections of the patient, but as being continually influenced in the way it expresses itself by contributions from the analyst.

The moment-to-moment transactions that take place in the analytic hour are reflective of and provide a window into the dynamic forces motivating both participants. Through his awareness of these interactions, as well as by means of his ongoing efforts at self-analysis, the analyst seeks to alert himself, not only to his transference feelings, but to the full range of his psychological experiences in the course of analyzing. He seeks, too, to put himself in touch with the influences, subtle and otherwise, that each personality is having on the other. For he realizes not only that the analytic situation inevitably involves the interplay of two psychologies by which it is continually shaped, but that the exploration of this dimension of analytic work is an important part of his technique.

What of the future? How can the communicative processes in analysis be further investigated? Several approaches to its study have shown promise. The oldest and most direct of these, careful observation in the clinical situation, has, in the hands of creative individuals, continued to be a rich source of new and stimulating ideas. Especially important have been observations concerning the analyst's physical and psychological experience while analyzing. These include not only the full range of his mental experiences as he works, but certain physiologic responses such as heart rate, muscular reactions, skin changes, and activity of particular secretory glands.

Comparatively neglected as a potentially valuable source of information about aspects of the psychology of the analyst at work have been his dreams. While dreams about patients are uncommon, ones that contain elements related to the analytic process are not rare. For the analyst, as well as the patient, the analytic hour may constitute the day residue that triggers a dream. The ongoing self-analysis of his dreams, therefore, may open a pathway to the understanding of attitudes and feelings toward his patients and the work of analyzing of which the therapist was previously unaware.

Thoughts and fantasies of the analyst's that occur outside of sessions are also phenomena which may yield useful information about his experiences in the treatment situation. Such phenomena have sometimes been spoken of as indicators of countertransference feelings which, escaping conscious awareness, arise in this way. The implication in this view is that such reactions constitute a formidable problem for the analyst and that the fantasies that surface outside the hours offer clues to these difficulties. While in certain situations this is undoubtedly true, such a perspective is a narrow one that unnecessarily restricts the understanding of such phenomena. In fact, like his other fantasies, those of the analysts that arise outside of sessions are complex phenomena that can provide insights not only into troublesome countertransference responses but into certain of his unconscious reactions to patients and the treatment situation. As a source of useful data, the investigation of such phenomena constitutes an important aspect of the analyst's self-analysis.

The study of nonverbal behavior in analysis is still in an early stage of development. Few analysts have trained themselves in its systematic use and, as a result, data deriving from this source is often overlooked in favor of that contained in the verbal material. Rarely are the nonverbal exchanges of patient and analyst discussed in supervision nor is this aspect of analytic work much emphasized in courses on technique. As a consequence, many graduating analysts have had little experience in the observation and interpretation of this dimension of analytic work. If our understanding of the range and complexity of the communicative process in analysis is to grow, it will be necessary to incorporate more teaching about its nonverbal aspects into our institute curriculums. Students must learn how to look as well as to listen (a process that in the first instance requires that they position themselves in such a way that they have a good view of the patient on the couch) and how to think analytically about material arising from nonverbal sources. They must also learn how to utilize their own spontaneous bodily movements and reactions as data in the analytic situation.

In understanding the complex way that humans communicate with each other, researchers and therapists in fields other than analysis have taken the lead. In fact, analysis lags far behind in studying these phenomena. Analysts in training could learn a good deal from studying the work of such authors as Birdwhistell (1952, 1963) and Scheflen (1963), whose pioneering researches into the world of nonverbal behavior have helped illuminate its role in the analytic process.

Slow, too, to develop in analytic research has been the use of audiovisual materials. While some important studies utilizing tape recorded analysis have been undertaken in recent years, the number of such projects has been small. The videotaping of analytic hours as a research technique has also been underutilized. Understandably, there is much objection to its use both on the grounds of confidentiality and because many colleagues believe that the introduction of a videocamera into the consulting room would result in an even greater distortion of the analytic process than takes place when analytic hours are tape recorded. While such arguments are cogent ones and not easily answered, it should be noted that the videotaping of psychotherapy has, in some training centers, become an invaluable teaching method and a promising research technique. Those who have had experience with this procedure assert that, carefully handled, the question of confidentiality does not pose an insuperable problem and that modern technology makes it possible for the videotaping to be done in so unobtrusive a way that the presence of the camera, after a period of adjustment to it, ceases to be a distorting factor in the treatment. Certainly it would be interesting and potentially valuable for analysts to investigate the possibility of using videotapes of analytic hours more extensively in their research. Should the wider use of this methodology prove feasible, it would unquestionably open up important new areas for study. No longer would colleagues interested in the communicative process be faced with the difficult task, after sessions, of reconstructing its essence. It would be possible for therapists to examine the exchanges, verbal and nonverbal, between themselves and patients on a frame-by-frame basis. The research opportunities inherent in the moment-to-moment review of such interactions seem limitless.

Whatever approaches are utilized, however, whether they be the use of sophisticated electronic equipment or the traditional method of clinical observation, continued investigation of the communicative process in analysis is an area of research that promises to be in the forefront of new developments in our field.

It has already had a significant impact on the way we think and work. No longer do the majority of analysts focus exclusively on the patient's words, with attention paid to countertransference responses only when they reveal themselves in troubling or disruptive ways. Rather, we function in an open, free-flowing, two-directional way that includes an ongoing effort to observe ourselves as well as our patients. Our analytic instrument has become a multichannel one that receives and processes data from multiple sources. Its increased capacities not only allow the analyst to take soundings from the depths with ever-greater sensitivity, but make it possible for him to decipher more quickly and accurately the covert messages that are an integral part of the treatment situation. And his improved ability to do so opens new pathways to the attainment of valuable insights into those metacommunications between himself and his patient that underlie all of the transactions of the analytic hour.

References

Arlow, J. A. (1969), Fantasy, memory and reality testing. *Psychoanal. Quart.*, 38:28–51.

———— (1988), Some technical problems of countertransference. In: *Counter-transference*, ed. E. Slakter. New York: Jason Aronson.

Balter, L., Lothane, Z., & Spencer, J. H. (1980), On the analyzing instrument. *Psychoanal. Quart.*, 49:474–502.

Baum, I. E. (1977), Countertransference and the vicissitudes of an analyst's development. *Psychoanal. Rev.*, 64:539–550.

Beiser, H. R. (1984), An example of self-analysis. *J. Amer. Psychoanal. Assn.*, 32:3–12.

Beres, D., & Arlow J. A. (1974), Fantasy and identification in empathy. *Psychoanal. Quart.*, 43:26–50.

Bernstein, I., & Glenn, J. (1978), The child analyst's emotional reactions to his patients. In: *Child Analysis and Therapy*, ed. J. Glenn. New York: Jason Aronson.

Bird, B. (1972), Notes on transference: Universal phenomenon and hardest part of analysis. *J. Amer. Psychoanal. Assn.*, 19:41–53.

Birdwhistell, R. L. (1952), *Introduction to Kinesics*. Louisville, KY: University of Louisville Press.

———— (1963), *The Kinesic Level in the Investigation of Emotions, Expression of the Emotions in Man*. New York: International Universities Press.

Blum, H. P. (1971), On the conception and development of the transference neurosis. *J. Amer. Psychoanal. Assn.*, 19:41–53.

———— (1980), The value of reconstruction in adult psychoanalysis. *Internat. J. Psycho-Anal.*, 61:39–52.

———— (1983), The position and value of extratransference interpretation. *J. Amer. Psychoanal. Assn.*, 31:587–619.

———— (1987), Countertransference: Concepts and controversies. In: *Countertransference*, ed. E. Slakter. New York: Jason Aronson.

Boesky, D. (1982), Acting out: A reconsideration of the concept. *Internat. J. Psycho-Anal.*, 63:39–55.

———— (1989), Enactments, Acting Out, and Considerations of Reality. Paper presented on Panel on Enactments, Meeting of the American Psychoanalytic Association.

Brenner, C. (1983), Transference and countertransference. In: *The Mind in Conflict*. New York: International Universities Press.

Breuer, J., & Freud, S. (1893–1895), Studies on Hysteria. *Standard Edition*, 2. London: Hogarth Press, 1962.

Burlingham, D. (1967), Empathy between infant and mother. *J. Amer. Psychoanal. Assn.*, 15:764–780.

Calder, K. (1980), An analyst's self-analysis. *J. Amer. Psychoanal. Assn.*, 28:5–20.

Calef, V., & Weinshel, E. (1981), Some clinical consequences of introjection: Gaslighting. *Psychoanal. Quart.*, 50:44–65.

Caruth, E. G. (1985), Secret bearer or secret barer. *Contemp. Psychoanal.*, 21:4, 548–562.

Deutsch, F. (1952), Analytic posturology. *Psychoanal. Quart.*, 21:196–214.

Deutsch, H. (1926), Occult processes occurring during psychoanalysis. In: *Psychoanalysis and the Occult*, ed. G. Devereux. New York: International Universities Press, 1953.

Fenichel, O. (1941), *Problems of Psychoanalytic Technique*. New York: Psychoanalytic Quarterly.

——— (1926), Identification. In: *Collected Papers*, First Series. New York: W.W. Norton, 1953.

Freud, A. (1954), Problems of technique in adult analysis. *Bull. Phila. Assn. Psychoanal.*, 4:44–70.

Freud, S. (1895), Frau Emmy von N. *Standard Edition*, 2:48–105. London: Hogarth Press, 1955.

——— (1905), A fragment of an analysis of a case of hysteria. *Standard Edition*, 7:1–22. London: Hogarth Press, 1953.

——— (1909). Notes upon a case of obsessional neurosis. *Standard Edition*, 10:155–318. London: Hogarth Press, 1955.

——— (1910). The future prospects of psychoanalytic therapy. *Standard Edition*, 11:141–151. London: Hogarth Press, 1957.

——— (1912), Recommendations to physicians practicing psychoanalysis. *Standard Edition*, 12:111–120. London: Hogarth Press, 1958.

——— (1913). On beginning the treatment. *Standard Edition*, 12:123–144. London: Hogarth Press, 1958.

——— (1915), The unconscious. *Standard Edition*, 14:166–204. London: Hogarth Press, 1957.

Gardner, M. R. (1983), *Self-Inquiry*. Boston: Atlantic-Little Brown.

Gill, M. M. (1982), Analysis of Transference. *Psychological Issues*, Monograph 53. New York: International Universities Press.

Glover, E. (1927), Transference and countertransference. In: *The Technique of Psychoanalysis*. New York: International Universities Press, 1955.

Gombrich, E. H. J. (1963), *Meditations on a Hobby Horse and Other Essays on the Theory of Art*. London: Phaidon.

Greenacre, P. (1959), Certain technical problems in the transference relationship. *J. Amer. Psychoanal. Assn.*, 7:484–502.

——— (1975). On reconstruction. *J. Amer. Psychoanal. Assn.*, 23:693–712.

Greenson, R. R. (1967), *The Technique and Practice of Psychoanalysis*. New York: International Universities Press.

Halpern, H. M., & Lesser, L. N. (1960), Empathy in infants, adults, and psychotherapists. *Psychoanal. & Psychoanalytic Rev.*, 47:32–42.

Heimann, P. (1950), On countertransference. *Internat. J. Psycho-Anal.*, 31:81–84.

Isakower, O. (1963a), Minutes of New York Psychoanalytic Institute faculty meeting, October 14, unpublished.

—— (1963b), Minutes of New York Psychoanalytic Institute faculty meeting, November 20, unpublished.

Jacobs, T. (1973), Posture, gesture and movement in the analyst: Cues to interpretation and countertransference. *J. Amer. Psychoanal. Assn.*, 21:77–92.

—— (1980), Secrets, alliances and family fictions: Some psychoanalytic observations. *J. Amer. Psychoanal. Assn.*, 28:1, 21–42.

—— (1986), On countertransference enactments. *J. Amer. Psychoanal. Assn.*, 34:2, 289–307.

Kernberg, O. (1976), *Object Relations Theory and Clinical Psychoanalysis*. New York: Jason Aronson.

—— (1980) *Internal World and External Reality: Object Relations Theory Applied*. New York: Jason Aronson.

Kestenberg, J. (1972), How children remember and parents forget. *Internat. J. Psychoanal. Psychother.*, 1:103–123.

Kohut, H. (1971), *The Analysis of the Self*. New York: International Universities Press.

—— (1977), *The Restoration of the Self*. New York: International Universities Press.

—— (1984), *How Does Analysis Cure?* Chicago: The University of Chicago Press.

Kramer, M. K. (1959), On the continuation of the analytic process after psychoanalysis (a self-observation). *Internat. J. Psycho-Anal.*, 41:147–156.

Kris, E. (1956), The personal myth. In: *Selected Papers*. New Haven, CT: Yale University Press, 1975, pp. 272–300.

Langs, R. (1975), The therapeutic relationship and deviations in technique. *Internat. J. Psychoanal. Psychother.*, 4:106–141.

Lipps, T. (1913), *Grundzuge der Psychologie. II. Die Einfuhling*, Leipsig.

Little, M. (1951), Countertransference and the patient's response to it. *Internat. J. Psycho-Anal.*, 32:32–40.

Loewald, H. C. (1960), On the therapeutic action of psychoanalysis. *Internat. J. Psychoanal.*, 41:16–33.

—— (1972), Freud's conception of the negative therapeutic reaction with comments on instinct theory. *Amer. Psychoanal. Assn.*, 20:235–245.

—— (1978), Instinct theory, object relations, and psychic structure formation. *J. Amer. Psychoanal. Assn.*, 26:493–506.

Malcove, L. (1975), The analytic situation: Toward a view of the supervisory experience. *J. Phila. Assn. Psychoanal.*, 2:1–19.

MacDougall, J. (1979), Primitive communication and the use of countertransference. In: *Countertransference*, eds. I. Epstein & A. Feiner. New York: Jason Aronson.

McLaughlin, J. T. (1975), The sleepy analyst: Some observations on states of consciousness in the analyst at work. *J. Amer. Psychoanal. Assn.*, 23:363–382.

—— (1981), Transference, psychic reality and countertransference. *Psychoanal. Quart.*, 50:639–664.

—— (1988), The analyst's insights. *Psychoanal. Quart.*, 57:370–388.

Michaels, L. J. (1985), Bearer of the secret. *Psychoanal. Inq.*, 5:1, 21–30.

Myerson, P. G. (1960), Awareness and stress. Postpsychoanalytic utilization of insight. *Internat. J. Psycho-Anal.*, 41:147–156.

Pick, I. B. (1985), Working through in the countertransference. *Internat. J. Psycho-Anal.*, 66:157–167.

Poland, W. (1986), The analyst's words. *Psychoanal. Quart.*, 55:244–271.

—— (1988), Insight and the analytic dyad. *Psychoanal. Quart.*, 57:244–271.

Racker, H. (1958), Counterresistance and interpretation. *J. Amer. Psychoanal. Assn.*, 6:215–221.

—— (1968), *Transference and Countertransference*. New York: International Universities Press.

Reich, A. (1951), On countertransference. *Internat. J. Psycho-Anal.*, 32:25–31.

—— (1960), Further remarks on countertransference. *Internat. J. Psycho-Anal.*, 41:389–395.

—— (1966). Empathy and. countertransference. In: *Annie Reich: Psychoanalytic Contributions*. New York: International Universities Press, 1973, pp. 344–360.

Reich, W. (1933), *Character Analysis*. New York: Orgone Institute Press, 1945.

Rustin, M. (1985), The social organizations of secrets: Towards a sociology of psychoanalysis. *Internat. Rev. Psychoanal.*, 12:2, 143–159.

Sandler, J. (1976), Countertransference and role-responsiveness. *Internat. Rev. Psychoanal.*, 3:32–37.

Schafer, R. (1959), Generative empathy in the treatment situation. *Psychoanal. Quart.*, 28: 342–373.

Scheflen, A. E. (1963), Communication and regulation in psychotherapy. *Psychiatry*, 26:2, 126–138.

Silverman, M. (1987), The myth of the perfectly analyzed analyst. In: *Countertransference*, ed. E. Slakter. New York: Jason Aronson.

Spruiell, V. (1984), The analyst at work. *Internat. J. Psycho-Anal.*, 65:13–29.

Stein, M. H. (1965), States of consciousness in the analytic situation including a note on the traumatic dream. In: *Drives, Affects, Behavior*, Vol. 2, ed. M. Schur. New York: International Universities Press, pp. 60–68.

—— (1981), The unobjectionable part of the transference. *J. Amer. Psychoanal. Assn.*, 29: 869–891.

Stolorow, R. D., Brandchaft, B., & Atwood, G. (1983), Intersubjectivity in psychoanalytic treatment. *Bull. Menn. Clinic*, 47:2, 117–128.

Stone, L. (1967), The psychoanalytic situation and transference: Postscript to an earlier communication. *J. Amer. Psychoanal. Assn.*, 15:3–55.

Waelder, R. (1960), *Basic Theory of Psychoanalysis*. New York: International Universities Press, pp. 107–108.

Winnicott, D. (1949), Hate in the countertransference. *Internat. J. Psycho-Anal.*, 30:69–75.

Wolf, E. (1979), Countertransference in disorders of the self. In: *Countertransference*, ed. I. Epstein & A. Feiner. New York: Jason Aronson, pp. 445–469.

Name Index

Alexander, F., 44
Arlow, J. A., xix, 142, 161, 175, 181, 227

Balter, L., et al., 118, 119, 227
Baum, I. E., 175, 227
Beiser, H. R., 175, 227
Beres, D., 181, 227
Bernstein, I., 181, 227
Bird, B., 76, 227
Birdwhistell, R. L., 103, 224, 227
Blum, H. P., 75, 131-132, 161, 174, 196-197, 227
Boesky, D., 31-32, 14-142, 227-228
Brenner, C., xix-xx, 76, 228
Breuer, J., 101, 228
Burlingham, D., 110, 111, 228

Calder, K., 175, 228
Calef, V., 53-54, 228
Caruth, E. G,, 51, 228

Deutsch, F., 102-103, 105, 228
Deutsch, H., 124, 181, 228

Fenichel, O., xiii, 110, 228
Freud, A., xiv, 228
Freud, S., xi, 101-102, 117, 120, 176, 179, 187-188, 197-198, 228

Gardner, M. R., 158, 175, 220, 228
Gill, M. M., 4, 152, 228
Glenn, J., 181, 227
Glover, E., 159, 160, 228
Gombrich, E. H. J., 104, 228
Greenacre, P., 75, 196, 228
Greenson, R. R., 104, 228

Halpern, H. M., 111, 229
Heimann, P., xviii, 158, 180, 229
Horowitz, M., xx

Isakower, O., 5, 117-119, 120, 229

Jacobs, T., 51, 229

Kernberg, O., 192, 229
Kestenberg, J., 207, 208, 211, 229
Kohut, H., 4, 76-77, 229
Kramer, M. K., 175, 229
Kris, E., 208, 229

Langs, R., 142, 229
Lesser, L. N., 111, 229
Lewin, B., 44
Lipps, T., 110, 229
Little, M., xviii, 158, 180, 229
Loewald, H. C., 221, 229

231

Subject Index

Abstinence, xiv, 143
Acting out, 141-142, 209
Actualization, 141-142
Adolescence, and transference neurosis, 60
Affects, 4, 193
Aggression, patient's, 87, 114, 147-148, 212, 213
    covert, 34, 44
Alliance(s)
    family, 201, 211, 212
    therapeutic, developing, 6, 7, 16, 47
Amnesia, 208. *See also* Remembering and forgetting
Analytic style, 44
Analyzing (or analytic) instrument, 117-120, 133-135, 225-226
    defined, 118
    as state of mind, 119
Anger
    analyst's, 36, 39, 151, 163, 169
    patient's, 44-45, 55, 84, 85, 147
Associations, 70, 107, 175
    free, 120, 124, 175
Attention
    evenly hovering, 118, 120, 125, 162, 220
    "free-floating," 143, 176

Audiovisual materials, 103, 224-225
Autonomic responses, 125-126, 147, 223. *See also* Nonverbal communication

Beginning of treatment. *See* Opening phase of analysis
"Body empathy," 111-112
Body language. *See* Nonverbal communication
Body movements, 101-105, 112-116, 224
    and empathy, 110, 111-112
    and listening, 104-105
    psychological factors and, 105
    See also Nonverbal communication

Center for Advanced Psychoanalytic Studies, xix
Child analysis, 54, 123, 181, 202
Classical vs. interpersonal analysis, 220-222. *See also* Interpersonal dimension of analysis
Collusion
    within families, 211, 212, 214
    patient-analyst, 51, 56, 68, 74, 153, 218
Communication, 4, 8, 102, 120-121, 133, 219-226

233

Seductive behavior, patient's, 165, 166-167, 168-169
Self, analyst's use of, 117-135
  and analytic instrument, 117-120, 133-135
  clinical examples, 126-134
  and countertransference, 122-123
Self-analysis, xiv, 115, 162, 164, 175, 222-223
  and countertransference, 141, 175-177
  Freud and, xi-xii, 176, 179-180
  techniques, 177
Self-object representations, 192, 198, 199. *See also* Object world, patient's
Self-object (or idealizing) transferences, 4, 76-77, 78
Separation issues, 131
  and family secrets, 215, 216
Sexual abuse, 34, 205-206
Siblings, 56, 86-89, 191-192
Silence(s), 7, 120, 128, 143
  analyst's, 145
Style, analytic, 44
Subtransference, 183
Superego, 76
Superego development, 213, 214-215
Supervision, 175

Tact and timing, in analysis, 4, 5
Temporal relationships, 97
Termination
  decision to terminate, 149-152
  interplay of enactments in, 48-49
  transference and, 94-95
Training analyst, 56-57, 61, 159
Transference, 4-6, 21-22, 52, 75-97, 185, 207, 217
  analyst's, 139-140 (*see also* Countertransference)
  and childhood trauma, 97
  clinical examples, 78-96, 127-128
  as compromise formation, 76
  and countertransference, xii, xx, 53, 149, 191, 222

defensive use of, 86
development of, 13, 51-52, 55-56, 77-78, 86
as ego function, 76
idealized, 190-191
negative, 13, 24-25, 81, 126
nonverbal cues and, 108-110, 127-128, 129-130
positive, 17, 21, 23, 142
primordial and mature, 76
relationships between, 75-97
self-object (or idealizing), 4, 76-77, 78
sibling, 86-87, 88
splitting of, 194
and termination, 149, 151
transformation of, 80-82, 84-85, 87, 89-96. *See also* Transference neurosis
Transference neurosis, 51, 52, 54, 73-74
  and adolescence, 60
  and analytic secrets, 58-61, 66-67, 70
  clinical examples, 54-61
  and countertransference, 53
  development of, 51-52, 56, 60
  traditional view of, 52
  and transactions, 52
  and written word, 68
  See also Transference
"Transference secret," 203, 207
Trauma, childhood, and transference relationships, 97

Unconscious, xiii, 133, 177

Videotaping, 103, 224-225
Visual associations, 144
Visual imagery, 125
Visualization of patient, 124, 125

Work blocks, 17, 18
Working through, 40, 148, 149
Written word, 68